STARTING AND CLOSING

STARTING AND CLOSING

Perseverance, Faith, and One More Year

John Smoltz
with Don Yaeger

wm

WILLIAM MORROW
An Imprint of HarperCollinsPublishers

Unless otherwise noted, all insert photographs are courtesy of the author with the exception of the following: the *Lansing State Journal* (bottom left and right on p. 6, and top left and right on p. 7); SEBO (top and center on p. 11); courtesy of the Boston Red Sox (bottom on p. 14, and all on p. 15); and courtesy of Tom Bommarito (all on p. 16).

HarperCollins books may be purchased for educational, business, or sales promotional use. For information please write: Special Markets Department, HarperCollins Publishers, 10 East 53rd Street, New York, NY 10022.

A hardcover edition of this book was published in 2012 by William Morrow, an imprint of HarperCollins Publishers.

FIRST WILLIAM MORROW PAPERBACK EDITION PUBLISHED 2013.

Library of Congress Cataloging-in-Publication Data has been applied for.

ISBN 978-0-06-212056-4

13 14 15 16 17   OV/RRD   10 9 8 7 6 5 4 3 2 1

To my wife, Kathryn, who helped me get through the final year of my career. Without her love and support, I am not sure I could have made it.

To my kids. Their support and understanding were essential as well.

To my family. My mom, dad, brother, and sister were, and have always been, awesome.

And last, to Dr. Joe Chandler. Without you and Dr. Jim Andrews, I don't know where I'd be. Your passion as a doctor is unmatched and your care is unreal. Without a doubt, you made it possible for me to play many years longer than anyone expected. JS

To Mom and Dad: As I heard often while working here with John, the real framework for success is built at home. Thanks for laying that foundation for me. I miss you both. DY

Contents

STARTING AND CLOSING

Chapter One

WHY NOT?

It's been more than two years since I picked up a baseball, but everyone still wants to know. Whether I'm standing in line for a movie with my kids, teeing it up at a golf tournament, or just hanging around a batting cage chatting with current players before a game, the questions are always the same.

Why?

Why did I come back from Tommy John surgery at age thirty-four with one year left on my contract? Why did I go to the bullpen after more than a decade as a starter? Why after three full seasons in the bullpen did I feel compelled to convince then–Atlanta general manager John Schuerholz to let me rejoin the Braves' starting rotation? Why did I put my body through all those surgeries and years of rehab? Why did I risk failing . . . for one more year?

Why?

By now I'm used to the questions. I guess that happens after spending more than twenty years standing by a locker and pulling on a uniform as my motives, my reasoning, and even my sanity at times were questioned, examined, and scrutinized. My career always seemed to invite people to wonder, *What the heck is this guy thinking?* The media, of course, tried to fill in the blanks and provide some answers, and countless reporters along the way have attempted to pin me down and define me as a baseball player. But let me tell you, sometimes they were wrong. I guess it's easy to be wrong about someone when you're trying to suggest what he should be doing or predict what he's going to do. And I guess from the perspective of most people, it always seemed like there was very little to gain and much to lose by a lot of the things I did.

In truth, my answer to all these questions is the same, and it's far simpler than many believe: *Why not?*

Why *not* do what you love for as long as you're physically able? Why *not* take risks, as long as they're calculated? Why *not* chase what some see as impossible? Why *not* believe in yourself? Why *not* dare to be great . . . even if it means being different?

Why not?

I'm here to tell you that understanding who I am and why I did what I did—or even why I do what I do today—is really very simple. You just need to know three things about me:

1. All I ever wanted to do was win.
2. I'm not afraid to fail.
3. I never did anything in my baseball career just to set a record, or to be able to say no one else has done what I have done.

All I ever wanted to do was win.

I decided I was going to be a professional baseball player when I was seven years old, and from the first day I picked up a baseball to the day I stopped playing, all I ever wanted to do was win. I truly enjoy competing and I really believe to this day that I can beat most people. It's really not an ego thing; it's just a belief that I have and I think it's really one of the keys to my success on the field and in life in general.

But at the same time it's not like I don't have any grip on reality and think I can do anything. Like if you ask me to ice-skate, I'm not going to fake it and say in four months I'll be able to ice-skate and possibly play on a hockey team. It may seem crazy that a guy from Michigan has never worn ice skates, but I seriously have never even put them on and don't think I could. So I don't believe things I know I can't possibly ever do. I am just really aware of what I am and am not capable of doing. I know my body and I know what I can do.

I wish I could put my finger on what makes me just know certain things about myself. You would think a lot of athletes know their bodies like this and have this type of confidence, but from my experience hanging around baseball clubhouses for more than twenty years, they really don't. They are all blessed with God-given abilities and tremendous talents, but very few of them ever achieve their highest potential. It seems to me that the majority of people—pro athletes and average Joes alike—are unwilling to break out of their comfort zones and risk the possibility of things not going well. We'll dig into this more here shortly, but for now let's just say I'm not one of those people.

Another thing I know about myself is how I learn. This sounds like a pretty basic concept considering most of us started school when we were about five years old. But seriously, knowing this is so important. Let me tell you, gone are the days when you could be an everyday big leaguer on raw talent alone. I guarantee you the guys who are able to stay in the majors and sustain careers are the ones who are constantly adjusting and developing their skills—whether it's a fastball pitcher tweaking his breaking-ball delivery, a contact hitter learning to hit the ball the other way, or a veteran infielder learning how to position himself to compensate for losing a step over the years—today's game demands players to adapt, overcome, or be sent down.

For me, when it came to working on new techniques like throwing sidearm or throwing a knuckleball, I was able to pick them up really quickly because I'm one of those guys who, if you show me something or tell me something and I *feel* it right away, I'll pick it up just like that. On the other hand, though, if I don't feel it, you could show me the trick to the greatest four-seam fastball in the majors and I'll just never be able to do it. I've got to see it or feel it for myself, or it just isn't going to happen. When it came down to it, knowing how I needed to approach new ideas really enabled me to take the mound many, many more times than I could have otherwise. Over and over again I found ways to work through injuries that would have likely just ended another guy's career. With me, it all really boiled down to doing whatever I could do to win.

From Little League to the big leagues, I have always wanted to win at all costs—not cheat to win, but seriously do whatever else it takes to win. Whatever the team needed me to do, I was always willing to do. If they asked me to lay down a bunt to move the runner to second base, I didn't allow myself any excuses. That's just not how my mind works. No, I stuck my bat out there and tried like heck to roll one down the first-base line. And if I popped it up or knocked it right back to the pitcher? Then I would be seriously upset with myself for not coming through when my team needed me. It's just my competitive nature. No matter the circumstance, I have always felt this great responsibility to my team. In my mind, there was always something I could do to help us win.

This will to win at all costs was really key to overcoming all the injuries I struggled with through the years. To me, the most important thing was always being able to make the next start; the pain was always secondary. My mind-set was always, "What can I do to work around the pain and still pitch effectively?" Mostly I did this by tinkering with my mechanics—changing a grip, changing my arm position, shortening my stride, just whatever it took.

Now, obviously, I'm human and I knew eventually there would come a point where I was just done, when the pain would be so unbearable that no matter what I tried, I just wasn't going to be effective anymore. I was always intent on exhausting all options before I got to that point; I was intent on trying every adjustment known to man to give myself a chance to go out there and contribute.

I pushed this strategy to the max in 1999 when I was really in the countdown to Tommy John surgery. I'll save the full story for a little later, but I basically taught myself how to pitch a whole new way, not really sidearm, but a low three-quarters delivery. I changed my complete delivery in one side session in the bullpen between games. I reinvented myself in the middle of a season. It was a huge risk to take, but I really thought I could be effective, and I was. Altering my delivery allowed me to continue my season and help my team down the stretch. I could have sat out and waited to feel better, but I never wanted to do that. I never wanted to play it safe. Had I played it safe, I would have missed pitching in five postseason games that year, including Game Four of the World Series. Taking the risk and making the adjustment gave me one more opportunity to win, and I would do it all again in a heartbeat.

I'm not afraid to fail.

I'm not afraid to fail. It doesn't sound like much, does it? But just think about this for a second. How many people can you think of right now who are out there, chasing down their dreams no matter what? Throughout my experiences in life thus far—from being a father and raising kids to coaching youth sports and observing elite athletes for more than two decades—one thing has become really obvious to me: We have a chronic fear of failure going on in this country right now.

Very few people today go out and, on their own desires, set a path toward their goals and then follow that path to its complete end. They don't let their natural ability be the determining factor. They let all the exterior things come into play—the doubts and the doubters—and they never reach their goals. Heck, a lot of them don't even get started. They never even give themselves a *chance* to fail. I'm telling you, I've seen more great athletes and more kids choke up or choke off an opportunity simply because they never even gave themselves a chance. They're too afraid to even risk the possibility. So many people are busy coming up with reasons why they can't do whatever it is they really want to do that many never even let themselves wonder, *why not?*

Now look, there's obviously a difference between not being in touch with reality and thinking you can do whatever you want. We can't all throw a ninety-eight-mile-per-hour fastball and we can't all run forty yards in 4.4 seconds. But we all have God-given talents, things that we excel at and enjoy doing. The thing is, talent is only one-half of the equation; it'll only get you so far. You also have to have the right mind-set. At some point you just have to decide, *All right, I'm going to go in with this game plan, and with the right plan I'm going to execute this. And if I fail, so be it. I'll learn something that will help me be successful the next time.*

In my career, learning how to deal with failure wasn't just a bonus that I kind of picked up along the way. Unfortunately, it was really a necessity. I'm one of those guys—and believe me, I wish it hadn't been this way, but I'm one of those guys who was always kind of digging out of a hole. More often than not, I was looking for a rally cry. With the exception of my first game in the big leagues, almost everything for me didn't go well right away. I won my first game, and then I failed miserably. Nothing ever seemed to come easy and

I was always battling. Along the way I was always telling myself, *John, you can rally from this.* Struggling through the tough times— the 2–11 stretches, the times when the bats seemed to go quiet every time I pitched—taught me never to get too carried away with success, and at the same time never to get too carried away with failure. The lessons were tough to learn, really tough, but they served me well in baseball and in life.

In some ways, not being afraid to fail really allowed me to get away with all my infamous tinkering. I'm certainly not the only pitcher who has ever worked on things in the bullpen or watched other guys pitch and picked up things here and there. Everyone does that. The difference is that very few guys ever even try new things in the game. Me? I *always* brought it to the game. Again, I just figured, Why not? There's no way to know if it's going to be effective until you bring it in the game.

Now, obviously there's risk involved here. You could fail. They could light you up like a Christmas tree on national TV. Been there, done that, and thankfully lived to tell about it. But I always thought, *What good does it do to just keep it in the bullpen?* You've got to have the guts to find out. You've got to be able to cross the line when it counts and be able to trust the thing you're working on. And if it doesn't work, you've got to trust that you can go back to the bullpen and find something that does. It all goes back to believing you can do it in the first place.

I'm telling you, in my baseball career some of the moments that should have done me in were actually motivators for me. When other guys might have just hung it up, for me it was always rally time. Take my second time out of the bullpen in 2002 as a closer. I stunk it up. There were reasons why I stank—another injury, of course—but I wasn't going to use it as an excuse. I still remember getting in my car after the game and just telling myself, *You know what, John, you gotta dig deep. You just gave up eight runs in your second game as a closer.*

Your season goals have just been shot. But you gotta get back in there and keep pitching. I wasn't afraid of the job and I wasn't afraid of the challenges, but I knew it wasn't going to be pretty for a while.

When I decide I am going to do something, I'm going to do it. When I take my mind to a place where I focus only on the task at hand and it's totally wrapped, it's all in. It isn't, "Maybe I can do it." No. If I fail, I'm failing all in.

If there is anything that I've learned in this journey, it's how to make the best out of really crappy situations. Whatever it is, just make the best out of it. It's easy to just give in to the negative thinking: Everything is stacked up against you, everyone is out to get you, and woe is me and all that. Doubts arise and it's natural to question yourself and think, *What am I doing?* But if I had ever given in to those doubts, if I had let the fear of failing dictate my career, I never would have known what I was truly capable of and I would still be wondering today, *What if?* Let me tell you, I'm sure thankful today to know.

I never did anything in baseball just to set a record, or to be able to say no one has done what I have done.

First of all, the reason no one had ever gone from being a starter to a closer and then back again is certainly not because there's never been anyone else capable of doing it. There are a handful of people I can think of right off the top of my head who have got the stuff and who could be effective at both. Guys like Randy Johnson, for one. But why would they? And would they if they were asked? I don't know. And of those capable of doing both, do you think any would consider switching midway through their careers? I mean, do you think if you went up to Mariano Rivera and asked him to start, he would? It's an interesting question.

My reasons for going to the bullpen and later rejoining the starting rotation had absolutely nothing to do with setting records or just trying to do something that no one else had done before. And honestly, if my primary motivation had been to be able to say something like that, I don't think I would have ever been successful.

When it came to closing, what a lot of people don't understand is that Atlanta really kind of leveraged me into it. I was basically told after the 2001 season that the only way I could stay with the Braves was to move to the bullpen.

Okay, time out. I guess we need to add another item to the list of things you need to know about me: (4) I lived and breathed and bled the Atlanta Braves. Atlanta was my baseball home and remains my home today. I wish I could have stayed forever with the Braves, but it just didn't work out that way for me.

As for going back to starting, the reason was actually simple. Records were not on my mind. Winning was on my mind.

All I ever wanted to do was win. I wasn't afraid to fail. I still thought I could pitch, and I wanted to be an Atlanta Brave. Those are the answers to 99 percent of the questions about my career. It's really as simple as that. For twenty-one long seasons, game after game, inning after inning, I kept coming back because despite what everyone else thought, I knew I could still do it. Had I not struggled through all the injuries, had I always waited for things to heal and for conditions to be perfect, I wouldn't have experienced half the success that I did over the course of my career. Certainly it made me the pitcher I was. When it came down to it, I pitched some of my greatest games in the worst of conditions. And at the end of the day, the results were all that mattered.

I loved it, and I don't know that I'd want it any other way.

Chapter Two

BURN NOTICE

Look, I've got to be honest here: I *never* wanted to write a book. Perhaps that isn't the best thing to admit right off the bat here, but it's true. My impression is that a lot of people write books just to pat themselves on the back and remind themselves of how great they are, and that's just *not* who I am or something I ever envisioned myself doing.

Now that I've had a couple years away from baseball to reflect, I finally realize there could be a bigger reason for me to write a book—one that is actually meaningful to others and not just gratifying to myself. And after much thought and much prayer, it became evident to me that despite my own misgivings, this is not only the right thing to do, but what I am being called to do: I feel a *burden* to write this book.

You see, it's hard for me to ignore all the things the good Lord has shown me and not make an attempt to try to show other people how to overcome and deal with failure in their own lives. I feel obligated in my heart to do what I can to pass on a little nugget of wisdom here or there. At the same time I realize nothing I have is of my own; whatever I have, God has put it in my heart and given me the desire to pursue it and think the way I think.

This book is not so much about finding a measure of success in baseball; it's about growing and learning how to be successful in *life*. Whether you're eight or eighty-eight, a baseball fan or foe, practically anyone who shares this human existence can relate to this book, because when you boil it down to one sentence, this book is really about a kid following an improbable dream.

In these pages I am going to talk about persevering through hard times, overcoming obstacles, and rallying from the uncomfortable depths of failure—since a life lived in pursuit of dreams is destined to involve a ton of failure—but I am also going to talk about faith.

The fact is, the things that I have accomplished in my life that are viewed as "great" mostly have to do with the peace that I have in my heart today; the peace that I never knew before I truly accepted Jesus Christ as my savior in 1995. Now, I'm not going to get into all the philosophical conversations, and I'm not going to cast judgment on those who don't believe. I simply want to make it very clear that my faith in God has been the primary thing that has sustained me all these years. All the glory and honor belongs not to me, but to Him.

Now, higher purposes aside, there are, admittedly, a few gratuitous things that go along with writing a book. One of these is the opportunity to set the record straight on a few things, especially one ridiculously false story that has followed me like a shadow my entire career. Before we get into this business of telling my side of the story, though, I want to be clear about my motives. I am not fishing for sympathy here or indicting the media either. I am simply presenting evidence that what you have read or heard about me before may or may not be true.

At the same time, if there's one thing I am delivering in this book, it's the truth. This is how things happened. And the truth is, never would I have imagined some of the things I have done, some of the things I didn't get to do, or some of the things that have happened to me. This is my life: it's real, it's authentic, and it's decidedly *not* perfect. It is what it is. I have made my fair share of mistakes in this journey and I'm not afraid to talk about them; I'm not afraid to use my life as an example to help others.

That's what this book is all about.

For reasons I'd like to forget, I will never forget spring training in 1990. Before I headed to the ballpark one morning, I had used a portable steamer to get a few wrinkles out of my shirt. I had it sitting on the bathroom counter at one point, and when I lifted up the steamer, it spit out some water and burned me on my neck. What began as an innocent, ho-hum scrape with domesticity literally changed my life.

At the time I didn't think much of it, but once I stepped foot into the clubhouse—with this burned spot on my neck, of all places—it became *the* topic of conversation. The guys immediately teed off on it. They were riding me and reincarnating every stupid hickey joke or story they had ever heard. I had no better story of my own to chip in but the truth, which unfortunately for me involved only a hot portable steamer, and not a hot young woman.

Unbeknownst to me at the time, a reporter was lurking about, literally loitering in the clubhouse. I never saw him, he never asked any questions—certainly never asked me about my "hickey"—but he went and wrote an article claiming that I had burned myself while attempting to iron my shirt . . . while *wearing* it!

I had no idea he had even written the story. Like a lot of other guys in spring training, I was completely consumed by and immersed in baseball: I was either at practice, driving to or from practice, thinking about my next practice, eating, or sleeping. It was just another day until I turned on the TV for a few minutes before I went to bed. *The Arsenio Hall Show* happened to be on and Arsenio was doing his monologue. He was going on about politics and whatnot, when he suddenly segued into baseball. Much to my horror, the next thing I heard him say was, "Well, no wonder the Braves can't win; this guy Joe Schmoltz"—he didn't even get my name right—"irons his shirt while wearing it!"

Have you ever had a moment in your life when you cannot *believe* what just happened? It's almost like an out-of-body experience. You desperately hope that you're just having a nightmare and soon you will wake up and things will go right back to normal. This was one of those moments for me. I just sat there, stunned.

Soon after, the phone calls started coming in; the first one from my dad. I knew he had already heard the story because he had the whole parent-who-is-currently-freaked-out tone in his voice when I answered.

"Hey Johnny, what happened?!" he said. "The news says you have third-degree burns!"

I guess, looking back, I should consider myself fortunate that it was only 1990, and thankfully nobody had Facebook, Twitter, or blogs back in those days. But even without the endless reach of today's social media platforms, the story took on a life of its own and basically cemented itself as an urban legend overnight. Thanks to one careless reporter, I have been forever tagged as the schmuck baseball player who burned himself while trying to iron a shirt while wearing it.

You might remember that even *Sports Illustrated* got in on the act and printed a cartoon of me with an iron on my chest. As soon as the issue hit the stands, I contacted them. I thought surely once *SI* heard my side of the story, they would do something about it, but my efforts were about as effective as standing at home and talking to my wall: It didn't change a thing. As far as I know, they never printed a retraction or anything. Nobody, not even a respected publication like *Sports Illustrated,* was interested in letting something like the truth get in the way of a good story.

The whole experience was just surreal and it left me, frankly, disillusioned. If you can imagine my room while I was growing up, it was literally wallpapered with *SI* covers. Every stitch of my wall was covered by a picture, or a graphic, or something from the magazine. I don't think I can adequately explain how it felt to see myself later actually in the magazine, made out to be the butt of this joke. Now look, I have a sense of humor and I can take a joke. If you want to roast me for something silly I have done, go ahead. I'm a big boy. But there's a difference here. I was being made fun of for something I never even did. It just wasn't funny anymore. That cartoon is the reason why I refuse to read *Sports Illustrated,* even to this day.

From the moment I first heard it on Arsenio to today, I have attempted to set things straight every time the question was raised. But it never made a difference. To this day, my burn story lives on like a Roundup-resistant weed: it just won't die. I seriously doubt it will die now even after this book. This story will be linked to me forever because it's already been written too many times. And I guess I get it now. The truth just wasn't the best story and people had a good time with it. It makes me wonder what it would have been like if I had just embraced it and tried to make the best of it. Maybe it could even have led to an endorsement deal. I can just see the commercial now: "Check out Rowenta's new portable steamer. It's so safe and easy, even John Smoltz can use it without worrying about missing his next start."

The truly ironic thing is that one of my teammates actually did this one time. He tried to use a hot iron to smooth out a wrinkle on his sleeve and burned his triceps. I know because he told us the story in the clubhouse one day. I just looked at him and the telltale singed outline of an iron on his upper arm and could only laugh. Here it was, probably ten years after the story, and this time it had actually happened. And I knew that this version would probably never get into the papers. (Which, of course, it didn't.)

Prior to this experience, I had been going about my business in pro baseball, doing my part to answer questions from reporters and assuming naively that things would be handled legitimately. This story basically served as a crash course in media awareness for me, quite literally my own "burn notice": I learned the hard way that you can't assume anything with the media.

From this point on, I was much more mindful of the tactics reporters employ on occasion to "get" their stories. You can't always prevent things like this from happening, but knowing what reporters are liable to do (namely, write a story without asking a lot of questions) makes you look twice at a guy standing silently in the corner of the clubhouse with press credentials hanging from his neck and a notepad in his hands writing feverishly. Especially right after someone has just played a prank on someone, or other, similar situations that can be widely misinterpreted. It can pay to engage these guys and ensure that they at least have their facts straight before they walk out with the wrong idea and something stupid ends up in the newspapers.

This is a side of pro sports that the general public has little sympathy for, in my opinion. It's as if most people figure, "Hey, athletes are making millions of dollars so public scrutiny is just the price they have to pay." Fans get a kick at laughing at us "overpaid bozos" (a phrase used to describe me and other athletes on the Bleacher Report's list of the Ten Dumbest Sports Injuries Ever; I'm number seven). I get it, but what a lot of people overlook, I think—and probably because they don't have to deal with it themselves—is that it can be incredibly painful to have your life played out in public. Especially when about half the time the stuff that's reported isn't even true and there's usually not much you can do about it. Sure, you can always hire a lawyer and take somebody to court, but at the end of the day it really doesn't change anything. People generally only remember the original story they heard. Who was right, who was wrong, and what the real story was in the first place often ends up buried in the small print and is largely ignored.

This is unfortunately just one of the many stories that have been printed about me over the course of my career that I feel wholly justified to take issue with. In the early days, I didn't handle these situations very well at all.

I'll never forget happening to run into the reporter who wrote the original burn story outside Holman Stadium in Vero Beach, Florida, the day after the story first broke. It was probably the maddest I have ever been and I took it out on him. I really aired him out. (For the record, he did apologize, but obviously that did little to alter the course of this story.) It wasn't my proudest moment, but that's how I handled that situation.

When it came to dealing with reporters and inaccurate stories, my natural inclination was to confront them, with the exception of this one time. I tried to do it in a respectful manner. It just went against every fiber in my body to know something was being said or written about me that was not true and to just ignore it. All I could think about was how hard I had worked to get to where I was, while on the other hand these reporters could spend a few minutes writing an untrue story—many times without even asking me about it directly—and seemingly undo it all. It was *galling*.

Thankfully, over time I did learn to temper my frustration and develop better methods of media engagement.

I remember one time I was riding home from the ballpark with Greg Olson, our catcher at the time, and we had the radio tuned in to one of the sports talk shows in Atlanta. The host was talking about the Braves' season thus far and discussing why we were struggling that particular year to gain the lead in our division. Now,

I'm fine with the armchair quarterbacking and "what if?" scenarios and all. That's just part of it—everybody thinks they can manage a baseball team better than the guys who are actually getting paid to do it. Sometimes players think so, too, believe me. Anyway, Greg and I were just sitting there listening to the fans' perspectives when all of a sudden, I guess to add some credibility to his comments, the host started talking as if he hung out in our clubhouse all the time and talked to players on a daily basis. Now, some reporters do this, but the problem was, this guy wasn't one of those guys. In fact, I was pretty sure I'd never seem him in the clubhouse before. So the longer we drove and the longer we listened, the more I got riled up.

Well, of course the next thing you know, somebody calls in and says something like "You know, John Smoltz is just not the same this year. Something's not right; it seems like he cares more about golf than pitching."

My mind immediately clicked into "Oh, here we go" mode. It was like I was bracing for impact, just waiting to hear what the host was going to say next. And I'll never forget this; he goes, "Yeah, you know, you're right. I've seen him in the clubhouse and noticed the same thing. It's like he doesn't seem engaged."

I looked over at Oly and I'm like, "Can you believe this?!" I could hardly contain myself as the conversation continued between the caller and the host, with the gist being that I wasn't the same pitcher this year and there was more to it than just not pitching well. Finally I just told Oly, "I'm calling him; I'm not going to let this guy get away with this. He's never been in our clubhouse, how can he make that comment?"

I started rifling through my bag for my cell phone, my mind buzzing with what I was going to say. Oly just shook his head and laughed at me. "You'll never get in!"

I just looked at him and said, "Trust me, when they hear who it is, I'll be the first one on."

So I called in, and sure enough, I went on the air with the guy. Now, thankfully I had the chance to calm down a bit before I actually went on and think about what I was going to say. Obviously an athlete calling in to a radio show all fired up is about as safe as swimming in shark-infested waters with an open wound. At the end of the day, you're lucky to survive without being eaten alive.

So I get on and say, "Hey this is John Smoltz. You know, hey, the fans are entitled to their opinions and I know a lot of them don't think we are going to be able to come back from this nine-and-a-half, ten-game lead of the Giants, but I'm telling you, we are going to catch them. We believe we are, and we are going to catch them. And while I'm on, I know you mentioned about my golf and this and that. I just wanted to tell you I've got a putting green in my backyard and anytime you want to come over and work on your putting stroke, you're more than welcome." And then I just added nonchalantly, "And as far as baseball goes, why is it that we've never seen you in our clubhouse?"

He said something like "Oh, I gotta get up early, you know, and . . . "—basically just fumbling around on air for an answer. As you might imagine, I didn't have to say much after that. Just to call him on the two or three things he had suggested he knew, I was able to—without getting nasty—just say, "Hey, when are we going to see you around the clubhouse?"

And then, literally the next day, he showed up. And we have been fine ever since.

Thankfully, that was one of the few times I chanced swimming with the sharks. As the years went by, I eventually learned that you just had to tune a lot of it out. People are going to write what they are going to write and say what they are going to say—whether it is accurate, slanted, biased, or just categorically false—and there's really not much you can do about it. For me, I finally came to a point where I was able to separate my own feelings of self-worth from whatever the papers were saying. I'd like to say life got a lot easier for me at this point, and I guess in some ways it did, but I don't think you are ever immune to letting it all get to you on occasion. I think the best you can hope for is a feeling somewhere between numb and disinterested.

Despite living with this reality that anything you say or do (or in some cases *don't* say or do) can and will be used against you in the court of public perception, I really tried to make an effort to put my best foot forward when it came to dealing with reporters. I was definitely cautious and wary at times, but I tried to avoid being guarded, and none of these experiences ever stopped me from making time for interviews. Regardless of whether I had just thrown a complete-game shutout or had just given up eight runs in two-thirds of an inning, I would face the questions. If I stank, I owned it. I didn't speak in clichés, I didn't give pat answers, and I always had something to say. I understood the role the media played and I grew accustomed to taking some shots and dealing with the aftertaste of an unfortunate story from time to time. It's just part of being in the spotlight of pro ball.

As I look back on my career today, I really wouldn't change my approach. I think it was best to be myself and take my lumps along the way, rather than just avoiding reporters and never engaging them. And really there's a serendipitous side to all of this, as I think my natural tendency to be open and forthright is really one of the reasons I was given the chance to get into broadcasting today.

I truly enjoy broadcasting and the opportunity it affords me to stay connected to the game I love. And I also know that dealing with all the not-so-pleasant criticism I faced throughout my own career helps make me a better broadcaster today. Because, believe me, I still remember what it was like to be picked apart by the guys sitting up in the booth.

Now, don't get me wrong here; it's not like I am up there giving anybody a pass. I call things like I see them. But I think guys like me, guys who have played before, tend naturally to have a better perspective when it comes to analyzing the game. When it comes to making sense of a perennial postseason team getting swept in their first playoff series, a hitter who can't seem to make contact to save his life, or a pitcher who has temporarily lost the area code for the strike zone, it helps to have been there and done that. Guys like me know what Yogi Berra was talking about when he said, "Baseball is ninety percent mental; the other half is physical." Sometimes, despite what the scoreboard says, you're not watching a better team beat a worse team. You're actually watching a superior team beat itself.

Unfortunately, my trials with the media would remain a constant theme throughout my career and, as it turns out, even today. I don't know why, but I always seem to attract false stories like some guys collect stray socks in the bottom of their locker.

While I have clearly fallen victim to an inaccurate or misleading story on occasion, I think it's safe to say that there isn't anything "out there" that would make somebody seriously question my character. I've never been linked to any scandals. There's no hint of steroids. There are no legitimate claims of cheating. And that's really what I am most proud of. I played baseball through several dodgy eras— the juiced bat, the juiced ball, the juiced strike zone, and the juiced body—but not once was I ever even tempted to mortgage everything I believed in for the chance to be more successful.

Steroids are a topic I think we're all tired of hearing about, frankly, but it's important to me to note that when it comes to performance-enhancing drugs and my career, I never saw anyone using them, I never heard anyone talk about using them, and I was never asked to use them myself. I don't know anything beyond the rumors and speculation we've all heard.

With that said, there are a few things about steroids I will readily admit. For starters, I never would have imagined the scope of the problem or that we'd still be dealing with steroids and other performance-enhancing drugs today in some form or fashion. Never when I was playing did I realize how prevalent steroid use really was, and beyond that, I was completely shocked to learn how many pitchers supposedly used them. I had no clue steroids would help pitchers to the degree that they have apparently helped some guys.

The one thing I have stood firmly for from the beginning is anything that will help eradicate steroid use from the game and restore competitive balance. Whether or not I feel it was the government's place to get involved and hold congressional hearings—which incidentally still ranks up there as one of the *saddest* things I've ever watched on TV—I certainly understand and share the collective angst to get steroids out of the sport, especially since they started trickling down to kids.

The steroid era has undeniably changed the game and I hate that fans have been given legitimate reasons to wonder and second-guess players who are putting up obscene stats or making seemingly miraculous jumps in body composition in short amounts of time. I hate it for the fans, but I especially hate it for the players who are out there injecting nothing more than their own motivation into improving their game or making their bodies stronger in the offseason.

If you ask me, one of the greatest tragedies in sports today is to be falsely accused of using any performance-enhancing drug, because once a player is tagged—correctly or incorrectly—there's really no redemption. A cloud of suspicion will haunt him his entire career, regardless of whether the suspicion is based on rumors and speculation or evidence and/or an admission. The reality is that an accused player is considered guilty until proven innocent. It's not fair, but it's the reality. And I'm sure glad I don't have to worry about it.

As you might have realized by now, this is not your typical autobiography. We're not starting in the beginning with "I was born in Warren, Michigan." We're focusing on my last year in the major leagues,

2009. For those of you who have followed my career, you know already that this was not my best year. I was trying to come back from major shoulder surgery at age forty-one, and my team, the beloved Braves, whom I so dearly wanted to end my career with, basically viewed me as the old trusted workhorse who was no longer useful to anyone. Nobody within the organization wanted to take me out behind the barn and put me down, but nobody wanted to sign me either. So I began anew with the Boston Red Sox, and that, my friends, is a story I'd much prefer to bury in the back of my mind and try to forget than to dig up and dissect in a book.

But as much as this is an autobiography, it isn't about me. (If it were all about me, I'd write a book about 1996, when I went 24–8 and won the Cy Young, only maybe I'd change the ending so we actually won the World Series that year.) This book is about the journey that God has put me on, the challenges I have faced, and the challenges I have overcome. I hope that by using my final year as a backdrop, I can teach somebody somewhere something. Whether it's a philosophy, a lifestyle, or things that I'll never know, that is my honest intention.

I like to ask people, "What's the most days in a row you've been happy?" I usually get this look like, "Not many." When they think about it, there aren't a whole lot of days they come up with because the reality of our lives today is that there all these things that can interrupt our happiness. But for me, those things, they're peripheral. Joy is central. You can have joy in the midst of some of the worst suffering.

I know because I've been there myself.

Chapter Three

SO YOU SAY I'VE GOT A CHANCE?!

"Wow, I don't feel that bad."

That was my first thought as I opened my eyes and started to come to after undergoing arthroscopic shoulder surgery on June 10, 2008. I had literally just started to wake up and take note of my surroundings, and almost on cue, a nurse came in the room.

Her eyes scanned the room as she approached the bed, visually inspecting my IV and the various monitors I was hooked up to, then she sort of mechanically grabbed my arm to read my bracelet as she said, "Name please."

I looked at her, at this busy lady who obviously meant business, and said slyly, "Bond. James Bond."

The nurse was not, in any way, amused. Beyond an almost inaudible sigh, she did not react at all. She just repeated her question, more emphatically this time, like she was speaking to a misbehaving adolescent boy: "Name please."

Meanwhile, my brother Mike, out of respect to the nurse, was trying like heck to bottle up his reaction. There we were, snickering like two schoolkids literally moments after I had just come out of anesthesia from a surgery that could very well mean the end of my baseball career. It was such a unique thing in so many ways because I never woke up in a good mood. This was the fifth surgery of my career, and in the past I had notoriously woken up in an awful state: sick to my stomach more often than not and just feeling downright miserable. I took my mood now as my first good omen in the long and winding journey that I hoped would lead me back to the mound.

Dr. Joe Chandler, the Atlanta Braves team physician and an orthopedic surgeon, came in next. He had traveled all the way down to Birmingham, Alabama, to collaborate with and assist Dr. James Andrews, the orthopedic surgeon who performed the operation. At this point in my career, Dr. Chandler was much more than my doctor, with all the injuries we had been through together since we both joined the Braves in 1987. Our relationship had grown beyond baseball and we had come to share in each other's joys and walk together through the struggles of daily life. He was in many ways more like a second father than just my doctor. I knew the man and he knew me. And he knew what I wanted to know before I asked the question.

"Well, what do you think?" I said as soon as he entered the room.

Dr. Chandler walked over to the bed and started hemming and hawing. I mean, he was talking, but not really saying anything. It was a whole lot of "Well . . . You know . . . I mean . . ."

I'm like, "Come on, just hit me with it. Give it to me straight, do I have a chance?"

And I'll never forget this: He said, very cautiously, as if the measured pace of the words would help me grasp the true reality of the situation, "We think with the way you work out, and the way you rehab, we think you've got a *chance*."

In all reality, that probably meant "you don't have a chance." But he went on to explain to me that when they opened up my shoulder, my labrum—which basically works like a rubber gasket, surrounding your socket and keeping your shoulder in place—looked like hamburger meat. They knew it was going to be bad, but it was far worse than even they had expected. It took nine anchors to basically tack my labrum back into place, the most Dr. Andrews remembered using, with the exception of a surgery he had performed on NFL quarterback Drew Brees. I listened to everything he had to say, but I had already heard all I needed to hear. "So you're telling me I've got a chance!" I'm telling you, it was a scene straight out of *Dumb and Dumber*.

From that point on, my motivation was simple: Every day I got up with the sole mission to get back and be able to be pitch again. I wanted nothing more than to pitch for the Atlanta Braves again in 2009, but I knew there'd be some tough decisions and I didn't know for sure if it was going to work out. I couldn't control whether or not the Braves wanted to sign me. I hoped things would work out, but in the end it wasn't just about trying to make it back to pitch for the Braves. It was about trying to make it back to pitch, period. I was chasing the same dream that had first caught fire in my heart at age seven. Here I was at age forty-one, and nothing, not even the threat of the Braves not wanting to sign me again, was going to be enough to extinguish that dream.

But in order to understand this, we've got to go to back to the beginning for a moment.

If somebody had told my parents in 1974 that their oldest child was going to be a major league pitcher, they wouldn't have believed it. And not only would they not have believed it; I'm not so sure they would have been happy about it. You see, I was born John Andrew Smoltz, a descendant of Italian immigrants, and my destiny was to be a professional accordion player.

Music wasn't just a hobby in my family. My mom's uncle owned a music shop and my mom and dad both gave accordion lessons there. My dad, John Adam Smoltz, was an electronics salesman in his day job, while my mom, Mary, stayed home with me; my little brother, Mike; and little sister, Bernadette. My dad played in a band and a lot of our weekend activities, especially in those early years, revolved around the accordion. If you were having a polka or an Oktoberfest in Warren, Michigan, and you needed an accordion player, you called the Smoltzes.

By age four, I was already being indoctrinated in the Smoltz family way. I took accordion lessons and I practiced every day. I worked hard at it, but I seemed to have the gift of a musical ear and, to a certain extent, it seemed to come naturally to me. Soon my parents were driving me all over the place to compete in contests and play recitals. As my parents tell me today, I would usually win, even against kids almost twice my age, and my parents could not have been more proud. Here I was, their first child, already the anointed leader of the next generation of proud accordionists. All was right in the world until I turned seven.

At age seven, I had one of those moments where I just suddenly knew what I wanted to do, and on the flip side, what I didn't want to do anymore. A dream was born that day. A dream that would initially disappoint my parents, but would fulfill my life in the long run.

As the story goes, we had pulled into a gas station to fill up our little AMC Pacer. As my mom stood there pumping gas, she struck up a conversation with me in the backseat.

She said, "Johnny," which is what my parents still call me to this day, "what are you going to do when you grow up?"

As she remembers it, I sat there, sort of considering the question thoughtfully, and then said, "Mom, I want to be a pro baseball player."

My mom would tell you today that she never seriously thought I would *ever* make the big leagues. Sports were not anything anyone in her family had ever done, but beyond that, while she may not have known much about sports, she knew enough to know it was a long shot at best. Thankfully she was kind of enough to always keep that opinion to herself.

But still, she looked at me and said, "Well, Johnny, that's a great dream, but you know, a lot of little boys want to play pro baseball, but not a lot of them ever get to do it. Maybe it would be a good idea if you had a backup plan, you know, if baseball didn't work out."

That seemed reasonable to me, so I thought about it for a second and then I said, "Okay, well, if I can't play baseball, maybe I could be a gas-station attendant."

To which my mom said, "Well, let's not tell your father that."

I obviously grew out of wanting to be a gas-station attendant one day, but it's safe to say really from that day forward my dream of playing pro ball became like an eternal flame in my heart. It would continue to stay lit through every obstacle I ever faced, from the light rain of a blown save to the torrential downpour of a multiple-game losing streak. All it knew how to do was burn.

Age seven would prove to be a turning point in my life. It was the time when I put down the accordion and picked up a baseball, and nothing has been the same for my family ever since.

I don't know if I can adequately explain how big a deal it was for my parents to let me quit the accordion. This was like the oldest son shunning the family business, and not because he wasn't capable, but because he wasn't interested. It was clear I had inherited the same musical gene that my parents were blessed with, and to my family it was a tough pill to swallow. My mom says to this day that she really thought her uncle was going to disown her and our entire family for allowing me to quit.

My parents, while disappointed with my decision, were, thankfully, rational about it. They knew my heart wasn't into the accordion, that I wasn't having fun playing the instrument. I cannot thank my parents enough for the opportunity they gave me to pursue and experience baseball. Their openness, their willingness to allow me to try something that was sort of from left field for our family—it was such a blessing to me.

From that day forward, I had one vision for my life. All the things I had learned by playing the accordion I translated into baseball. But the difference was I not only had a talent for baseball, I also had a *passion* for baseball. Nobody had to push me to go out and practice. For some reason, even at seven, it was almost ingrained in me that this is what I was supposed to do. I had such a visionary, dream-type mind-set; I never stopped to consider all the reasons why I might not make it. I just always believed I was going to make it and I always practiced like I would.

When I got a little older, I basically laid claim to the brick wall right outside our screen door on the front of our home in Lansing, where we moved when I was in the fifth grade. I'd mark the outline of the strike zone on the wall with tape and then I would literally stand at the curb, because that was as far back as I could go without being in the street, and I would pitch against that brick wall with a rubber ball for hours and hours. Every once in a while I would throw a wild pitch, missing the wall entirely, and the ball would ricochet off our aluminum screen door, which drove my mom nuts. Whenever she heard that telltale *clank*, she would yell something like "Johnny, you better learn to throw strikes!"

I taught myself everything. I didn't go to camps. I'd watch TV, look at a book, see a grip, and go outside and try to emulate it. It was the only way I had ever known to achieve (witness the accordion playing) and I just worked and worked. It was just second nature to me to go out there and pitch every day.

One of my favorite things to do was to watch a game on TV and then go out and pitch it. I really didn't waste my time with regular-season games, though; I went right to the postseason. In my mind, it was always the seventh game of the World Series and I was pitching for the Detroit Tigers. I imagined myself pitching every big game known to man.

I put the pressure on myself so much, so often, that I think I prepared myself for moments like when I went out to pitch Game Seven of the 1991 World Series against the Minnesota Twins. It was like living out my wildest dream—a dream I had been envisioning since I was seven years old—and everything I had ever imagined, down to being matched up against the very guy I had spent my childhood idolizing, longtime Detroit Tiger Jack Morris, who was now pitching for the Twins.

I can still, to this day, remember standing on the side of the mound in the bullpen during warm-ups, being struck by this sense of déjà vu. I'm standing there getting ready to pitch and I'm almost confused by the mix of emotions I'm experiencing. It was part nerves and part "man, I have done this *so* many times." What finally clicked things into perspective for me was watching this little girl—she couldn't have been more than seven years old—sing the National Anthem right before the game.

I remember Leo Mazzone, the Braves' pitching coach, looking at me and the expression on my face and asking, "Are you nervous?"

And I was like, "Not anymore."

He goes, "Why?"

And I said, "If that little girl can sing the National Anthem and she's seven years old, then I can pitch the seventh game of the World Series."

Once the game started, I felt like I was right back at the brick wall, living out my dream. It really was like the entire game was meant to be—except for the final score.

We lost the game, and the World Series, but I had never felt more comfortable in a situation I was not prepared for. I had *no* experience in any postseason before, but there I was drawing on this huge vat of confidence that I had unknowingly gained through all those years throwing simulated Game Sevens against the brick wall. And I'm not lying when I tell you that year after year, it was always the same way. The postseason always felt like the place where I was supposed to be. And I wanted the opportunity to be in that spot every single time. In some way, it became an obsession for me in my career to find ways to get there again.

That game defined what I always believed. Even if we'd had a pitcher on our staff who was 20–0 in the regular season and I was 14–6 or something, I would have gone to my manager and said, "Give me the ball." It's just an inner desire, not a cockiness. I want to be *the* guy. And if I fail, then I'll learn from it.

In real life, I fared pretty well with my postseason record, but it was no comparison to my career brick-wall win-loss record, which stands at 99–1. I threw that one loss in there just to keep it real . . . I mean who goes undefeated their whole life? That's just not probable.

My ability to dream and follow through with hard work was only one part of my childhood that helped me big-time in the big leagues. There were many other things that growing up in Michigan with my family taught me, but the one that played out time and time again was pretty simple: never forgetting to have fun and never forgetting the sheer joy that can come from mixing it up with your teammates. And more often than not, this works to bring everyone together. It certainly did for my friends and family and it's something I still value to this day. I guess looking back, I really should be grateful for Michigan winters.

I love to compete, I love a good challenge, and I love to have fun, and that's pretty much all I did as a kid. And I'm telling you, I had a blast. If it was warm enough to be outside and I wasn't playing baseball, I was probably playing basketball or football. I would organize teams and rules to make things interesting and I was usually angling for a way to set up my side as underdog. I just have always wanted to beat other people at their best and I would actually go out of my way to help my opponents and make them better, even if it could end up costing me when I was competing against them. Winning is never sweeter than when no one expects you to win.

The thing about growing up in Michigan, though, was there were only certain months of the year that the weather allowed for hours upon hours of outdoor fun. There was always winter to contend with.

When winter came and forced our activities inside, it forced us to be creative. Sure we watched some TV and played some video games (for the record, Baseball Stars is the best Nintendo game ever made to this day), but mostly we would play games that didn't involve electronics. I think all of those winters we spent in the basement contributed to the uncanny ability I have to think up games; they sort of made me into this MacGyver of impromptu ways to kill time and have some fun.

One of the all-time-favorite basement games that I came up with was Ping-Pong baseball. This game involved a plastic oar (the type you'd use for a little canoe) for a bat, a Ping-Pong ball, and our Ping-Pong table. We didn't have that much room in the basement, maybe twenty or thirty feet, so the hitter would stand on one side of the room near the stairs, where we had a strike zone taped up to the wall, and the pitcher would stand behind the table. You could pitch it straight to the hitter, or you could skip it off the table first. If you didn't hit the ball in the air, you were out. If you did get a hold of one, wherever it impacted the wall determined the outcome. So, for example, if you drove one into the curtains over the windows: home run. If you cleared the curtains and tagged the space between the windows and the ceiling: grand-slam home run.

Over the years I perfected this nasty pitch that my opponents would only let me throw once per at-bat. I'd put the ball between my fingers and flick it in a way where it would go straight up and straight down, like a big, huge curveball. I'm telling you I had the meanest Ping-Pong breaking ball of all time.

We took our games pretty seriously—my best friend, Chuck Cascarilla, and I would keep a log for all our stats for Ping-Pong all year—but we kept it fair and we kept it fun. There was always schmack-talk and perhaps some disputes over calls—like my brother, Mike, swears to this day that he beat me at Ping-Pong baseball one time with a walk off grand slam, but it was a triple, I assure you. For as competitive as we were, we were good sports about it.

Much to my parents' chagrin, all of their children ended up playing sports. I played baseball and basketball. Mike played football and Bernadette played softball and basketball. But sports and playing games and competing fairly helped us all grow and have fun together. And it has been a common thread throughout our lives.

For example, I endured years of good-natured garbage dished up by my little sister, Bernadette, while she was playing softball for Michigan State. She loved nothing more than to call me after a game and say, "Hey Smoltzy, I went two-for-three with a home run today. What did *you* do?" I finally got a reprieve on May 3, 1989, when I hit my first career home run.

I never lost the feeling of being a kid. I never lost the youthful desire of playing games and getting after it even today, and I have found light in some of the darkest moments of my life and baseball career by never forgetting to have fun. And in 2008, it was no different. Take it from me, rehab is a grind. It's getting up every day and pushing yourself, willing yourself to move that one degree farther than you could the day before. I'm not sure if I would have been able to embrace the process with as much patience if I hadn't been finding ways to make it a game or make it fun for myself. That's just who I am. In a lot of ways, I'm a big goofy kid trapped in this aging, adult body.

I wasn't born to play baseball, I wasn't made to play baseball, but Dr. Andrews had given this seemingly ordinary kid from Michigan the *chance* to keep doing the thing he loved most for just a little while longer.

Chapter Four

ONCE A TIGER

Shoulder surgery was really always an inevitable reality in my career, but one that I willfully fought, delayed, and postponed until the bitter end. I didn't know it coming into the year, but 2008 would prove to be that bitter end.

In 2008, I was coming off a great year, and I actually went into spring training fairly healthy. But then one day in camp, my left foot slipped just slightly as I threw a pitch in the bullpen and it was just enough to overextend my arm as it came over the top and tweak my shoulder. It turned out to be the straw that broke the camel's back.

Here's the thing, though, I'm not the kind of guy who just stops when the camel buckles under the weight of that last straw. I must explore all options, every last resort, before I call it. In this case, it took me five more starts and one forgettable appearance as a closer to convince me that the camel, or rather my shoulder, was officially done.

April 2008 turned out to be my own version of *The Good, the Bad and the Ugly*. My shoulder had gotten to the point where I couldn't bear to throw between starts and it would take a much longer time than normal in the bullpen before games just to get it moving and warmed up. Once I got it moving, there were two things that helped sustain my effort: the natural rush I would experience while pitching a major league game—and Novocain.

In the early innings, my shoulder was not an issue, as far as being able to do what I needed to do on the mound. But by the time I got to the fifth or sixth inning, it would start feeling heavy. The painkiller would be wearing off and my shoulder would get harder and harder to manipulate. On only one occasion in the month of April did I pitch into the seventh inning—that was on April 22, and adrenaline had a little something to do with it.

Coming into 2008, the public relations guys were tracking my strikeouts like a countdown to the New Year. Every game I pitched inched me closer to the three-thousand-strikeout plateau. It was a big deal, in part because if I could make it, I would be the first pitcher in franchise history to do it. To tell the truth, though, I was far more concerned with my shoulder at the time than my statistic for career strikeouts. I was so frustrated with how it felt that I spent practically no time thinking about the pending milestone. And I really didn't stop to think about it, or even grasp the magnitude of it, until I found myself in the moment.

We were at home against the Washington Nationals that day and I remember from the very start of the game, whenever I got two strikes on a hitter, the crowd went nuts. Everybody was anticipating a strikeout, and in that first inning, I caught myself trying a little too hard to deliver. I didn't actually strike anyone out until the top of the second, but once I got that first one, it really helped me relax. The crowd was still into it, but in my mind I had broken free of the pressure of the moment and got into a groove. The magic number soon stood at one.

When Felípe López came up as the second batter in the top of the third and I worked the count to 2–2, Turner Field was on fire. I just tried to ignore the noise and the anticipation and make my pitch. Felípe was batting left-handed, and if you threw a slider or a curveball down and in, you could sometimes get him to swing over the top of it. From the moment I released the ball, I knew I had executed my pitch—I could see it start to tail in toward him. When he swung through it and the ball landed in Brian McCann's glove, the emotion I felt was more relief than elation. *Okay, good. That part is over,* I thought. *Now I can focus on getting the win.*

But everybody was standing up and going nuts. I mean it was really something, for a regular-season game in April. That's when it really started to hit me that it was such a big deal. I had been so focused on the condition of my shoulder that when the moment finally came I really didn't know what to do. I remember hugging Brian and shaking some guys' hands, and that's about it. And of course I remember the crowd. But stuff like this, numbers and statistics and records, it truly wasn't anything I ever paid attention to.

Now, I'd be lying if I told you I don't remember my first strikeout, against Darryl Strawberry, but I couldn't tell you anything about my one-thousandth strikeout unless I looked it up. I don't remember my two-thousandth strikeout either, but I do remember that particular game because I hit a three-run homer off Dave Eiland that night. I do remember my two-hundredth win, because I was pitching against Tom Glavine and the New York Mets. But that's just the way I am; I didn't ever get too caught up in my own stats.

As I stood there on the mound, what I really wanted was everybody to just sit down so I could get back to pitching. If there was one thought going through my head or one prayer going through my mind, it was something like *Please Lord, don't let my shoulder fall off right now.*

Maybe if I had been healthier, I would have been able to enjoy it more. It's just hard to describe the way the year was going. It was filled with these moments of *Wow, I'm pitching well early on, but I don't know if I can continue.* I was throwing some of my best stuff, but only when my shoulder was, let's just say, Novacained up. When the painkiller wore down, it was torturous, wanting to keep pitching so badly, knowing that I had a lot left in the tank, but also knowing realistically that the end was near for that year.

After the adrenaline wore off on April 22, I was like, *wow.* It literally felt like I had been run over by a truck. I attempted to make one more start against the Mets, which was ironic because I started my career pitching against the Mets at Shea Stadium, and here I was, quite possibly ending my career as a Braves starter there twenty years later. There's a lot of history between me and the Mets, but there wasn't much to remember about that day. I limped through four innings then just sort of knew I was finally done.

I went on the DL shortly after and spent the next month or so weighing my options and seeing how my shoulder responded to a little rest. I remember being down-and-out for a little while mentally, just trying to deal with the decision I knew I had to make. I attempted to make one last-ditch comeback in the bullpen, but all that amounted to was notching one last miserable inning in 2008, on June 2 against the Florida Marlins, in which I gave up not only the tying run, but the go-ahead run. Those runs proved to be the final nails in my coffin.

During the month of May, in between my last start against the Mets and my first blown save in three years against the Marlins, I was weighing all the pros and cons of my situation. I talked with everyone I could about what was best for me: my manager, my pitching coach, my doctors, my trainers, you name it. I was truly interested in hearing all sides and perspectives. I have made it a habit in life to surround myself with people who don't just tell me what they think I want to hear. I could always count on the people who were in my corner to tell me the truth, whether I had realized it yet myself or not.

Many people told me things that helped push me in the right direction, but it was the Braves team chaplain at the time, Tim Cash, whose words really hit home. "John, who are you kidding?" he said bluntly.

After listening to what all the experts had to say and trying to remove all my emotions from the decision, I ultimately made a solid decision based on prayer. I knew in my heart that I had gone as far as I could go and I decided I didn't want to limp my way through an entire season like I was. It would have been a grind and it would have had a horrible ending, so I decided to have surgery.

I think a lot of people at this point really thought this was the end for me. Fans, the media, maybe even the Braves. But in my mind, the situation could not have been more different. My decision to have surgery was an acknowledgment that I still wasn't done pitching. I wasn't ready to retire. Everything about surgery, down to the push to get it done as soon as physically possible—which turned out to be eight days after my last appearance—was planned with one single thought in my mind: how to set myself up in the best position to be able to rehab and play the following year.

I truly believed I could come back and pitch, but there were doubts in my mind that involved the Braves and how they fit into this picture. I wanted so badly to have the opportunity to finish my career in Atlanta, but at the same time I fully realized that this was one part of the equation I couldn't completely control. Where I would be in 2009 I didn't know, but if there was one thing I did put my trust in, it was that the Lord had a plan for me. It might not work out the way I wanted—my will and God's will might not be aligned in this case—but I was willing to walk the path and see what happened. And I knew if I followed my heart and I trusted in the Lord, He would not lead me astray.

I knew this because I had been down this path before. All I had to do was remind myself of 1987, when I had been *devastated* to find out I was headed to Atlanta. I learned way back then to trust that everything happens for a reason, even if we ourselves are not always capable of realizing it or appreciating it at the time.

We've already covered that it was my dream to play professional baseball. The *ultimate* dream come true, the version that came with nuts, whipped cream, and a cherry on top, was to play professional baseball for the Detroit Tigers.

Growing up in Michigan, I naturally gravitated to the Tigers for obvious reasons. It was the hometown team and we could listen to broadcasts of their games on the radio, but there was also a unique family tie that really sealed it for me. I had the amazing opportunity to grow up with a grandfather who worked for the Tigers.

My late grandfather, John Frank Smoltz, my dad's father, worked for the Tigers in various roles over the course of nearly thirty years. He'd been an usher, he'd worked on the grounds crew, and he'd even worked the press room, checking media credentials and so forth. Practically my favorite thing to do in life was to just hang out with him at the stadium and walk in his shadow while he worked. To be able to get that little sneak peak, that little taste or vision of what my life could be like, was unbelievable. To be on the field, at times practically within reach of all these players who I absolutely *idolized,* like Alan Trammell, Lou Whitaker, Jack Morris, Kirk Gibson, and Lance Parrish, was really something. I never called attention to myself or bothered players for autographs. I just stayed in the background, watching, listening, and observing everything that was going on around me.

We lived almost two hours away from Tiger Stadium, but it never really felt that far, and I seized practically every opportunity that arose to go there and just hang out with my grandfather. Thankfully my parents have always been up for road trips.

The other obvious benefit to having a grandfather who worked for the Tigers was tickets. I definitely had the extraordinary opportunity to watch a lot of games and from some really great seats. And this was never truer than during the 1984 World Series.

I was a junior in high school when the Detroit Tigers made it to the World Series that year. It was incredible; the entire state was infected with Tigermania and it was the one time in my life that my parents allowed baseball to take slightly more precedence than school; at least temporarily. Maybe if the Tigers made it all the time it wouldn't have been such a big deal, but the Tigers in the World Series, even these days, is only likely to happen once every twenty-or-so odd years. So I skipped everything at school that week—including homecoming—to go to the home games with my brother and my dad. I was only seventeen years old at the time, but it was an experience I will never forget.

The most memorable moments came from Game Five. We were sitting about twenty-one rows up, thanks to Grandpa, of course, and in the bottom of the eighth we were so close to the field that I could literally read the lips of Rich "Goose" Gossage, the pitcher for the San Diego Padres, when his manager, Dick Williams, came out to the mound to talk about what to do about Kirk Gibson. Gibson, due up next, was coming up to bat with runners on second and third and one out, and he had already homered earlier in the game. With the Padres down 4–5 to the Tigers, Williams, I suspected, was probably coming out to discuss intentionally walking Gibson.

"I want to pitch to him," I watched Goose tell his manager.

As the story goes, Goose did pitch to him. Gibson took the first pitch for a ball, but he sent the second pitch over the right-field wall for a three-run home run! The Tigers went on to win not only the game but the Series that night. It was so unbelievable to have been there and seen it all unfold before my very eyes. I have had the chance since to make a few baseball memories of my own, but I will never forget the pure, sweet sound of Kirk Gibson's bat making contact in the bottom of the eighth as long as I live.

Tiger Stadium was already going nuts in the top of the ninth and with each out recorded, the volume increased. By the time Tony Gwynn popped out to left field for the final out, it was downright pandemonium. Fans started rushing onto the field and soon they were literally tearing up the grass and throwing it into the stands. The three of us sort of looked at each other for a second, and then without a word my brother and I started snatching up hunks of grass. We ended up with two or three bags of sod and were just beside ourselves. We drove home elated by the win and with our own physical piece of Tiger history.

We carefully planted our sacred infield turf in the backyard. Eventually my parents added a big Tigers statue to stand watch over our Tiger grass, thereby completing the Smoltz Memorial to the Tigers' '84 Series victory. What we didn't know then was the very next year I would be drafted by the Tigers. And three years after that, well, let's just say the Tiger grass didn't make the cut to Atlanta.

The next three years would include some dramatic twists of fate that shaped how my career looks today. It's remarkable, when I think about it, how everything worked out in the end.

Going into the 1985 draft, I wasn't sure what to wish for, to be quite honest. I had already signed a letter of intent to accept a full scholarship to play baseball the next year at Michigan State, right there in Lansing, but that wasn't even the best part. The baseball coach was open to letting me also give college basketball a try. Here I was on the verge of playing the two sports I loved the most at my favorite school in my hometown. And the icing on the cake was my best friend, Chuck, was going to be in town as well, with plans to attend a community college nearby. Life that next year could very well resemble life right now: school, baseball, basketball, and my friends and family.

And then, on the other hand, there was the draft. The scouts we had talked to had projected me to be taken in the early rounds, anywhere between the first and fourth. But it didn't happen. The phone didn't ring until the twenty-second round. Of all teams, it was the Detroit Tigers on the other end of the line. In a lot of ways it was amazing and gratifying and yet, at the same time, really disappointing. Getting the call from the Tigers was awesome, but the twenty-second round just wasn't going to cut it. The only way I was going to go play pro ball right now, and skip the opportunity to go to college, was if I could get signed for first-round money. School was just too important.

So that was that. It was encouraging to get drafted out of high school, but I was surely headed to college now, I thought. What I didn't know was that I was about to embark upon a summer baseball season unlike any I'd ever experienced, and it would prove to be pivotal to my future with the Tigers. Without a doubt, the summer of 1985 changed my destiny.

I kicked off the summer with the All-American Amateur Baseball Association national tournament in Johnstown, Pennsylvania, with my team from Lansing. Then I got picked up by another team and went and played in the Stan Musial World Series. And after that, just when an unbelievable summer couldn't get any better, I got picked up for the Junior Olympics and ended up pitching against Chinese-Taipei and Cuba for Team USA.

While the opportunities were tremendous, I didn't actually have much success on these grand stages of amateur baseball. This was most especially true at the Junior Olympics, where I pitched in the gold medal game for Team USA against Cuba. We were up 1–0 and I was cruising, taking the game to two outs in the eighth before Cuba scored two runs at the plate, *bang bang*, just like that. And that's how the game would end: Cuba 2, USA 1. One second I was pitching my way to a gold medal and the very next it was silver. Never had I been more discouraged than when I gave up those two runs in my USA jersey; I felt I had let my entire country down.

I lost some heartbreaking games in these huge tournaments, but it was against the greatest competition I could play against. And I progressed so fast that summer, seriously by leaps and bounds, that the Tigers took notice of their twenty-second-round pick out of high school. At the end of that stretch, the Tigers contacted us and struck up negotiations.

My dad and I were invited to Tiger Stadium, and they put me in uniform before a game, and I got to walk around and meet all the players who I had been watching from afar all those years— Trammell, Whitaker, Morris, Gibson, and Parrish. Once the game started, I changed out of uniform and my dad and I went upstairs and talked with the front office. They handed us a piece of paper with an offer on it and told us to take it home and think it over. My hopes were riding so high at that moment, right up until I looked at the number on the page. The offer was so ridiculously low, it just wasn't worth considering when you weighed it against the opportunity I had to go to college.

The next two weeks were a teeter-totter of emotions. My dad, acting as my agent, continued to talk and negotiate with the Tigers and I worked on getting ready for school just in case. The whole time I was thinking, *Am I going to college? Am I not going to college?*

It came down to the last couple days before school was supposed to start and things were still in the air with the Tigers. Meanwhile, on the college front, everything was lined up: I had my dorm room, I had worked out my schedule, and my first class was set to begin at 8 A.M. Monday. It looked like I was going to be a freshman in college in a few days right up until the phone rang on Sunday night and the Tigers came through with their final offer. The numbers were finally in the first round neighborhood that we had been aiming for. My parents and I talked it through, and at about ten o'clock that Sunday night, I signed a contract that made me a Detroit Tiger.

I still think about this time in my life today. What if that hour had slipped by and I had gone to college? What would my career look like? What would my life look like? It's an interesting thing to sit and ponder, but it's not like I would go back and change things. I may regret a few things in my career, but this is certainly not one of them.

From this point on, I was on my journey to becoming a major league pitcher and it seemed almost too good to be true. To be getting a chance at the big leagues right of high school *and* for the Tigers. I thought I was starring in my own fairy tale until August 12, 1987, rolled around.

In 1987, I was playing Double-A ball for the now-defunct Glens Falls, New York Tigers. Things were not going well for me or the team. We were a ragtag collection of prospects and we weren't playing our best. We had loads of potential, but we all had a lot to learn. And on top of that, some key guys were out with injuries. All of which meant we were in dead last that August.

Back in those days at Glens Falls, let's just say there wasn't a lot of money being spent on minor league development. It was sort of bare-bones baseball. We had only a couple bona fide coaches, and not one pitching coach. And there I was, in the midst of a 4–10 season with a 5.68 ERA. I was just another prospect, plodding along, trying to figure out my way.

On August 12, I was sitting in the dugout watching a game on an off day and I got a message about a phone call. The note said simply, "Call your dad." I was immediately a little freaked out, as I thought surely something was wrong at home. Why else would I get a note to call my dad during a game?

I got into the clubhouse after the game and called my dad first thing. I was a little panicked and started out the conversation, "Dad, what is it? What's wrong?"

He proceeded to tell me that I had been traded for Doyle Alexander. I was actually relieved; I just thought it was a case of my dad being my dad, calling in a practical joke just to mess with me.

"Whatever, Dad, quit being funny."

But he was adamant. "No, Johnny, I'm not joking," he said. "I just heard it on the news. Do you want me to come out there and help you move?"

At this point I was starting to get a little angry. He had gone a bit too far with his little joke as far as I was concerned. So I said, "Dad, if this is a joke, I'm going to . . . I mean, I can't *believe* you're even trying to pull a joke like this!"

It was right about this time that I started to take a closer look at the piece of paper in my hand. I suddenly realized it wasn't just one phone message, but two. Right behind the note that said "call Dad" was another that said "call Detroit front office."

A pit was already forming in my stomach and I just said, "Dad, I think I'm gonna have to call you back."

I called the club next, and when they confirmed the news that they had traded me for Doyle Alexander, I was devastated. They told me I would be going to the Richmond Braves, the Triple-A affiliate of the Atlanta Braves.

I was speechless. I handed the phone to my manager and he couldn't believe it either. Soon I was packing up all my stuff and walking out of the Glens Falls clubhouse for the last time.

As I got in my car and started heading south on I-87, I couldn't help but think I was headed in the wrong direction, but the drive to Richmond was actually good for me because I needed the time to be alone with my thoughts and process for myself what the trade meant. I was twenty years old and my initial reaction to the trade was not just disappointment about my now-shattered dream of playing for the Detroit Tigers, but also this horrible feeling of not being wanted.

It took me something like twelve hours to get to Virginia and I just kept thinking what a bad turn of luck it was. Here I was leaving a team that had recently won the World Series and was in the hunt again this year, and now I was suddenly headed to a new place that I knew practically nothing about. And the one thing I did know was that the Braves organization was god-awful and had been god-awful for quite some time.

About the time I pulled into the parking lot for The Diamond and sat there in my car almost drooling over the brand-new Triple-A stadium before me (remember I was coming from Glens Falls), I had one of those "now wait a minute" moments. As I got my bearings and got adjusted to my new surroundings, it was actually easier than I thought to embrace the change.

I began to realize my time with the Tigers wasn't all it was cracked up to be. Here I thought when I got into the minor leagues there were going to be all these coaches and all this attention on getting better, but it just wasn't the case back then for Detroit in the places I played. In Class A we had one manager, but there was no other coach on the team. Without a lot of direction, it really was a tough, tough environment for a player in the developmental stage of his career. When I got traded to Atlanta, all of that changed.

In Richmond, they had a multitude of coaches that paid attention to the details, and it really made the difference for me. The mentoring I received from the pitching coaches who tutored me that season and during instructional league the following fall taught me basic principles about pitching in the major leagues and helped transform me into the pitcher I always thought I could be. And it all happened much faster than even I expected; certainly faster than it would have happened with Detroit.

To say the least, my first game in Triple-A was a big deal to my parents and my family. I was a little nervous, seeing all those folks in the stands, including Carl Wagner, my summer baseball coach, and Bobby Cox, then the Braves general manager, who had made the trade, but gone were the misgivings *about* the trade and the feeling of not being valued. Now I just felt humbled and incredibly excited.

But unfortunately for me, initially in Richmond, I found myself in a little bit over my head. I hadn't been very good in Double-A and there I was days later facing off against the best team in Triple-A, the Tidewater Tides, an affiliate of the New York Mets, my first time out. In short, it didn't go too well. But it was just another start, just another step in my journey to the major leagues.

Admittedly, despite the trade and the initial feeling surrounding it, I was still a Tigers fan through and through. As the season went on, Doyle ended up going 9–0 for them down the stretch and helped the Tigers make it to the playoffs. Here I was on the other end of the trade, finding myself rooting for the Tigers and Doyle, until it came to the point where I sort of had to stop myself. I remember sitting there watching a game and thinking, *Whoa, this trade is going to look really bad if I do nothing and Doyle goes on to bring home a championship for Detroit.* Thankfully, over time, I think I made good on the trade for Atlanta.

I thought I was living a dream when I was with Detroit for those first couple years. I wanted so badly the chance to pitch in my hometown. The following that I had in Lansing, Michigan the proximity; my grandfather working on the grounds crew in Tiger Stadium—it was your ultimate feel-good story. When I got the call that I had been traded, I thought life as I knew it was over. And it was, to be truthful, but I had to just settle down and reinforce my ultimate goal, which was to get to the big leagues, and whether it was with Detroit, Atlanta, or Toronto, it didn't matter. And the truly ironic thing was that thanks to Ted Turner and the Turner Broadcasting System, my parents were going to get to see me play baseball a whole lot more than they would have if I had been playing for the Detroit Tigers.

In one year I had gone from being a part of my hometown team, a team that was on the brink of competing for another championship, to this team that just was not very good, but had a guy named Dale Murphy on it. In all reality, it was probably the greatest thing that could have happened to me. No, check that. I *know* it was the greatest thing that ever happened to me.

On the other hand, my trade to Atlanta was not the greatest thing that ever happened to the Tiger grass in my backyard. The beloved Tiger grass caught the brunt of my dad's own anger over the trade. To this day, I don't know how it met its death—by shovel or bare hands—but when I came home from Atlanta the first time, it was dug up and gone and we've never spoken about it again.

Chapter Five

PERSEVERANCE

I'm not lying when I tell you I can remember almost every day after shoulder surgery. I can't tell you much about my other rehabs from my four elbow surgeries, including my yearlong recovery from Tommy John surgery, but my memories after shoulder surgery are vividly clear. It was such a tough surgery, such a tough injury, and it took such an incredibly long time to do *anything* at first.

When I say "anything," I do mean anything. In the beginning, one of the first challenges of any day was simply changing my shirt. As I sat there, struggling to manipulate a shirt around my stiff and painful shoulder, I didn't let myself dwell on the oppressive reality of the situation. As I wriggled my head into my shirt, careful not to torque my shoulder, I didn't let myself wallow in the obvious fact that my road back to the major leagues was so long that it had to begin first with conquering the now-tedious tasks of daily life. I was so intent on coming back and pitching again, I had so much to prove to myself, that I just trudged forward almost blindly. Odds be darned.

Every single day after surgery revolved around getting back onto the mound. Even during those early days—when the pain was so arresting that even sitting still in my favorite recliner hurt—I physically willed myself to get up and literally start moving in whatever way I could.

In those early weeks, about all I could really stand to do was go putt. It became my routine that after icing my shoulder, I would go outside to my practice green right behind my house. I would stand there for a few minutes, letting my shoulder thaw out and warm up in the heat of the Atlanta summer, and then I would start making tiny putting strokes. I couldn't move much at all in the beginning. We're talking about being able to draw the putter back maybe an inch or two at a time. All I worked on in the beginning was trying to attain that pendulum-swinging motion, back and forth, nice and easy. And I would do it over and over and over again, *tick tock, tick tock*.

Every day, religiously, I went out and worked on it. It became a daily game, a daily competition for me, to see how far I could swing. Putting golf balls provided two things I sorely needed: progress I could measure and the chance to have a little fun.

The doctors had given me a post-procedure protocol to follow, and follow it I did, but I knew their program wasn't enough for me. I knew if there was any chance of pitching again next year, I had to be more aggressive. I employed the help of Peter Hughes, one of the trainers who had been working with me for the last ten to twelve years of my career, and together we got after it. We approached rehab in a fairly unconventional way, but we never did anything counter to what the doctors were having me do. There's a distinct difference between pushing the envelope and being a little reckless. There's a fine line between being aggressive and potentially hurting yourself, and we always respected that line.

When it came down to it, rehab was an art and a science that my trainers and I had been perfecting since the beginning of my career, and not by choice.

We traded Doyle Alexander for this?!

Those were the thoughts racing through Dr. Joe Chandler's mind as he examined me for the very first time in August 1987, days after I had been traded to the Atlanta Braves.

Unbeknownst to me at the time, while the Braves' team physician performed my routine physical, cycling through all my body parts, he grew more and more alarmed. Every joint—not just my shoulder, but my elbows, knees, ankles, and hips—was double-jointed and hyper-mobile. My shoulder was actually so loose he could dislocate it four different ways on the exam table. There was no way around it: From a medical standpoint, my physical makeup was not suited for pitching in the major leagues.

Dr. Chandler was completely baffled. Why in the world would Atlanta ever agree to trade a proven veteran with nice, tight joints like Doyle for me, a six-foot-three, 210-pound Gumby? But that was before he ever saw me pitch. It wasn't until he saw me on the mound that he started to understand.

You see, the natural looseness in my joints was part of my gift with the baseball. I exploited it with every pitch, tapping into that extraordinary flexibility throughout my entire motion. If you think of a pitcher's arm as being a slingshot, I could draw that elastic band back a few degrees farther than most guys. It doesn't sound like much, but the fact that I could cock my elbow and shoulder back so far translated into my ability to throw a baseball 98 mph. That's where the external flexibility in my shoulder came into play. I also had internal flexibility, which meant that I was able to stay on the ball, or keep it in my hand, a split second longer than most guys before releasing it. I could extend my shoulder well past the normal stopping point, allowing me to be able to locate pitches with a fairly high degree of precision. Essentially, thanks to the hypermobility in my joints, I could throw a fastball on the outside corner pretty much anytime I wanted. Dr. Chandler likes to describe my pitching as a "God-given gift of neuromuscular balance and control." I would just say I have always been able to manipulate a baseball in ways that other guys couldn't.

After he saw me on the mound, Dr. Chandler got it: My looseness was an incredible blessing; it was a big part of what made me the pitcher I was. But medical science still told him another story: My joints were likely to be my curse someday.

The deck was stacked against me, physically speaking, before I ever began my big-league career. On the one hand, there was my unique physical makeup, this incredible looseness in my joints, and on the other hand, there was a lingering injury from high school that I would contend with throughout my entire career.

As a freshman in high school, I had suffered a pretty serious injury in the first game of a doubleheader. While I was running from first to second base during the game, something popped in my groin and it felt like I had been shot in the leg. I literally tumbled to the ground and rolled. The second baseman tagged me out and all the guys laughed at me because they thought it was just a spectacular trip. Unfortunately, it wasn't a case of being clumsy; I had pulled something in my groin and it was bad.

Injury or not, my coach was not about to put me on the bench for the second game. I had played shortstop in the first game, but I was supposed to pitch in the second. He told me to just wrap my leg and keep walking, in order to keep it from tightening up. So, like a dummy, I listened to him. I wrapped it and walked the rest of the entire first game so I could stay loose and still be able to pitch. Honestly, I knew at the time it wasn't the smartest thing to do, but that's just how important baseball was to me—and obviously to my coach, too—back then. He should have known better, for sure, but I can't deny my part in it. I was the one who walked that entire game, falling down occasionally whenever I would slightly tweak it again, but still going out and pitching five innings on it. It was not my smartest move of all time.

Every time the other team would bunt or hit a soft roller back in my direction that would cause me to run after the ball, I'd fall. Suffice to say, by the time I went to see a doctor after the game, I had done such damage to my groin area that I was out for seven or eight weeks.

Something about the location of the injury and the fact that my hips are so prone to sublux, or dislocate, left me with some chronic instability in my lower body. In those first years in the big leagues, it was not uncommon for me to be walking along and just fall to the ground for no apparent reason. There were certain movements that would trigger it, and pain would shoot through my leg and I would just drop to my knees. Other times, it would feel like something popped out of place slightly. Like on the mound, I always had to be really careful about reaching over to pick up the rosin bag. More often than not, when I bent over, I would feel something shift slightly out of alignment and I just wouldn't be able to pitch right afterward.

The Braves knew that they had acquired a young pitcher with a dynamic arm, but they obviously had some concerns about the long-term sustainability of what I was doing. It wasn't helping my cause that over the course of a season there would be about twelve or thirteen times when I threw a pitch that wasn't exactly mechanically sound and my shoulder would dislocate slightly on the mound. Even I knew it didn't look good whenever I had to come back in from pitching an inning and hang from the roof of the dugout as I carefully worked my shoulder back into place.

The Braves understandably wanted to take a proactive stance toward protecting the investment they had made in me and were interested in pursuing options that would help sustain my pitching career. For them, the most logical course of action was surgery. They thought it was critical to go in and try to counter the looseness and surgically alter my shoulder joint.

While I completely understood and frankly shared their concerns, I was totally against surgery as the first course of action. I always viewed surgery as the kiss of death for my career and I avoided it like the plague as a matter of course. As I look back now, maybe there were times I was overly stubborn about it, but right there at that point in my career, I am absolutely convinced I did the right thing. My loose joints allowed me to do what I did, and be the pitcher I was; shoulder surgery at this point would have changed *everything*.

That said, I knew I had to do something, so I enlisted the help of my agent at the time, Myles Shoda, and he ended up introducing me to Chris Verna. Chris was hailed as a nonconventional trainer, which maybe would have concerned some people, but I was up for trying anything short of surgery. And honestly, it sounded like a good fit to me because I certainly had a nontraditional body. Chris turned out to be an absolute guru; he's just one of those guys who can look at a body the way an architect looks at a building. I would never have played for as long as I did without Chris Verna and later Peter Hughes. I have no idea what my career would have turned into, or even if there would have been one.

Chris had come in to address my shoulder issue, but he didn't come in and just work on that joint exclusively. Chris examined my entire body, noting not only the looseness in my joints, but also the muscular imbalances throughout my body, and the peculiar aftermath of my high school groin injury. Chris looked at my body as a whole and quickly realized that the key to unlocking some of my shoulder issues was first to unlock my hips.

Before I started working with Chris, pitching coaches had always told me that I needed to improve the way I finished pitches. Meaning, when I would throw a pitch early in my career, I was likely to be almost falling off the mound and almost spinning out like a car hitting the brakes at the last second. I knew what they wanted me to do and why I needed to do it, not only to be more mechanically sound, but also to finish in a better defensive position, but the problem was I just couldn't ever physically do it. Chris helped me understand not only why I was struggling with this, but how I could fix it. Chris helped me change my body so I could change my mechanics.

Without getting into all of it, Chris showed me that I had been relying on the bigger muscles in my hips and the external rotation in the joint. The key was developing and working on the smaller muscles in my groin, and getting me to be able to rotate internally as well. By doing this, he helped me be able to better sync up my hips and my shoulder so that my shoulder wasn't constantly being overexerted.

Chris drew up a plan to systematically address all of these problems and we began to attack my weaknesses with an aggressive regimen of stretching and strengthening. Working with Chris, I started to gain the proper rotational flexibility in all my joints, and it made such a difference. He was able to strengthen my shoulder in a way I never thought possible. Working with Chris, I came to know my body inside and out and I became attuned to how things should feel and where things should be. Knowing my body like this and having someone like Chris by my side would prove critical time and time again throughout my career when it came to deciphering what was ailing me and what I could do to overcome it.

We made remarkable progress that first off-season, allowing my shoulder to go from dislocating thirteen times that year to only two times the next. And eventually it never happened again. Chris helped me get my shoulder to a place where it could stand the test of time. In addition, he figured out a way to manipulate my hips back into position whenever they did sublux. This was a critical discovery because despite all the work I did to prevent it, it was something that continued to plague me throughout my career. I eventually had to teach the Braves' trainers the technique that Chris had perfected so whenever or wherever my hips got out of alignment—like on the road in Los Angeles, thirty minutes before game time—they could get them back in place. I can't tell you how many games I would have missed in my career had I never figured this out.

When it comes to what I had to do to be successful, I know there are people who have worked harder than me, but I don't think there are many. My body was always a burden that I had to deal with, but understanding the burden made it an asset for me. It made it possible for me to push my body in ways that just didn't seem possible to some people.

When it came down to it, I really had no choice. If I wanted to have a baseball career, there were certain things that I had to do. All the strengthening and stretching basically bought me time, allowing me to squeeze as many innings and as many years out of my body as I possibly could. But Dr. Chandler would always be right in the end. My loose joints would eventually become my curse.

Throughout the course of my career in pro baseball I suffered more injuries than I care to admit. They have varied from your typical, run-of-the-mill nicks, bumps, and bruises to those that required surgical intervention on five different occasions. It's hard to say definitively what caused everything, because truthfully, there are a lot of dynamics to consider. Not the least of which was my habit of avoiding surgery and the disabled list at all costs.

Obviously, I was a pitcher who came with some physical baggage: namely, my genetic predisposition to incredibly loose joints and the groin injury from high school. In addition to those two factors, I endured the same reality that all pitchers face, the fact that the profession of pitching is going to naturally create discomforts from time to time. My response to those discomforts was to make adjustments to override them and pitch through pain as a matter of course.

If you liken my professional career to a game of dominoes, it seemed like a lot of times there was one thing affecting another thing, which affected another thing. I would do whatever it took to take the mound, altering one part of my delivery to override one particular ache or pain, which sometimes caused a whole other problem down the road. It's safe to say mine was a career at times held together with duct tape and bailing wire.

On top of the domino effect of all the factors I just described, I would also argue that the problems that plagued my elbow starting in 1992 up until the time I had Tommy John surgery in 2000 were at least in part the product of continual postseason play. During that time period, the Atlanta Braves not only made the playoffs, but we made deep runs in the playoffs, making it all the way to the World Series four times.

The privilege of playing in the postseason is accompanied by the price of playing in the postseason. I just got done broadcasting parts of the 2011 playoffs for TBS, and people listening at home probably got tired of me making this point, but it's absolutely true: Pitching one inning in the postseason is like pitching two or three in the regular season. It's that much more stress and that much more important. I always pitched a postseason game as if it was my last game ever because it always could be. You never knew how many opportunities you were going to have to get the ball in October. Getting after it like it was my last time out meant I was constantly reaching into the upper ranges of my velocity and throwing the fastest fastballs I could muster. And those pitches, the ones that you are really trying to zing in there, are the ones that really start to take their toll after a while.

The fact is that if you go to the World Series, you play an additional month of baseball and endure a whole additional month of wear and tear on your body. During the run-up to the Series, a starting pitcher could possibly pitch five times; that's about the most you can reasonably fit in, and after that, you're spent. You're so completely exhausted that it's going to take a lot longer to recover. But since the World Series typically ends on almost the last day in October, the one thing you don't have the luxury of is time. You can really only afford to take November completely off, because by late December it's time to start the whole process all over again. Pretty soon it's February and spring training is only a couple weeks away. That's just not a lot of time for the body to rest and heal.

I wouldn't be so inclined to point to the postseason if I was prone to bad mechanics, or if I made a habit of throwing pitches that banged my elbow all the time, but that really wasn't the case. Now, granted, things might have been different if I had just thrown eighty-five or eighty-seven miles an hour; I might not have had as many problems. But I probably wouldn't have as many wins as I had in the postseason either.

At the end of the day, I did what I had to do to sustain the run and deal with my injuries, and I realize there were consequences to the way I approached it. But at the same time, knowing what I know now, I wouldn't change a single thing. Make no mistake about it, I would have gone to the postseason every year if given the opportunity, even if it meant shortening my career. In the end, I was a unique pitcher who had some amazing opportunities and I was never going to let the pain in my elbow deprive me of the opportunity to pitch in the postseason.

Well, until 2000 anyway.

My elbow was basically destined to be a victim from the beginning. From the velocity of the pitches I liked to throw to the unique ability I had to torque my shoulder, which in turn put enormous pressure on my elbow, my elbow was simply not going to be able to withstand everything.

From 1992 to 1998, I could feel the trouble brewing in my elbow.

The pain wasn't severe to the point where you'd see me grimace a lot; that really came later. This was a gradual buildup, a gradual progression over time, as my ulnar collateral ligament grew more and more inflamed. It came to a point where I just knew when I got ready to release the ball, I was going to feel a nice sting; my elbow was going to let me know that I'd just thrown a pitch.

Finesse pitches always hurt me more than the velocity pitches. I would always feel it more when I threw a slider, a curveball, or a changeup, because those pitches required me to put that little spin on the ball with my fingers. It was that fine movement, similar to turning a doorknob, that would trigger the pain in my elbow. So, with that said, I would oftentimes choose to use velocity to work around the pain, choosing to just throw fastballs instead.

There's also a lot to be said for the adrenaline I felt during a game. I certainly was blessed with a high pain tolerance, but I was perhaps also blessed with an abundance of adrenaline. I always found that once I got heated up in the moment, I could sustain a lot of discomfort. It was when I had to sit down and cool off and wake up the next day that things got a little difficult. Everyday movements like putting a golf tee in the ground, or even using my right hand to grab the bill of my baseball cap and adjust it—those things would *kill* me. I know it seems a little crazy, but even when those things were unbearable, I could still throw a baseball 94 mph because I could overcome that little intricate movement during the game.

As I continued to pitch, my elbow continued to deteriorate, and my symptoms followed suit. There came a point in 1994 where I woke up in Denver and I could not even fully extend my elbow; it was basically locked in this ninety-degree angle. Of course, I tried to figure out a way to pitch with it, but eventually the team had to scratch my start and send me back to Atlanta to see Dr. Chandler. I was actually incredibly fortunate to have this happen the day before the strike that year, so I was given the gift of time to address the issue.

Dr. Chandler told me it was likely that my elbow was suffering from bone chips and bone spurs and he recommended surgery to go in and remove them. But early on in the strike, when there was this sense that there still might be a chance to resume the season, I was against surgery. I applied myself to figuring out whatever I could do to try to work with my elbow and get it back in shape to play again, but things didn't look promising. Dr. Chandler would drain fluid off of it, up to 15 cc's at a time, every other week, but it would just keep filling right back up. Fortunately for me, the strike eventually canceled the rest of the season and the postseason, so I elected to go forward with my first elbow surgery to clean up my bone chips and bone spurs. Thanks to the strike, I was able to have surgery in what would otherwise have been the middle of the season, allowing me enough time to heal and recover and not miss any time the next season. As a fan of baseball, I hated the work stoppage, but I have to admit the timing of the strike could not have been better for my elbow.

In these early years of dealing with my elbow woes, some people thought that I was a hypochondriac—that the pain was just in my head. It was a label that I grew out of over time, thankfully, and rightfully so, because I was by no means a hypochondriac. But I knew my Achilles' heel was always what everybody saw. Let's face it, when you're watching someone throw the ball ninety-three or ninety-four miles an hour, it can be hard to believe there can be anything wrong with him. And honestly, if I had been on the other side, I probably would have been saying the same thing. And that's frustrating because I knew I felt it and I knew it was real. In a way, I always felt reassured when the doctors opened me up, and went in and did surgery and told me what they saw, because it reaffirmed the truth of what I was feeling and what was causing it.

I would eventually have one more surgery performed to remove bone chips and bone spurs. It was after this second procedure, performed in December 1997, that Dr. Chandler started really explaining to me that these bone chips and bone spurs that my elbow was producing were a precursor to an underlying problem: My ulnar collateral ligament was compromised. What I really needed was Tommy John surgery.

When I heard the words *Tommy John surgery*, all I heard was "one year out of the game." I didn't know how I would recover from surgery at this point, almost a decade into my career, and I wasn't interested in finding out until it was absolutely the last option. Sure, my UCL was probably partially torn, but plenty of pitchers had pitched with a partially torn UCL before. Nolan Ryan for one. And here's the thing: I could still throw the ball ninety-three or ninety-four miles an hour. I wasn't about to take an entire year off to have surgery just to be pain-free if I could still throw ninety-four. As long as I could still be effective, I could care less about the pain. In my mind, it was only time to have surgery if I could no longer contribute to the team.

Toward the bitter end in 1999, there were days when the pain was so great that I was very limited with my pitch selection. The fact is, I couldn't repeat a slider too many times when my elbow was really inflamed. At times, there was a pretty narrow lane that I stayed in in order to compete, but that didn't mean I couldn't win. When I got out on the mound, my elbow was not going to be an excuse; I was going to pitch until they took the ball from me. I don't claim to be tougher than anybody else, but when it comes to competing, I always found a way to get my mind off the pain and a way to get the job done.

I would sometimes get criticized for the way I pitched a baseball game, by certain broadcasters or members of the media, but they didn't know what was really going on. They had no idea that there were things I couldn't physically bear to do on the mound. It would have been nice to be able to defend myself or even explain myself, but I wasn't about to say anything. If a hitter had known I was vulnerable, if the other team knew I was limited in what I could do, it certainly would have affected my game and my effectiveness. The people who needed to know—my trainer, my doctor, my pitching coach, my manager—all knew. But nobody knew on the other side.

The 1999 season would prove to be the most painful. Eventually it got so bad I couldn't even come over the top anymore to release the ball as I had always done. I had finally reached the point where I wasn't able to override the pain with velocity, and this is where I really had to get creative. I basically had to reinvent myself as a pitcher to work around my elbow.

I finally went to Leo Mazzone, the Braves' pitching coach, and told him I had to do something else and I wanted to try dropping my delivery down and throwing more sidearm. Leo gave me the green light and I got to work on my latest great idea.

As it turns out, I had one side session in which to work on it before I took the mound against the Houston Astros. A side session, by the way, is a short workout done between starts in the bullpen—we're talking maybe forty, sixty pitches max. Anyway, I just started messing with it, inventing pitches, throwing from different angles, really just using my imagination and figuring out what might work. At the end of the session, I turned to Leo and said, "At least it doesn't hurt, I gotta go with it." And he goes, "Go ahead." Thank God I had a pitching coach who was obviously extremely tolerant with me and all my new ideas.

So here I am, about to make my next start and about to throw with this low three-quarters delivery in a game for the very first time. Now, obviously the Astros had no idea I had been working on this and I will never forget throwing that first pitch to Craig Biggio. I blew one right past him and he just stood there with his bat on his shoulder and looked at me like "You gotta be kidding me!" He turned around to look at the dugout as if to say, *Where'd this come from?!* I pitched the whole game with this new arm slot, going seven innings, allowing eleven hits but only two runs. I had found another way to adjust and be successful, and I ran with it the rest of the season, making ten more starts down the stretch. My 3–3 record really doesn't capture how well I was pitching with my low three-quarters delivery, but what does is my ERA. When I started the game against the Astros, it stood at 3.57, but from that point on, with only two slight upticks, it was headed in a steady slide, bottoming out at 3.19 for the season.

When we ended up making the World Series in 1999, I didn't get a chance to pitch until Game Four, when we were already down three games to none to the New York Yankees. I wanted so badly to notch a win for our team, and maybe change our fate, that I just decided, *The heck with the pain, I'm coming over the top again.* So I did.

It was a gritty performance, but I still managed a quality outing on the biggest stage of baseball, striking out eleven and giving up six hits and three earned runs in seven innings. Unfortunately, we only managed to put up one run, and we would eventually lose the game and be swept out of the Series—a Series that was much closer than we get credit for. It turned to be the only elimination game I ever lost. I put everything that I had in the game to try and keep it going, but you just have to tip your hat to the Yankees.

After that game, I had to take a hard look at what my next year in baseball was going to be like. In my assessment, I couldn't go through another year like I just went through, but I had already made the determination in my mind that I wasn't going to have Tommy John surgery. So the question was "What's the next best thing for me?" The next thing for me, as I saw it, was going to be the knuckleball.

I had flirted with the knuckleball at times during 1999, and while it showed promise, I knew it wasn't ready for me to rely on as a permanent part of my pitch selection. At this point in the off-season, that was about to change. My thinking was, if I could pair a really good knuckleball with my still-good fastball (which I could still throw with limited discomfort), I just might have an effective combination.

So with that said, I spent hours and hours at an indoor facility near my house, beating up a poor catcher, and throwing knuckleball after knuckleball after knuckleball. It was frustrating, it was painstaking, but I felt confident that with enough time and attention I could really develop a major league knuckleball.

When spring training rolled around, I told my manager, Bobby Cox, and pitching coach, Leo Mazzone, "Look, I have no other options; you are going to have to bear with me, but I am going to work all spring on knuckleballs."

When I told the catchers about my new pitch, I warned them it was nasty. I told them they better go get bigger gloves and they all laughed; they were generally amused by me and my new idea right up until I threw my first knuckleball of spring training and promptly plunked Eddie Pérez in his opposite arm. He never even got a glove on it. They weren't quite so amused after that. Like I said, it was nasty, and I needed to practice.

All the work I had put into perfecting a knuckleball unfortunately did not translate into one more season for me. I didn't make it any further than my first spring training game. I never felt anything pop in my elbow, but about two hours after the game, the pain was unbelievable. I knew I had really done something when I couldn't even bear to use a fork or rest my elbow on a table. The doctors did an MRI and the results were conclusive: My ligament was finally torn. The time for Tommy John surgery had arrived.

In my career, I think it's safe to say I went as far and as long as I could in the effort to adapt and overcome discomfort and pain. Sometimes my adjustments worked and sometimes they didn't. Sometimes there were consequences to contend with down the road, but it was always my choice to continue to pitch. That's just the way I handled it. As an athlete, you know that whenever you're not feeling 100 percent right, the outcome could be something less than what you want. At that point you have two choices. You can adapt and overcome the pain, or you can shut it down. By shutting it down, you eliminate the

STARTING AND CLOSING | 69

chance that failure will happen, but you also eliminate the chance that success could happen.

I never ever wanted to shut it down and I was never interested in playing it safe. There's obviously a time to be strategic and act conservatively, but if I had played it safe, I never would have experienced half of what I experienced in my career. I think if you get in the habit of playing it safe all the time, you risk suffocating yourself and the greatness that can come out of you. I think you can miss out on some things. No one wants to get knocked down, but sometimes you've got to get nicked and beat up a little bit before you can experience what lies ahead; it makes you tougher.

As it was, I think I missed the least amount of time that I could have missed with five surgeries. I missed all of 2000 after Tommy John; there's no way to avoid that. But when you think about the big picture and five total surgeries, I really didn't miss that much time.

The number one golden rule in baseball is you can't make the club in the tub, but I think I might be the first exception to that rule. I had to invest a lot of time in the trainers' room, way more than I would have liked, but it was essential to keeping me at the level I needed to be in in order to pitch. On that note, I would be remiss not to recognize Dave Pursley, Jeff Porter, and Jim Lovell, the trainers for the Atlanta Braves during my time, for their patience with me. The time they spent with me was invaluable.

I honestly had to do things outside the box; I had to work very hard and incorporate nontraditional methods because I had a very nontraditional body. And I was incredibly fortunate to have a man like Dr. Chandler with me in this journey. His willingness to think outside the box as an orthopedic surgeon was *crucial* for me. I spent more time with him than with my family at times trying to solve this puzzle of a body.

Pitching through pain helped make me the pitcher that I was and it gave me the opportunity to experience some of the greatest moments of my career. I am absolutely serious when I say that I pitched some of my greatest games in some of my worst conditions.

The principles I used to push myself through adversity in my career are applicable in real life in many ways, whether you are trying to start a new career, get out of debt, or even run a 5K for the first time. I think most people can get started down the right road, but then it seems like the natural tendency is to give up at the first sign of trouble, or the first taste of failure. It's really easy to convince ourselves that once we've reached a certain point, we aren't capable of going any further. I think my pitching career stands as proof that those limits are mostly in your mind; we all have that capacity to surprise ourselves and attain or achieve things we never thought were possible.

Chapter Six

BULLPEN BUSINESS

I guarantee I would never have made it back to pitching after shoulder surgery if I hadn't spent my entire career figuring out ways to push through pain, adapt, and overcome. The rehab process from shoulder surgery was so long and so tedious that I don't know if I'd have been able to overcome everything quite as well as I did if I hadn't approached things the way I did.

As I said, rehab can be a grind. Even the most motivated people can get bored doing the same stretches and exercises over and over again. I know *I* did, so I tapped into the creativity I honed during Michigan winters and tried to always find ways to keep things fun and interesting. When it came to rehab, I just did things that made sense to me. And whenever I could work in doing something I loved to do anyway, it was a huge bonus. Maybe I did things that were a little bit aggressive, but I was always in tune with my body.

Perhaps one of the more unorthodox parts of my rehab program after shoulder surgery was fitting in time to mow my lawn. I stumbled upon mowing as a recovery technique sort of by accident. I happen to be one of those guys who just loves to ride around on a tractor and cut the grass. I don't know why, I just enjoy it. So for me, I can't tell you how satisfying it was to finally be healed enough to be able to get up on my lawn mower for the first time. Not only was it nice to get out and do something I enjoyed doing, but it was a relief to feel useful and productive for a change. I pride myself on taking care of my family and my property, and early on after surgery, I could barely change a lightbulb. I soon realized, though, that mental gratification wasn't the only thing I stood to gain from mowing.

When I gripped the steering wheel the first time after surgery, I could feel this trembling motion travel up my arm and into my shoulder. I really can't tell you what it was doing for me, but it just felt good and it *felt* like it was doing something for me. It takes me seven and a half hours to mow my entire lawn, and sometimes, during the summer especially, it can be hard to keep up with it. Rest assured that this was never the case during my rehab. And that constant vibration, that little pulsating motion—I'm convinced that it helped me heal.

Another part of my rehab program that would probably be considered a little unusual was my actual throwing progression. While it's absolutely true that every single thing I did during rehab was done with the intention of getting me back to being able to throw a baseball, I didn't actually work on throwing a baseball before I had already worked on throwing a football. In my mind, throwing a football was actually a natural precursor to throwing a baseball. You don't use your whole range of motion like you do when you throw a baseball and you can just toss it nice and easy and still get that movement in your shoulder. And I love to throw a football anyway, so this was a no-brainer addition to my recovery plan.

Throwing footballs also served as another useful measuring stick when it came to judging my progress. The first time I was healthy enough to even attempt throwing a football, I couldn't lob it more than ten yards. I still remember standing there and just feeling depressed, really almost pathetic. I mean, ten yards is *nothing*.

But every day I kept working at it. From a distance, maybe it looked like a mindless game of catch with my trainer Peter Hughes, but it was really a mental and physical workout for me. I really concentrated on my mechanics as I threw and focused on rebuilding the muscle memory in my shoulder so I could naturally repeat a smooth, steady throwing motion.

As I got stronger, I was able to gradually lengthen out my tosses. Whenever I got some air under one, I would make Pete stay right where he caught it so I could come pace it off. Inevitably I would think the ball had traveled farther than it did. And inevitably I would soon be chastising myself: *Thirty-eight yards?! Are you kidding me? Come on!* Throwing was serious business to me.

I eventually reached my goal of being able to throw a football fifty yards, and I did take some pride in that, but it was still frustrating knowing I used to be able to really chuck it a lot farther. I'm really not exaggerating when I say there used to be a time in my life when I could throw a football seventy, seventy-five yards no problem. It's just something I was always able to do. I've always been able to throw a baseball really hard and a football really long. Well, before surgery anyway.

When I was finally physically ready to throw a baseball for the first time, I'm not going to lie: There was a *ton* of apprehension. Mentally, I wasn't quite prepared for the moment not to go well. I was so anxious; I remember just standing there just hoping that everything would feel all right.

When I rocked back on my right leg for the first time with a baseball in my right hand, I was struck by this almost overwhelming feeling of nostalgia. Once my weight had shifted back, my body just took over and knew what to do. As my arm and shoulder rose together and cocked back behind me, I half expected to feel something—pain or tightness—or God forbid, hear something—like *snap, crackle,* or *pop*—but there was nothing but the old feeling of my muscles working together in the way they always had. As I followed through and released the ball nice and easy, I just broke into a smile. It was in that moment that I truly knew I would be able to pitch again in 2009.

I never doubted that I wouldn't make it back to pitching, but when you are recovering from a major surgery, it's hard to predict how many setbacks you're going to encounter along the way. The amazing thing is I never had an issue really, and it's remarkable when you think about it, because the odds were practically insurmountable. Shoulder surgery for any pitcher would more than likely end their career. For me, at age forty-one, it was not only more than likely; it was practically a done deal.

It wasn't the first time it really looked like my career might be over, and it also wasn't the first time that things were headed in a direction that I never intended. The parallels between 2009 and 2001 would prove to be eerily similar, but thankfully odds and uncertainty were all things I had conquered before.

"I'm done. I quit. I just can't do this anymore."

It was June 9, 2001. The visitors' clubhouse at Yankee Stadium. As the starting rosters of the Atlanta Braves and the New York Yankees took the field to start the top of the fourth inning, I was certainly not where I thought I'd be at this moment in time. Instead of sitting in the dugout with my jacket slung over my right shoulder, trying to keep my arm warm as our guys came up to bat, I was slumped in my chair in the clubhouse, staring at my locker and hopelessly rubbing my right elbow. Having just finished ranting out loud about my likely retirement, I sat there thinking, *How the heck did I get here?*

It's not like I was suffering from short-term memory loss; I was certainly aware of why I was no longer in the game. My manager, Bobby Cox, had just yanked me after only three innings. It had been an uneven performance, to say the least. I had managed to squeeze in one lone good inning in between two dismal ones. I had thrown seventy pitches—although forty-one had been strikes—and given up six hits and four runs, all earned, thus inflating my ERA to nearly 6.0.

The third inning had gone so poorly that when Yankee catcher Todd Greene mercifully hit a routine fly ball to right field for the third out of the inning, even I knew what was coming. All I had to do was glance at Bobby as I strode off the mound and headed toward the dugout; I saw the look on his face and I knew my day was done. He was talking to me as I walked down the steps into the dugout, but I don't remember actually hearing what he said. It was like I was temporarily deafened by my own frustration. I was so mad. No, I wasn't just mad; I was literally *fighting* mad. I made a beeline for the door leading to the clubhouse, battling the impulse to take my anger out on anything in my path until I was out of sight of the TV cameras.

When I finally got to the safe haven of the clubhouse, I stormed over to my locker, ripped off my uniform, and threw everything on the ground. When my glove had the audacity to ricochet a good ten feet away, I stomped over, retrieved it, and violently launched it back toward my locker. Nobody had a radar gun handy at the moment, but I'm telling you, that thing had some juice on it. It was easily the hardest thing I had thrown all afternoon. As I watched my "Wilson heater" hurtle through the air, I felt a little better, almost relieved, but the feeling was oh so very brief. About the time I heard the satisfying *thwack* of my glove crashing into the back of my locker, I let out an involuntary sound of my own: the unmistakable yelp of pain. I instinctively grabbed my right elbow and slunk down in my chair, completely defeated.

So, in a very literal sense, that's how I came to be seated in front of my locker. What my mind was really busy chewing on was the bigger picture: What had it all been for? The surgery, the entire last year spent on the disabled list, all the rehab, all the hours and hours of preparing to pitch again. How in the world was I here, nursing my elbow after another poor start in my fifth time out this season? Not only had I not yet regained my usual form, it seemed like I was regressing every time I picked up a ball. And the icing on this cake of self-pity was that my elbow hurt worse right now than it ever had before. It was just *unbelievable*. And I just thought, *Well, that's it.* Obviously, the surgery and all the work had been for nothing. As far as I was concerned, you could stick a fork in me: I was done.

The trainers and coaching staff had wisely kept their distance while I did my best Happy Gilmore impression. Now, as I calmed down and regained my senses, they began to approach me. I honestly wasn't in the mood to listen to anybody, but somehow they managed to talk me out of retiring on the spot. Everyone agreed that I should just take some time and head down to Birmingham to see Dr. Andrews again. The more I listened, the more the fog of anger seemed to lift and I started to think a little less emotionally. By the time the game ended, I was ready to run everything by Bobby. He was immediately on board with the plan. Everyone seemed to agree that the best course of action was to let the experts take another look at my right elbow before any decisions were made about how many innings were left in it. For once, I wasn't holding my breath.

Of course, as the story goes, it was not the end for me. I got down to Birmingham, went through all the exams, and—sure enough—Dr. Andrews told me I just had severe tendonitis. The surgically repaired ligament was still intact, but it was inflamed and irritated. He told me, "You're fine, just wait it out." All the staff members agreed, telling me essentially that with enough rest and therapy, my elbow should be back to normal soon. Whatever *normal* was, at this point.

As I boarded the plane back home, I was grateful but sullen. I was certainly relieved that my career was not yet over, but I was brooding over the additional delays now forecasted before my eventual return. I didn't want to wait anymore. I don't wait well under any circumstance, let alone coming off an entire *year* of waiting. My idle meter was already pegged and here I was flying back to Atlanta to go hurry up and sit on the bench.

I did try to wait it out for a while. I went to the park every day, did my physical therapy, got my treatment, and then sat on the bench and tried to be the best teammate I could be. I tried to be okay with it, to make peace with my situation, but the longer I sat there in the dugout, the more worthless I felt. Watching all the guys go out and bust their butts every day—hustling down to first just in case the shortstop bobbled their routine line drive, backing up throws, and diving into the bleachers to try to snag foul balls—it just ate at me. Especially as I sat there with the modern-day buffet of dugout eats—an array of sunflower seeds, bubble gum, and peanuts—at arm's reach: I felt like such a slug, and my appetite for all of it, especially the sweet and salty snacks, quickly waned.

Ultimately, I would sit there staring out at the field and brainstorming my situation. Was there any way to get back on the mound sooner rather than later? Was there any way to contribute to the team in a meaningful way this year instead of spending another season on the bench? Finally, I worked out a plan in my head and I went to see my manager.

"Bobby," I said as I sat down in his office. "I want to go to the minor leagues and start rehabbing as a reliever."

Bobby sort of smirked and then just shook his head. "Nope," he said. "I'm going to wait for you as a starter."

I had expected this reaction. For years, I had been offering to help out in the bullpen, especially in the postseason, but Bobby was always against it. He had only taken me up on my offer twice, and with mixed results. I made my first two relief appearances in 1999.

The first time I came out for the ninth inning of Game Two of the National League Championship Series against the New York Mets. I pitched well, retiring three batters in succession, and earned my first save. But when Bobby called on me again in Game Six, I got lit up. I surrendered four runs on four hits—two doubles, a single, and a two-run homer to Mike Piazza—in one-third of an inning. I was in and out of the game so fast that fans who happened to be up hitting the restroom or grabbing another beer at the time probably didn't even realize I had come in at all.

Undeterred by one shaky past performance, I continued to sell my plan, laying out my case like a lawyer presenting his evidence to the judge. "Bobby, I can't start right now. There is just nothing. I just don't have it back yet," I said. "But I can help you guys as a reliever, I'm telling you."

I could tell by the look on his face that he was still not convinced this was a good idea, and my hopes were sinking by the second. I seriously felt almost physically ill as I sat there visualizing myself riding the bench for the foreseeable future, when he finally broke the silence. "Well, look, you can go give it a try," he said. "But," he quickly added, "I'd rather wait on you to come back and start."

That's the eternal optimist in Bobby. But I knew that if I was going to help *this* team *this* year, it would have to be out of the bullpen.

I sat there for a second, sort of taking in the irony of the moment. There I was sitting in my manager's office, thanking God that I had convinced him to send me down to the minors. Here I was at another point in my career that I could never have foreseen or imagined. But all I knew to do was to try to make the best of things and I knew going down to the minors presented me with the best chance of contributing to the team this season. And really anything at this point, even the minors, beat sitting on the bench.

So with Bobby's reluctant endorsement, I went to the minor leagues. It was a completely different experience for me, and I am not even talking about getting back on the buses after more than a decade in the bigs. I'm talking about coming out of the bullpen. It was so different from starting, but the limited work—one to two innings at a shot—was perfect for where I was in my recovery. It really helped me ease back into throwing hard while still facing real batters.

My arm still wasn't ready to go six or seven innings, but I could certainly put in one or two innings of work every other day. Eventually I could pitch on back-to-back nights. As my arm began to strengthen and shore up, my confidence followed. Soon I got to the point where I could throw three days in a row. After that, it wasn't long before I got called back up and was on a flight bound for Atlanta. I was eager to get back to business and prove to my team and myself that I still had something to contribute this season.

The first time I got a chance to talk to Bobby, he was as noncommittal about using me as a reliever as he'd been before. He just said, "Look, I don't know when I'm going to use you, but the first chance I can, I'll work you into the game." That was certainly good enough for me.

The first chance came on July 22. We were up 8–2 at home against the Montreal Expos and Greg Maddux had pitched eight solid innings. Right after he recorded his twenty-fourth out, the phone rang in the bullpen: Bobby was calling for me. I was pumped. I jumped up and started warming up to come out for the ninth. As I stepped out the door, the place went nuts. I came in and pitched a perfect inning, recording three outs in only nine pitches. I had good stuff and my fastball was whistling in at 98 mph. I struck out left fielder Brad Wilkerson to end the game and got mobbed by my teammates. It was awesome. I still remember the look on Bobby's face when I shook hands with him after the game. He just sort of shook his head and said, "Whoa." I think it was right about then that Bobby started to warm up to the idea of having me in the bullpen.

It was just one inning and just one part of the process of figuring out how to pitch effectively in relief, but I did take the time to stop and savor the moment. For the first time in more than a year, I sat in front of my locker after a game completely satisfied with my performance on the field. For the first time that season, I had a game in the books that I could draw confidence from. For the first time in a long time, it felt like things were getting back to normal, even if it was a new normal.

My outings continued to be strong through the remainder of the season, and after bouncing around from working the sixth, seventh, or eighth inning, I finally settled into the closer spot. I ended up saving ten games down the stretch and two more in the postseason. Things went better than even I had expected and I was really proud of the fact that I had taken the risk and found a way to make it work for the betterment of my team.

The problem with my newfound success in the bullpen was that it seemed to be a double-edged sword—everyone seemed to fall in love with it and just started assuming that was where I needed to stay. It seemed as if my career as a starter was almost completely forgotten overnight. Some people were even saying I should have been closing all along. I couldn't believe it. In less than one full season in the bullpen, people had forgotten about the more than two thousand innings I had pitched as a starter, not to mention the 159 regular-season wins and the Cy Young Award I had earned. It was really depressing. As I look back now, all the comments about my future as a closer should have served as a harbinger of things for me, especially as I entered the off-season on the final days of my current contract. Little did I know that I was embarking on what I now fondly refer to as the Off-Season from Hell.

My mom always used to tell me, "John, be careful what you ask for." When it comes to closing, let me tell you, it would have been best for me to listen to Mom. The closing experiment was obviously my idea—I mean, to the point that I had to sell my manager on it at first. But for me, it was just something I was doing to help contribute in the short term. What started out innocently enough ended up sealing my fate as a starter, though, as the Braves front office must have decided somewhere along the line that it was also a very advantageous move for the club's bottom line.

I was about to find out, as we began the process of negotiating my new contract, that General Manager John Schuerholz and I were not on the same page with regard to where I best fit into the Braves' future plans: in the bullpen or in the rotation. The million-dollar question—quite literally in this case—would soon be raised. Did I want to be an Atlanta Brave or did I want to be a starting pitcher? I was about to find out I couldn't have both.

Baseball is a business, no bones about it. For a player, as soon as we sign any contract—for the minors or the majors—we are liable to get traded, released, or otherwise scuttled off to another team, to another league, to another city in another state, with just a moment's notice. When making personnel decisions, baseball GMs don't see us as guys married to wives with good jobs in the area or with kids with their best friends next door and good schools down the street. Admittedly, they really can't if they are going to be as effective as possible. Yet however you look at it, we are really more like pieces on a big chessboard that get shifted to and fro to try to elicit the desired effect: the right pieces in the right places at the right time to make a championship run. Now, I knew all that; I understood it and had come to expect this reality, but I also thought at this point in my career that there would be some . . . I don't even know the best word here . . . *consideration,* I guess, for the fourteen years in which I had literally sacrificed myself for the good of the Atlanta Braves.

I had naively thought my next contract would be easy. I still wanted to be a Brave and I was coming off a season in which I had proven I still had good stuff. I wasn't coming in with a laundry list of unreasonable demands. All I was asking for was a contract that would allow me to resume my real job with the Braves: starting.

As much as a part of me would like to go through and detail all the things that were said to me throughout the negotiations with the Braves, I'm just not going to do it, and for a host of reasons. Not the least of which is that I don't think it accomplishes much to drag out all the things that were said by either party. These types of discussions are best done behind closed doors and kept behind closed doors.

I also want to be clear that while it's safe to say that I have never quite understood or in many cases agreed with John Schuerholz over the years, when it comes down to it, as a player I always respected his position as general manager of the Braves. I respected the hard decisions he had to make every year about who was staying, who was going, and what he could get in return. When it comes down to it, John Schuerholz was paid to make shrewd business decisions, not decisions that made everybody—including me—feel good.

The only part of this negotiation that I think is instructive to bring up is that John told me from the very beginning of the negotiations that "our starting rotation is set, but we want you as closer." It was as shocking to me then as it is even now. He was saying there was no room for me as a starter in Atlanta—it wasn't even an option. If I didn't agree to be a closer, our relationship was over. It was comments along this line that effectively stalled negotiations with the Braves and led to my becoming a free agent.

There were two things that really made this negotiation difficult for me. First, the New York Yankees offered me a five-year deal as a starter for $23 million *more* than the two-year deal the Braves were offering me to close. And second, while it seemed like the Braves were saying that closing would be better for my arm and health, I was suspicious that there was a little more to the story. My sense was that maybe I was really being asked to sign a deal that would only send me to the bullpen for a year.

You see, the next year Greg Maddux's contract would be up. With the way he was pitching, it was going to take a lot of money to keep him in Atlanta. I had a feeling that the Braves were already anticipating the possibility of not being able to re-sign Greg, and if that did happen, they could just ask me to start again since they knew I would always do whatever the team asked me to do. But therein lay the rub: they would then have the luxury of having me in the starting rotation on a closer's (much smaller) salary.

This time, the negotiations came down to the wire. I was literally moments away from signing with the Yankees when the Braves came through with a last-minute adjustment and I became a Brave again. In the end, I signed a three-year deal as a closer with a clause that said that if I did start again, I would get a certain incentive per start. I knew the clause would effectively lock me into closing, but I had decided during the negotiation process that this was probably for the best, at least at that stage anyway. When it came down to it, above all else, it was far more important for me to remain in Atlanta . . . and everyone, including the Braves front office, knew that. Clearly I lost leverage by being so open about my feelings. But at least now I would have a contract that offered incentives if the opportunity did arise for me to rejoin the rotation.

One thing I really want to point out is that I was never trying to get the Braves to make me the highest-paid pitcher in baseball. If it was all about the money, I could have saved myself a lot of trouble and just donned the pinstripes. This was really about wanting to stay with the Braves and wanting to sign a contract that made sense for what they were asking me to do.

Ultimately I made the decision, and not begrudgingly, to stay in Atlanta. Once I signed the contract, the tension was over for me. The process, though it had thrown me for a loop, was now over and my focus was now on embracing this change, on embracing what my team was asking me to do. It was bittersweet because my first love was always starting, but when it came down to it, it wasn't about me. It was about doing whatever it took to help my team win.

So off to the bullpen I went for the next three years.

I figured once the contract had been ironed out, surely the worst of my problems were over for the off-season. Now I could kick back a bit, relax, and start getting ready to throw again. Boy, I couldn't have been more wrong. I was merely beginning part two of the Off-Season from Hell, starring one of the worst injuries of my entire career. It wasn't my elbow again, or my shoulder, and I hadn't even been doing any ironing. Instead it was nothing more dramatic than that little piece of anatomy that separates us humans and primates from the rest of the species on the planet: my opposable thumb. To be more specific, my right thumb, which had been helping me grip and release a baseball since I was old enough to pick one up.

For as long as I can remember, I have always had this ridge on the right side of my right thumb, where the fleshy-meaty part meets my nail. It never was an issue and it never bothered me. I always had a normal-looking nail and everything, so I just assumed it was nothing to worry about. But as the years went on, that little ridge started to hurt every once in a while. And now, in 2002, I had enough with the nagging pain and wanted to do something about it.

So I went to see the docs and everyone decided it was time to cut it open and see what was going on in there. They just used a local anesthetic, so I was wide-awake for the whole procedure, including the part where everyone gasped and the doctor said, "Oh my gosh! Look what's in there!"

Now, this was one of those times when you have to stop and think for a second: *Do I* really *want to look?* It's like when one of your kids yells from the bathroom, "Hey, Dad! Come take a look at this!" You really have to take a moment and ask yourself, *Do I really want to know?*

Well, I looked. My swollen thumb—about the size of fingerling potato at this point, and I am only slightly exaggerating—was spewing forth pus. I mean, it was just unnatural. It turns out that all along, my nail was slightly deformed and had gradually been growing into my thumb, eventually leading to the festering digit attached to my hand. It's a common thing to have an ingrown nail—I think most people have had one from time to time—but almost *nobody* has one for years and years—like more than a decade—and tries to throw a major league fastball.

Anyway, so they ended up cutting half my nail off. It would be the first of four different procedures during the off-season to try to get my thumb back to normal. To make matters worse, after undergoing all these procedures, I developed a staph infection. Spring training was now right around the corner and instead of logging hours on the mound, I was spending my days at the hospital. At one point I was in so much pain I had to get nerve blocks just to sleep. Yep, I could tell already: It was going be another stellar year for Smoltz.

So, long story short, I finally kicked the staph infection and reported to spring training. Because of the thumb—and what was supposed to be a "minor" procedure—I had never been less prepared for the start of a baseball season as I was that year. Not only had I not spent any time throwing, I still couldn't even pick up a ball. And I do mean that literally. My thumb was still so painful I couldn't bear to actually wrap my fingers around one and grip it in my right hand. I couldn't stand to toss a Wiffle Ball underhand to one of my kids, let alone reach back and try to fire a fastball in the mid-to-upper nineties.

I just kept nursing my thumb back to health—rest, ice, anti-inflammatory meds, rinse, and repeat. After weeks of nursing it with patience that nearly put me over the edge, I could at last pick up a ball, and finally, I started throwing again. I started out just throwing in the bullpen and then I managed to get up to six or seven innings of spring training work, which is *nothing*. There I was, about to enter my first year as "The Closer" and I wasn't ready. Not only had I not totally adjusted to the routine of working day to day out of the bullpen, I had to fake like I was ready to pitch on the mound. Now, there's a recipe for success if I've ever heard one.

Truthfully, if I hadn't had fourteen years of experiences to pull from, there's no way I could have started that year on any roster. But in the end, the challenge of that off-season likely played a vital role in preparing me for the challenges of being a closer for the first time.

Let me tell you, there's no way to fake it in the big leagues. Hitters at the pro level are too good, and they reminded me of that right away. In my second game out as a closer, I got rocked. It was April 6 and I came in for the top of the ninth against the New York Mets. The game was tied 2–2 and the very bottom of the Mets' lineup was due up to bat. It should have been just another day at the office. Well, it turned out to be one of those shoulda, coulda, woulda deals. Before I knew what had happened, I had given up eight runs in two-thirds of an inning. Bobby had to bring in Aaron Small to get the final out and I heard some boos as I walked off the mound. My ERA had gone from 0.0 to 43.20 in about ten minutes. It was unbelievable.

That miserable outing was a humbling experience, to say the least. The media jumped all over me. It seemed like everyone had something to say about it. One friend even called to tell me, "Hey John, only fifty more innings and you can get your ERA back to three." Nice. Everyone was questioning me and my ability to get it done, but besides my coaches and teammates, nobody knew the real story behind it. Nobody in the press knew about my thumb and I certainly wasn't going to let anyone in on it. For one thing, I wasn't going to hide behind my injury or use it as an excuse, but I also wasn't going to let anyone on another team know that I wasn't quite ready or that I didn't think I could get the job done.

It really had gotten to the point where it was natural to assess the situation and think that I had nothing to gain and everything to lose with this deal, with trying to figure out how to be the closer and work around my thumb. But I really wasn't thinking about that. I was only thinking, *John, it's rally time.* I just did what I did best when the chips were down: I put my head down and I worked through it.

As things progressed, I finally determined that I was just going to have to learn how to throw all my pitches again. My fastball, my slider, my curveball, you name it—I was seriously going to have to go back to the basics. It sounds crazy, doesn't it? How one ingrown thumbnail could wreak such havoc? But I think any pitcher would agree, the thumb on your throwing arm is as critical to your delivery as your elbow, your shoulder, or anything else, for that matter. The mechanical motion of pitching requires every part of your body to work in sync. If just one piece is slightly off, it sets off a chain reaction that affects another thing, which affects another thing, and so on and so forth.

I wish it had been different. I wish it had been easy, but it wasn't. For the entire first month, every day was a battle, a new challenge. But every day I learned something new and I got better, both as a pitcher and as a person. I never thought I couldn't hack it; I never thought it wouldn't work, but even I couldn't have predicted what would happen after I survived those torturous early weeks in April. I went from being booed to being lights-out; I would finish the season leading all of baseball by recording fifty-five saves and earn the National League's Rolaids Relief Man Award. In my first full season as a closer, I had darn near broken Bobby Thigpen's record for the all-time most saves in a single season. *All-time.*

The next two years in the bullpen would be not be as stunning statistically, but I definitely had two more solid seasons, finishing 2003 with forty-five saves and 2004 with forty-four.

The transformation from starting pitcher to closer was such a tough, tough transition. It was really like playing right-handed your whole career and then learning how to play left-handed temporarily. It proved to be the ultimate challenge. When my ingrown nail flared up, things moved beyond "ultimate" to this *Mission: Impossible* category.

But all along, through all the trials, I never doubted that I would find a way to make it work. Looking back, it was another one of those times when I had to step out of my comfort zone, embrace the change that was happening in my life (even though it was against my own wishes), and try to make the best of the situation. I failed a ton, sometimes on a daily basis, but I just kept on learning. And that's really one of the secrets to my success. I didn't ever look at failure as a reason or an opportunity to quit. I always looked at it as an opportunity to grow. And grow I did, night after night, in Atlanta's bullpen.

Chapter Seven

CLOSING FOR DUMMIES

People don't often believe me when I tell them that the transition from starting to closing was, without a doubt, one of the toughest obstacles I had to face in my entire career. Some people think I must be joking considering some of the injuries I've faced, or the major surgeries I found ways to come back from. Other people just don't understand how there could be such a difference between starting and closing. I mean, it's all pitching, right? The short answer to that question is "Yes and no."

I guess it can be hard to understand if you've never pitched before, because, as with most things in life, proximity and perspective matter. In reality, starting and closing are alike in the way a portobello mushroom and a white truffle are alike. Now, I'm no chef, but I have sat on the couch next to my wife enough times to know those guys on the Food Network would have a heart attack if you said they were the same. The same thing goes for pitchers when it comes to starting and closing. After having done both now, I can assure you, they are like night and day.

After many failed attempts at trying to describe the difference between starting and closing to people who don't know much about pitching, I finally came up with an analogy that seems to help. It goes something like this: Say you are at work. You go get in your car and start to drive home. You drive the speed limit and get back to your house, no problem. That's starting. That's structured. You knew where you were going and you were absolutely comfortable getting in the car and going there. Now go back to work and try it again, only this time, when you get in your car, get it up to a hundred miles an hour immediately, and this time, no matter what, don't let up on the gas until you arrive home. Along the way try to avoid the following likely scenarios: causing an accident, running off the road, and harming yourself and/or anybody else. Now, how did you feel? Were you in control? Were you confident that you were going to arrive home safe and sound? Well, *that's* closing. And now you also know why there are a limited number of guys who can do it.

When I first went down to the minors to start rehabbing as a reliever, I had to abandon a lot of things that I had grown accustomed to as a starter—not the least of which was my old routine. That may not sound like much, but it was really one of things that I hated most about closing. I make no bones about it; I'm a structured guy. I like to schedule things; I like to know what I'm doing today, tomorrow, next week, etc. So starting was perfect for me, since I knew I would pitch every fifth day during the season, barring things like bad weather or injuries that occasionally added or took away a day here and there. Most of the time you could count on four stress-less days in between starts because, besides watching tape or studying your next opponent, there is little else you can do to help your team win. So you sit back, you watch, you learn. You're a teammate. Then, on the fifth day, you pour everything you have into the game.

Over time, your body gets used to this buildup to game time and then the downtime in between, especially mentally. I really thrived on it.

Closing could not have been more different. From one day to the next, I never had any idea when I would be called upon to pitch. When I went to bed at night, I had no idea if I would pitch the next day. When I got up in the morning, I still didn't know. When I got to the park, same story. By the fifth inning, I might have an idea, but I still didn't know for sure. A lot of times it would be nearly ten o'clock at night before I would know. Maybe it doesn't sound like that big of a deal, but it proved to be a huge challenge for me. Closing took away one of the things I liked most about starting: knowing when I was pitching next. I was never in control of the rotation per se; my manager was, obviously, but knowing the schedule sort of gave me a false sense of control. By going to the bullpen, I sacrificed two things that really helped me tick: knowing what was coming and feeling like I was in control.

It took me a while to adjust to this new reality and I quickly learned that one of my biggest obstacles was simply going to be time. In pro baseball, all the players are expected to be at the park every day at a certain time, regardless of whether you're a starting player, a bench player, or a reliever who may or may not pitch that day. So for me, as a closer, this meant on the average day there would be at least six hours from the time I walked through the door to the time I *might* pitch. I think we've been over this already, but it's worth repeating: I do not wait well.

So how do I kill six hours, prepare myself to pitch in case I am called upon, yet still stay sane in the process? Should I concentrate on the game or watch it from a distance? Should I avoid it entirely? These were the things I had to work out if this closing thing was going to work. What I really needed was my own *Closing for Dummies* book, but the one I found at Barnes & Noble had to do with real estate, not pitching.

Anyway . . . so I knew challenge number one would be coming up with a new routine that would enable me to survive six hours without letting all the uncertainty drive me up the wall and still be ready to pitch if/when called upon.

Challenge number two was going to be the actual bullpen itself.

When the 2002 season began in Atlanta, the indoor bullpen at Turner Field was small and sparse. It was basically an oversize storage area with some folding chairs in it where the relief pitchers and catchers could go to get out of the sun when they weren't watching the game or warming up in the practice area cut out of the right-field stands. Now, by "get out of the sun," don't think I'm implying the space was air-conditioned, because it wasn't. The only respite available from the sultry Atlanta summer was shade.

Well, after spending one game in the bullpen, I knew that just wasn't going to work for me. So I sat down with Bobby and told him, "Look, I'm not saying I am better than everyone else. That's not it at all. I just can't sit there all night and still be in prime condition to come out and close. I just can't do it." Bobby didn't give me any grief about it at all. I think at this point in my career he trusted the fact that I knew what I needed to do (or in this case couldn't do) to be ready to pitch.

So next I started hanging out in the clubhouse and watching the first half of the game on TV. This didn't work either because I had the tendency to get too wrapped up in the game. For example, if the game wasn't going well, I would get really upset because I knew I wasn't going to pitch. (Sounds crazy, I know, but you have to remember I always want the ball. Always.) Or, on the other hand, if it was close, I'd be expending all this energy and getting all worked up about a game I had absolutely no control over. Eventually I found a way to sort of monitor the game—mostly so I'd have a feel for the strike zone in case I did pitch later—but not sit there hanging on every pitch or swing of the bat. Basically, I tried to keep my mind away from it for five innings after I had a good idea of what kind of strike zone the home-plate ump was calling. During this time, I would start getting my body warmed up and ready to go. I would jog and stretch, basically try to get loose, and then head down to the bullpen for the sixth.

After trying out this approach for a little while, I got an even better idea. (A man can do a lot of thinking in six hours of nightly purgatory.) I decided it was time for the bullpen to get an Extreme Makeover. I just looked at the guys and told them, "Dang it, we're going to have fun down here."

When you do something this nontraditional, you give others built-in excuses to predict failure. Some people seemed to be skeptical at first. The common thought was, "This is not going to work; you're going to be too relaxed." Good grief, I seriously cannot even write that line without laughing. First of all, I don't think anyone has *ever* accused me of being too relaxed. Second of all, there's no reason why relief pitchers can't relax during the game, be professional, and still be focused when they get the call.

The Braves allowed me to feng shui the bullpen; but when it came down to making it happen, I ended up personally footing the bill for the entire project. When I weighed the monetary investment it was going to require against the opportunity to have a space that would help me and the other guys be ready when Bobby picked up the phone, it wasn't even close. Spending some money to help myself be primed for a long outing? That made good financial sense to me.

By the time I was done with it, the Braves' bullpen was the Taj Mahal of major league bullpens. It was a thing of beauty. We tore down a wall, put in a new air duct for a/c, and brought in six reclining chairs and a refrigerator. Now, don't get me wrong, it wasn't Happy Hour all the time down there. We had rules. First of all, rookies couldn't come in and just hang out. We'd let them in on occasion, especially if it was really hot, but it wasn't an open invitation. Another rule was that if you needed to take a nap, you could take a nap, but you couldn't get carried away. We just approached things with common sense. We had a veteran bullpen and we all seemed to flourish once we had a new place to chill, literally. It cost me $28,000 for the wall and air duct alone, but I would do it all again in a heartbeat.

Once the new bullpen was open for business, I changed my routine slightly. I still stayed in the clubhouse for the first five innings, but then I would come down and sit in my recliner for two innings and relax. By "my" recliner, I literally mean I took my favorite recliner from home and transplanted it in the bullpen. I never really intended it to be a permanent donation—it was seriously my favorite chair of all time—but after I moved it down there, my wife didn't want it in the house anymore. The last time I checked, it was still there, ably helping the next generation of Braves' relievers sit through games in relative peace and comfort until the phone rings.

It may seem extreme to go to such lengths to create my own happy place, but I just have this tendency to get too wrapped up in things if I'm not careful. Really the worst thing I can do is overthink. When I was a starter, I tried not to think about pitching at all in the hours before I took the mound. By that point I had already done the work—I had looked at the charts, I had watched the video, I had met with the pitching coach, etc. I figured out early on that I had to get all my prep work done on the days in between starts so I could come in on the day I pitched and just try to relax. When it came to closing, this became a little more challenging, but I eventually figured out how to be prepared yet still keep myself from obsessing on game days.

Going through this process of figuring out a new routine was really vital to my success. I knew I had to figure out a way to get myself in the right mind-set night after night. Not surprisingly, the same principle I followed in starting proved to be true for closing: The more I didn't think about pitching, the better off I often was. That's just what I had to do; it's just what worked for me. Other guys had other routines—some guys had to pitch the game the night before in their head before they went to bed. To each his own, you know. There's no one set way to be successful, but for me and what made me tick, I needed to do certain things.

The bullpen and my mind-set weren't the only things that required some refurnishing to make my move to the bullpen successful. I still had a lot to figure out about the art of closing.

Thankfully I had several things going for me in this department. One, I had already pitched for more than a decade in the majors. Starting and closing are different, as I have already pointed out, but certainly there are still principles that apply to both disciplines. So while a lot of it was new to me, it wasn't like I was a complete rookie. The other great thing I had going for me was that we just happened to have a group of veteran guys in the bullpen at the time and they were always willing to let me pick their brains. We had three former closers on our staff—Darren Holmes, Steve Reed, and Mike Remlinger—and those guys were always there for me, helping me along the way.

That was a good thing, because thanks to my thumb injury, the one thing I didn't have was the luxury of time. I didn't have the benefit of spring training to work things out. The season started and I basically had to learn on the job. And fast. It was sort of like trying to put your mouth around the end of a garden hose. You really only get a few good swallows before you get drenched trying to keep up with the flow of the water. I came to the park every day and did my best to be a sponge and soak up as much as I could every night. The lessons were hard—especially when my mistakes were liable to be played on a seemingly endless loop on ESPN's *SportsCenter* or *Baseball Tonight* for the next twenty-four hours. But eventually I started to get the hang of it and the pace seemed to slow down. Everything was still going 100 mph, but eventually it began to *feel* more like 70 mph. And I could handle 70 mph, no problem.

So there I was, finally settling in as the Closer, and there's still something else to worry about: I didn't have a walk-in song yet. You know, a specific song they play when I walk out to the mound from the bullpen when we're playing at home. Now I could really care less, but the public relations guys kept giving me a hard time about it. It's not that I'm not into music or anything; I just wasn't going to waste my time thinking about what they should be playing on the speakers when I walked out the door. At the moment I had bigger issues on my mind, namely, how I was going to pitch after I walked out the door. So, finally, I just told them, "Look, I don't even know what to pick and I don't really care. Pick something. If it sticks, it sticks." I was really hoping it would just work itself out.

So the season went on and I never really paid too much attention to what was playing as I'd take the field. Everything was fine until one day I walked out the door and I noticed "Dancing Queen" was being played. Seriously. I started laughing on my way to the mound. Now, I did say I didn't care, and nothing against ABBA (I actually have one of their CDs), but "Dancing Queen" is *not* the song you want to have in the back of your mind when you're staring down a hitter. It does absolutely nothing for your fastball, trust me.

So the game ended up going okay; I think I got a save actually, and I was just hoping nobody had noticed the music, or if they did, they had forgotten about it by the time the game was over. Yeah, not so much. I really took some heat from the guys. The music guy actually came all the way down to the clubhouse to apologize to me. Apparently it wasn't intentional at all; the guy had just made a mistake. The whole thing really didn't rile me up, but it did make one thing obvious: The time had come for me to do something about "The Song."

So I rounded up the guys from the bullpen and told them, "Guys, you're going to have to do something. I'm putting you in charge of the song. Pick anything you want, but I'm telling you 'Dancing Queen' can't be it."

So the bullpen guys got together and picked something out. The next day they came back and told me, "You're not going to believe it the next time you come out the door." They wouldn't tell me what it was but said, "We're going to blow you away."

That comment landed me precisely in the situation I was trying to avoid all along: thinking about the dang song. Now I was champing at the bit for my next time out just because I wanted to find out what they had cooked up. Great. Well, finally, a couple days later I got my chance. I opened the door, and after about thirteen steps, I had to put my glove over my mouth because I was laughing my butt off. AC/DC's "Thunderstruck" was absolutely rocking Turner Field. They had lightning bolts on the screen and everything. The funny thing is, if you know me, I'm not a heavy-metal guy at all. But there was no turning back now.

As I said, I didn't care in the beginning, but now I was hooked. The next thing you know, I'm tracking down the PR people myself and having them put together a little mix for me. From that point on, every time I opened the door, the *Star Wars* theme song would play while I walked through the outfield. Once I stepped on the infield, it switched to "Thunderstruck." It ended up being the coolest thing in the world to me. The fans seemed to love it, too. And I guess I have "Dancing Queen" to thank for it all.

So now I had figured out my routine, refurnished the bullpen, and I had my own walk-in song. All I had left to worry about was what I was actually getting paid to do: to get my team safely out of games in the ninth inning. This is probably going to sound a little silly, but one of the first things I knew I had to do when I moved to the bullpen was *not forget about pitching*.

As a starter, you come into a game expecting to face the other team's lineup several times. The entire game you are thinking about matchups and how to exploit hitters' bad habits and/or weaknesses. The sequence of pitches you throw to a guy in the first inning, and their relative outcome, affect how you approach the same batter in subsequent innings. Effective pitching requires effective execution certainly, but it also comes down to working out a sound game plan with your catcher and knowing what to throw to what guy on what count.

Meanwhile, as a closer, with usually only one inning of work expected, it's really easy to forget about all this, about pitching, and just throw. Since you are only going to face each hitter once, it changes the complexion of everything. You aren't concerned with future matchups, you're really only concerned with getting outs any way you can. Sometimes closers, especially power pitchers like me who can really get something on the ball, can get lulled into just throwing as hard as they can, without taking into full account what a hitter may or may not be expecting. It's easier than you might think to stop concentrating, get lazy, and just reach back, grunt, and let it go. I had seen this happen to guys before. They might get away with it a couple times, but in the end, the results could be disastrous. I tried to make a conscientious effort to avoid this tendency and always keep *pitching,* not throwing, out of the bullpen.

Now, at the same time, that's not to say I wasn't throwing hard. I was actually throwing as hard as I had ever thrown, with my fastball humming in at 96, 97, even 98 mph. My resurgence in velocity actually caused some folks to raise their eyebrows and wonder if the extra couple miles per hour I had regained were all thanks to my surgically repaired elbow. The myth in baseball is that if you've had a bad ligament and you get a new one, you're going to throw harder. But that just isn't the case. Tommy John surgery didn't give me a 98 mph fastball. It was there before, but when you pitch hurt for so long, you don't have ninety-eight left in your arm. Also, as a starter, I always used to have to tone it down and not use my extra gear so that I could last the whole game. These are adjustments you have to make to keep your fastball hopping toward the end of games when your pitch count is topping out at 110, 120 pitches or more. When I was a closer, endurance and maintaining my velocity were never issues, so I could go in and use my extra gear right away.

One advantage my experience as a starter gave me was an edge, a certain cockiness or bravado or swagger. I had already earned that through my previous fourteen years of starting. If I had been a rookie or a guy who had never found much success as a starter, I wouldn't have had that edge. It would have been harder to approach closing with as much confidence as I did.

Now, with that said, the funny thing is that when I was walking out the door of the bullpen and taking the field, I wasn't actually thinking, *I'm coming in here to take you guys down.* People ask me about this all the time actually—they want to know what I was thinking that helped me be successful. Everyone is always shocked by the answer I give: I thought I was going to give it up. When I walked out of the door, I thought I was going to give it up. About this time the same people are usually looking at me trying to decide if I am messing with them or serious. Once they find out I'm serious, they want to know why in the world I would have such a negative thought process going on in my mind. But to me, it wasn't a negative thought process. I know it sounds contradictory, but let me explain.

When I told myself, *John, you could give it up today,* it was a motivator to myself to stay on task. I put the pressure on myself, and it really helped me focus. Now look, it's not like I had to do this all the time; I mean, if you can't get amped up for a game that's tied or one in which your team is leading by one lone run, then you really shouldn't even be on the field. I'm talking about the games where you are coming in to get three outs and your team is leading by four and five runs. In those situations, it can be easy to start thinking, *All right, let's get this over with* or *Man, my six-year-old son could get us out of this game.* Once you start taking outs for granted, things are liable to turn ugly fast. Before you know it, you'll have just thrown your fifth pitch and the bases are loaded with no outs.

Welcome back to your 100 mph commute—it's time to buckle your seat belt.

I was determined to be more mentally tough on the mound than my opponent. That was part of my edge. I would always be telling myself something like, *You could possibly give it up today, so get after it John. This is three outs you've got to get.* That's what I used to get myself locked in. I always seem to perform best under pressure.

Other guys had other ways of approaching it. I've heard guys talk about using all kinds of things—visualizing their kids getting abducted, their wife or girlfriend being threatened by another man, their mint-condition 1967 Shelby GT getting vandalized—just whatever it took to get themselves worked up and have that little bit of adrenaline pumping through their veins. Some guys used anger to be successful. I used failure. I wouldn't suggest it for everybody, because some people don't function well under pressure, but it's what worked for me.

I've always used this analogy that there's this beast within all of us. The beast basically represents your impulsive tendencies or instinctive behaviors that determine how you respond in times of stress and crises. It's what you are liable to do when the pressure is on. It's not a bad beast per se, but it's a beast that wants to get out and do what it wants to do. In order to be successful, you've got to learn what your beast is, what it wants to do, and how to tame it.

Like when I play golf, I've learned there's no word for *lay up* in my beast's vocabulary. My beast could care less about the odds or recommended safe shots, particularly on long par fives. My beast constantly eggs me on and tells me, "Pick up your driver, John. Darn those bunkers, you can reach that green in two!"

When it came to closing, I learned the hard way that when I walked out of that door, I had to channel my beast in a very peculiar way to be successful: by simply telling myself over and over again, *John, you could give it up. You could give it up right here.*

Thankfully, more often than not, I didn't.

For all the challenges that closing presented, there were certainly things that I did love about it. I loved the incredible rush of adrenaline as I walked out the door and took the field. I loved being the guy my team called when the game was on the line. I loved coming in and getting my team out of jams.

There were also parts that I *hated* about closing. Most of all, I hated waiting around and seeing if the other guys, our starters, could be effective. I wanted to be in their shoes. I wanted to be going head-to-head with Randy Johnson, Curt Schilling, and Jack Morris. I loved those moments; I missed those moments. Through all the innings in the bullpen, I really never let go of starting.

And after three years of doing what Atlanta had asked me to do—and having to largely stand by and watch my team falter in postseason after postseason, I was ready to ask for something from the Braves: another chance to start.

This wasn't just some passing thought. I had really started seriously thinking about it midway through the 2004 season, and since that time I had devoted a lot of time and effort to exploring the idea from all sides. While my personal preference was certainly to start, it was essential to me to first ensure that my desire to start didn't in any way go against what my doctors, coaches, or trainers thought was best for me and my arm. Given my age and the arm problems I had already faced, I wanted to find out from them if one position, starting or closing, offered me any better chance at sustainability.

It proved to be a difficult question to answer objectively. We were basically in uncharted baseball territory and there was little scientific or medical evidence to support one position over the other. It became a really subjective question. When you really sat down and weighed the pros and cons of the two positions, it almost seemed like it was a draw—that the perceived benefits of one balanced the perceived disadvantages of the other. But over the course of three years of closing, I had realized closing had two distinct drawbacks: the lack of true rest and the long-term impacts of throwing as hard as I could as often as I was.

After I weighed all the available evidence and spoke with my trainers and doctors, it was obvious to me that closing was worse for me physically than starting. So I started preparing myself to make my case to Bobby and the front office that I should get ready to do what no one in the history of the game had done successfully—to go from starting to closing and then BACK to starting. My argument was going to come down to two key points:

Our rotation needed power: The truth of the matter is the one thing that had always propelled us into the postseason year after year, strong starting pitching, had gone by the wayside shortly after I moved to the 'pen. To add insult to injury, Tom Glavine left for the New York Mets after the 2002 season and Greg Maddux went back to the Chicago Cubs after 2003. I didn't harbor any grand illusions that my return to the rotation was the only thing we needed in order to mount another championship run, but I really felt it could be part of the solution. I also knew that without some power in the rotation, they wouldn't need me as a closer because there were going to be fewer games where we were in position to win.

Closing wasn't better for my arm: My original assignment to the bullpen was motivated, at least initially, by the mind-set that it would be a better way to rehab my arm coming back from Tommy John surgery. From that point on, I think it was just always assumed that shorter outings from the bullpen would be better for sustaining my career than returning to the rotation. After three years of closing, I was no longer convinced that this was the case.

When I came in to a game, I was there to throw as hard as I could and to record outs immediately. In 1996, I pitched nearly 300 innings—253 in the regular season and 38 in the postseason. I didn't think I could be more spent than that. After one year of closing, I realized I was more mentally and physically exhausted than I'd been in 1996. The cruising speed I pitched at as a starter was more sustainable than the quick spurts of max effort required as a closer.

There was also the issue of daily wear and tear and the lack of true rest to consider. As a closer, I was sometimes called into games four days in a row. In the three years I had spent in the bullpen, I had only had two designated off days where I sat there in tennis shoes and truly had a rest day. Every other day I was lacing up my spikes for a possible appointment on the mound.

And then, there was all the warming up. When I first began closing, I would throw around forty, fifty pitches before going in to pitch one inning. I realized quickly that my arm was going to fall off if I didn't make a drastic change. I soon learned to settle for fifteen pitches in the 'pen and then the eight I would get out on the mound once I got called into the game. This strategy would save my arm in the long run.

This may not sound like much, but I think what a lot of people don't realize—myself included when I was a starter—is how many times you get up to warm up and do not end up in the game. Sure, they're warm-up pitches, but let me tell you, they add up. I was called in to seventy-seven games my first full year in the bullpen, but I warmed up more than *140* different times. And that number isn't a total for the year—that's just when I gave up counting. In one game alone, I warmed up seven different times. We were in Minnesota and the game went fifteen innings, I believe. That's an extreme example, but there were plenty of games in which four to five warm-up sessions were very possible.

When it came down to it, there was no way to predict the future, but I had done my homework. All the doctors and trainers had weighed in and the one thing we could all agree upon was that starting was certainly no worse on my body than what I was already doing in the bullpen—which is all I needed to hear. I was already convinced that I could do it, and now there was no reason for me not to try. I had no idea what my statistics might look like, but I believed with everything I had that I could be successful as a starter again.

That is, if I was given the chance.

Chapter Eight

ME AND THE HOMEBOYS UPSTAIRS

It was October 11, 2004, and I had just returned to the clubhouse from the bullpen after watching us lose yet another National League Division Series. I hadn't so much as picked up a ball all night in our 12–3 losing effort against the Houston Astros, a team we ourselves had historically sent packing in the opening round of the playoffs, and it was eating at me. As I went through the housekeeping motions of wrapping up another season, storing my gear and deciding what equipment to take home or leave in my locker, I was already thinking about next season. About how I hoped things would be different, and not just in the postseason.

It was obvious that we didn't have what it took in the starting rotation anymore, and it was absolutely brutal for me to sit in the bullpen, watching my team fall short in the postseason, knowing that I could still start and knowing that *maybe* with me in the rotation, things could have been different. Maybe it would be us packing for a flight to St. Louis that night to face the Cardinals in the National League Championship Series.

Watching this last series play out—and only being able to contribute five innings in two games—was enough to convince me to do something about it. I vowed to myself right then to find an opportunity to engage my general manager, John Schuerholz, sometime during the off-season. I felt burdened to look him in the eyes and share with him what I knew: that I truly felt I could contribute much more to the Atlanta Braves as a starter than as a closer. I didn't know what would happen, but I figured it was worth a shot.

I approached John shortly after that and just asked him if he would be up for meeting for lunch sometime to discuss some things I thought might make us better. He agreed and he seemed genuinely interested in the idea. I was really encouraged by his attitude. As the years went by and I grew to know the Atlanta organization inside and out, this was the kind of conversation that I truly liked to have, to just have the opportunity to share with my general manager the perspective I had as a player on some things that might make us better and help him make the big decisions. It only happened a couple of times, but whenever it did I was grateful for the opportunity.

When I sat down for lunch with John at McCormick & Schmick's restaurant in Atlanta that off-season, I had not only done my homework about the position change and its expected impact on my arm, but I had also made peace with the situation. No doubt I was there to lobby for my return to the starting rotation, but in my heart and mind I was prepared to do whatever the GM thought was best for the team. When we began to talk, I wasn't emotional, but I was emphatic. I was emphatic that I should be back in the rotation.

John opened the lunch with a question that had been a long time coming, to my mind. He asked me, "John, what do you think makes us better? You as a starter, or you as a closer?"

Basically I told him the facts don't lie. That although I had really enjoyed the opportunity to close games for the team, we just weren't winning. We hadn't won a series in the postseason since I went to the bullpen full time, not one series. In all the years I had started in the playoffs, we had never *lost* a first-round division series. "So if you're truly asking me, what makes us better," I said, "what makes us best is me as a starter. Hands down."

John had his doubts at first, but he really seemed to warm up to the idea as we talked things over and he got a sense of how confident I was that I could start again. Once we had kicked around the merits of moving me to the rotation, the next topic was the bullpen. My move to the rotation would obviously help address a need in the rotation, but John would need to find a closer to take my place. Here's where I knew the timing of everything could be an issue. Neither of us could predict if or when John would be able to find a closer, and we didn't have the luxury of time to just wait and see. If there was any chance that I might be starting, I had to switch gears right now.

So before we left the restaurant, I said, "I'll tell you what I'm going to do, John. I will train to start. If you get a closer, then I'll go ahead and start. But if you don't get a closer, then I'll close. But I can't train to close, and then turn around to start. It just doesn't work that way."

Now, there was one more thing I had to ask John Schuerholz about: a new contract. As things stood, I would enter the 2005 season with one year left on my current contract. I was not in any way interested in going through another year of proving that I not only wanted to stay in Atlanta, but that it was worth it to the Braves to keep me here. I didn't want to be a free agent at the end of the next season again; I really wanted the opportunity to sign a longer-term contract that would allow me hopefully to finish my career in Atlanta. When I brought this up, John didn't flinch. He just said he would try to make it happen for me. First, he'd work on the closer piece, and then we'd discuss my contract. That sounded *perfect* to me.

This was by far the easiest and most amicable discussion I had ever had with my general manager regarding my role within the Braves organization, and I was really optimistic about the outcome. There were no guarantees that any part of our plan would work out as intended, but things were looking better than I could ever have imagined.

Not too long after that lunch, John called me at home to deliver some news: He had just acquired relief pitcher Danny Kolb from Milwaukee. Danny was coming off two years as a closer with the Brewers and his numbers looked promising: The previous year he had saved thirty-nine games and been selected to play on the All-Star team. The plan appeared to be taking shape. The next hurdle would be negotiating another contract.

As affable as John Schuerholz had seemed to be during our lunch-time strategy session, when it came time to commit money to the deal and make my return to the rotation official, there were still a lot of doubts. Looking back, I certainly understand and respect that there was no precedent for a thirty-seven-year-old pitcher with some arm issues to be able to successfully transition from being a closer to a starter again. And beyond that, there's obviously some justifiable doubt that a general manager has to have when a player is getting older. No GM wants to be the guy responsible for signing a veteran to a longer deal only to find out the hard way a year later that the guy didn't have two or three good playing years left.

John asked me, "What makes you think you can still throw two hundred innings a year?"

As far as I was concerned, there *was* solid evidence that I could do it. I had been proving myself to him and overcoming doubts my entire career. I understood his having doubts. What I was proposing was unheard of, and taking risks like that isn't often good business, but I think if John had had a better idea of what drove me—the engine that was ticking inside, my desire to want to do this—I think it might have lessened his doubt.

The relationship I had with John Schuerholz can be hard to explain. It's safe to say we didn't talk very much, but it's not like we despised each other either. Really, for the most part, our relationship was nonexistent if we were not negotiating a contract; he did his thing and I did mine. It was unfortunate and really disappointing to feel as disconnected as I felt to such a big part of an organization I truly loved, but it's almost like it had been destined to be that way from the very beginning. To say that John Schuerholz and I got off on the wrong foot would be the understatement of my career.

When I first came to the Braves, Bobby Cox was the general manager, and my first contract negotiation was simple, straightforward, and easy. Then, after three years, when John came in and established himself as the new general manager, it was like a complete regime change in the front office. John was intent on implementing the same system he had used as the GM in Kansas City, and it caught me off guard to say the least.

You see, I was one of the players caught in the middle of this change. Here I had been indoctrinated according to Bobby's way, and there were certain expectations for both sides that had already been discussed and understood. Now everything had changed, and I was stuck in a place where John basically wanted to start the process all over again.

I was literally days away from being eligible for arbitration, which would have allowed me some leverage as a player to try to settle my contract dispute with the team, but John didn't want to make an exception for me and he didn't have to. I didn't think it was right, and my agent didn't think it was right, but in reality there wasn't much I could do about it.

At that precise moment in time I had few options besides verbally appealing to John to basically make an exception and asking to be grandfathered into his new system. I met with John, face-to-face, to make my case. He explained his position and didn't budge. So my agent at the time, Ed Keating, advised me to do one of the toughest things I could ever imagine doing: He advised me to walk out of camp, as it really was the only way I could make a statement. This was not an easy decision, but at the time I listened to my agent.

Walking out is one of the few regrets I have about my career. I felt fairly confident that it would work, but it didn't in so many ways, causing a rift in my relationship with John. I'm not sure what a player–GM relationship is supposed to look like, but I didn't help my chances of building a positive one by the way things started out.

Because we were at a stalemate, John ended up just renewing my contract, which meant I was going to be taking a pay cut from what I made the previous year, despite going 14–11 on a team that had lost almost a hundred games in 1990. It was a tough pill to swallow in so many ways, as all I really accomplished was to damage my relationship with my new general manager.

As I look back on it, in all fairness to John Schuerholz, it's easy to see how he saw things differently from his perspective. Here he is the new GM and this young kid tries to hold out for more money. I'm convinced that the seeds of our relationship were sown right there in 1991.

In the off-season of 2004, more than a decade had passed since my first negotiation with John Schuerholz, but time had done little to improve our relationship. So as we attempted to negotiate a contract that would allow me to return to the starting rotation, I was forced to convince him that I was capable of delivering for him yet again. The discussion was becoming somewhat tiresome to me because in my mind, there *wasn't* any doubt.

It was hard to explain, but I *knew* I had it in me. So much of this game is won or lost in your mind-set and I knew that my mind—and my body—were capable.

"John," I said, "look at my track record. I've done this for fourteen years. I can go out there and pitch two hundred innings in my sleep."

Thankfully, we finally agreed to terms and I signed another three-year contract. And with the exception of my first start on Opening Day, that next year was really an unbelievable one. I pitched as good a stretch of baseball as I had ever done in my entire career. Really, it seemed like the older I got, the better pitcher I was becoming. In 2005, I pitched 237 innings (including the postseason), leading the whole team by 34 innings, was among the league leaders in ERA, and I was the only guy on the staff to win a playoff game.

Yet my record was still only 14–7, which, while not bad, was indicative of a rough season for our bullpen. I think it was eight times I left a game that season with a lead that the bullpen lost. When this part of the plan failed to pan out, the media went looking for explanations. This was tough for me because there were some perceptions being floated around in various news articles that I knew were just not accurate. Some stories claimed that I was responsible for the demise of the bullpen. Others insinuated that I had forced John Schuerholz's hand—that I had basically bullied myself back into the rotation—but that just wasn't the case. In my mind, I had given him the ultimate luxury of all GMs: the option to use me in either role.

I understood that people had fallen in love with the idea of me as a closer, but when it came down to it, nobody seemed to understand that we weren't accomplishing anything—at least in the playoffs—with me in the bullpen. I think the record shows that my return to the rotation had a bigger, more positive impact on the Braves than I could have had as a closer—though admittedly, and unfortunately, it didn't translate into another championship.

Like I said before, it can be hard to describe the relationship John Schuerholz and I had. It's not like we spent years sniping at each other, but it's not like there wasn't an undercurrent of tension at times either.

Any feelings or observations that I had about my GM, though, I always tried to keep to myself. The first time I saw a reaction from him that surprised me resulted from an interview shortly after the All-Star break in 2006 when a reporter asked me a question about what our team needed to do to get back in the playoff picture that year. We had sunk to the bottom of our division on June 18, but had been busy clawing our way back into the race—bolstered in part by a seven-game winning streak from July 8 to July 18. My answer to the reporter was simply, "Now that we're playing good, I hope management will do whatever it takes."

What I was trying to say and how it was interpreted were two very different things. I was just trying to acknowledge that it was our job as players to get us back into the race in order to allow management the opportunity to make changes. I meant my words to be complimentary, but John Schuerholz certainly didn't take them that way.

When the media asked John about my comments, it was obvious by his answer that he misunderstood what I was trying to say. He used that forum to remind me what he had accomplished in the past as the GM, but he never talked me about it directly. How he handled it didn't sit well with me because in my mind I had made a comment that any competitive player would make. But I let it go and just made a mental note to change my media tactics when it came to John. I vowed not just to watch what I said (as I always had), but not to say anything at all. Well, that's what I tried to do anyway.

Later that same season, Jeff Schultz, a columnist from the *Atlanta Journal-Constitution,* interviewed me after a game. It started out innocently enough, but then he wanted to know what I thought the Braves needed to do, what changes we needed to make this season in order to reach the postseason. Specifically, the question was: "If you were GM, what kind of moves would you make to improve this team?" I knew where he was going with this. I knew no matter how I answered the question, John Schuerholz was going to take it personally and I attempted to plead the Fifth.

"Oh, no, no, no," I said, "I will *never* do that again."

Jeff said, "Why not?"

"When I answered this question in the past, he gets all over me," I said.

"Who is he?"

"Come on. Homeboy upstairs. You know who I'm talking about."

Now, those who know me know that it's just in my personality to say things like that, to just be a little sarcastic. I didn't mean anything by it. I certainly didn't mean any disrespect to John. But there it was, and I couldn't take it back. I really should have known better than to say something like that to a reporter, but I seriously didn't think the newspaper would run with it.

In reality, it would have been better for me if I had just walked away when Jeff started leading me down that path. Let me digress for just a second here. This is one thing that probably burned me more times than it should have—I was always very generous with my time. In retrospect, I probably spent too much time with reporters. I think reporters sometimes took advantage of the fact that I would be open and honest. It really seems like if a reporter had a point he wanted to make, he would often use me to make it. So what begins as Jeff Schultz vs. John Schuerholz morphs into John Smoltz vs. John Schuerholz in the paper.

The next day, when I walked into the clubhouse, Bobby called me into his office. "John wants to see you right away," he said, and handed me a copy of the newspaper.

I never looked at the paper—and when I say this, I mean never as in except in meetings like this where someone was taking exception with something I had said. Needless to say, my blood pressure was already rising before I even read the article, and sure enough there it was, plain as day: John Smoltz calling John Schuerholz the homeboy upstairs. Great.

About five minutes later, as I headed upstairs, I knew said Homeboy was not going to be happy. I felt like a little kid making the long walk to the principal's office; I knew what was coming and it wasn't going to be pretty.

John took one look at me, pointed to the paper, and said, "I thought we had a better relationship than this."

John proceeded to go through this whole dissertation about how disrespectful I had been, about what his colleagues thought about it. Finally, I said, "Time out, John. Look, I meant no disrespect. I'm sorry this guy did what he did, but I was referring to you in the third person."

We were in his office for a long time that day and we both had the chance to get a few things off our chests. The last thing I remember saying to him was something like "I guarantee you will never see another comment from me in the paper about anything regarding the team or you. Nothing. But don't tell me you thought we had a better relationship than this. We don't even talk."

I'm certainly man enough to admit that I have made some mistakes in my day, and I obviously do regret my choice of words in this case, but it certainly was never my intent at any time to undermine or disrespect my general manager.

I used to think, as perhaps many people did, that me and the Braves—we were forever linked. I mean, I was barely old enough to walk into a bar and order a beer the first time I took the mound for Atlanta. I literally grew up under the lights of Atlanta-Fulton County Stadium and later Turner Field, and I always dreamed that one day I would retire under them, too. But, of course, that dream never materialized.

Despite any hard feelings that at times existed between me and my general manager, the fact is I always loved being an Atlanta Brave. I loved playing for Bobby Cox. I had the time of my life in Atlanta and it was an amazing thing to be on a team that had gone from among the very worst in baseball to the very best. John Schuerholz and the Atlanta Braves gave me an opportunity to compete in the playoffs fourteen straight years, and it was never hard for me to remember why I wanted to stay, even in late 2008. Really, right up until the moment I signed with the Boston Red Sox, I still wanted to be a Brave.

I'm going to revisit my divorce with the Braves for one main reason—to explain what it taught me and what it could teach someone else. The fact is, in life, and especially in today's economy, we aren't always able to completely control our environment. Sometimes you have to do things you don't want to do. Sometimes you've got to move and change jobs. You can wish all you want for things to be different, but the truth is that oftentimes we have little control over the cards we are dealt. You can choose to be bitter, or you can choose to move on and be better. For me, I did feel bitter at first with the way things ended, but I chose to saddle up and move on.

When I elected to have shoulder surgery in June 2008, I held a press conference. I think for a lot of people it seemed like farewell. I never once said I wasn't coming back, but the tenor of the conversation seemed to gravitate toward this feeling like, "You know, he's had a good long run. Maybe it's time to just call it a day."

To this day, I really believe that if I had suddenly had a change of heart during the press conference and had just looked at John Schuerholz, who was now the Braves president, and Frank Wren, who had been promoted to general manager from assistant general manager, and said, "You know what, guys? I think I'm done," they would have been relieved. They would have said some nice things about me, we all would have said our good-byes, and we would have walked away peacefully. Things would have been different.

The problem was, I *wasn't* done yet. I still harbored the passion and the desire to pitch in the major leagues and I still thought I could. I wasn't somebody who was just trying to hang on or didn't know when it was time to quit. And this wasn't a "trivial pursuit" to try to accumulate more numbers. This was about reaching one last time for the same dream I'd been dreaming since I was seven years old.

I wanted the opportunity to go out on my own terms and I knew full well that by doing so I was running the risk that it might not happen with the Braves. But when it came down it, my decision to come back after surgery wasn't just about the Braves. This was something I needed to do for myself.

I went through my entire rehab without any contact with the Atlanta Braves, contractwise. I became a free agent after the World Series in October and I honestly didn't know what to think. I wasn't foolish enough to think that no news was good news in this case, but I still hadn't given up hope that we might be able to work something out.

I worked harder than I had ever worked in my entire life to come back from shoulder surgery, and at five and a half months I was at a place I never thought I could be, even in my wildest dreams. Even though the Braves still hadn't expressed any interest in signing me, I really wanted Bobby Cox to at least come see me and be aware of the progress I had made. He not only agreed to come, but he brought the Braves' current pitching coach, Roger McDowell, along with him. I thought maybe, just maybe, if they liked what they saw, I would still have a chance with the Braves.

When Bobby came to see me throw, I felt like I was sixteen years old again, trying out for the very first time in my life. There I was, standing on the mound, nervous as all get-out, because I wanted so badly to show him that I wasn't kidding anybody, that I wasn't kidding myself. I really had healed and I was capable of coming back and pitching for him.

When Bobby saw me throw, he just went, "Oh my gosh." Bobby was never was one to blow smoke, and I could tell I had really impressed him. He knew how significant this moment was. Somewhere within me I really thought that this might do it for the Braves; when I impressed Bobby, I thought to myself, *Maybe there's a chance.*

But in the end, the Braves made it clear that I was no longer a part of their plans. When we did negotiate one last time, they presented me an offer that was filled with incentive clauses that were just unattainable.

It would have been easier to take if they had just told me they wanted to go in a different direction. I would have respected that. It still would have stung, but I would have appreciated their honesty.

At this point I wasn't going to convince them one final time that I deserved another chance. My agent just said, "Okay, that's fine," and I never said a word. In my mind, there was little left to say. The whole time I had been hoping like a little kid that it might still work out with the Braves, and when it didn't, it was a sad, sad day.

Almost immediately I started wondering how all of this would play out. I honestly wanted this new direction to work for everybody, and I really hoped we could all part peacefully. For my part, I wasn't planning on saying *anything;* I just wanted to be able to walk away and start over with a new team. But at the same time I knew that at some point I was probably going to have to respond to whatever way the Braves chose to break this news.

Once the Braves made their decision to go in a different direction, things happened pretty quickly, because the Boston Red Sox had already offered me a contract. With the Red Sox, I didn't even have to throw a pitch and I was guaranteed $5.5 million. My agent spoke to John Schuerholz and told him the news, and that was that.

Well, I *wish* that had been that anyway. Parting ways with the Braves obviously didn't pan out as peacefully as I had hoped.

When the Braves' organization later painted a completely different scenario of why I left—which was not accurate—I was forced to react. As embittered as I might have been, though, I just responded with the truth—that the offer the Braves made me was not even *close* to the offer the Red Sox gave me.

It should have ended much better, it *could have* ended much better, and it's really a shame that it didn't. But all I could do was pick up and move on and start dealing with my new reality:

I was no longer an Atlanta Brave.

Chapter Nine

NO DECISION

Nineteen ninety-five was a huge year for me. I mean *huge*. It was literally as if my whole life had led up to this year, and I finally reached a place where I realized, *That's it; my life will never be the same again.*

Of course, 1995 happens to be the one and only year that the Atlanta Braves won the World Series during our fourteen-year reign as division champions. A one-hitter by Tom Glavine and a solo home run by David Justice in Game Six proved to be enough not only to finish off the Cleveland Indians, but to remove the stigma of a notorious losing legacy in the World Series. When we hoisted the Commissioner's Trophy high above our heads at Atlanta-Fulton County Stadium on October 28, we literally lifted our team out of the chronicles of inglorious baseball teams. We were no longer in danger of becoming baseball's version of the Buffalo Bills; we were finally champions.

Certainly, the World Series win in 1995 was significant in my life. It was a landmark achievement not only for the entire Braves' organization, but for every player who filled the roster at the time. But winning the World Series actually pales in comparison to the life-changing event that I am describing. I'm talking about the day I truly became a Christian.

Parts of that day remain etched in my memory like they happened yesterday, as if preserved in a neatly labeled Mason jar and tucked away on a shelf in the corner of my mind. The words that were spoken, the intuitive feeling of transformation in my heart—those things have stood the test of time. Other details have been lost to the years, lost to the cobwebs on those shelves—like what I ordered for lunch and even when exactly it happened. (I'd honestly be hard-pressed to pick out the date even if you gave me a calendar.) What I can tell you is that I was at a Bennigan's in Atlanta having lunch with then-Braves chaplain Walt Wiley.

Walt was a guy who was very nonconfrontational; he embraced everyone's thoughts and allowed each of us to experience God in our own way, all the while ensuring that everything was grounded in the truth. He led our regular Bible-study sessions, and his subdued-yet-steady manner was a huge influence on me. I owe a great deal not only to Walt, but to the two chaplains who followed him, Mike McCoy and Tim Cash, during my tenure with the Braves. As a pro baseball player, you spend so much time at the park, you miss out on normal opportunities to worship and attend church. These chaplains did a great job of coming down to the field and feeding our souls and talking about things relevant to our faith and baseball, to the lives we were living.

I am grateful that these three chaplains somehow saw the man I was and also the man I could be. I was fortunate to have not only the chaplains, but also some great teammates like Sid Bream, Jose Alvarez, and Marty Clary, who were really looking after my heart from the beginning. These guys were all incredibly influential in my faith journey and collectively inspired me to seek out my own answers to life's big questions. I started thinking about things I had never really thought about before, like my own existence, and why we are here on earth. What is this whole faith-based anything?

I've got to be honest here: I used to have—I don't know the best way to say this—I guess I mean that I had a misguided view of born-again Christians (which is more than a little ironic considering I call myself one today). Some of the folks I came across who ardently professed to be born-again—I was just taken aback by their testimonies. It wasn't as if I was skeptical of their newfound faith; it's that I was critical of their past. More often than not, I would walk away thinking something like *How dare they?* How dare these people tell me how to live my life when a lot of them have been down these really bad roads, made horrible decisions, and truly hurt people? And now all of a sudden they're going to tell me how to live my life? And I'm not even a bad guy! I just couldn't seem to get beyond the things some of these people had said or done in the past.

But I had a lot of questions and I was always searching for answers. I guess you could say I had a certain kind of hunger to get to the bottom of it all. I was earnestly interested in what other people thought and believed and rarely passed up an opportunity to discuss such matters with someone, even relative strangers on occasion. My appetite for knowledge led to one pretty awkward, yet ultimately defining moment in my faith and in my life. I'm talking about the first time I met Richie Hughes.

It was 1992 and I was interested in starting an annual youth baseball camp in Atlanta. I needed to find someone who could not only help me get the idea off the ground, but could also run the camp the way I wanted it run: with integrity and with a focus on learning the fundamentals of the game while also giving kids lessons about life. I saw the camp as an opportunity not only to teach baseball, but also to talk about other things: having goals, having dreams, and also just having fun. The kind of fun I knew growing up—getting outside and playing, not sitting in front of the TV or playing video games all the time. It was incredibly important to me to find a partner I could entrust with this vision. My agent, Lonnie Cooper, suggested Richie.

Richie is a huge part of my life today, but I had actually only known him for about sixty seconds when I asked him something like "So what's the deal with these born-again Christians?"

We were standing in his office at Mount Paran Christian School in nearby Kennesaw, Georgia, where he was currently serving as the basketball coach. After we had made our introductions, I just stood there looking around his office and the items on display and I asked him, "Is this a Catholic school?"

He said, "No, it's a Christian school," which led me straight into the aforementioned question. Now, the ironic thing is that I didn't realize that I was asking the question to a man who would later become an ordained minister in the Church of God. So you can imagine the look on my face when he says, "Well, I am one."

We've all heard it said a million times, but it bears repeating here: "God works in mysterious ways." For me to ask that question to Richie at that moment in my life . . . well, you just couldn't have scripted it any better. Obviously, his answer caught me off guard. He went on to share a little bit of his own testimony and I just stood there listening. That's how our relationship started and it only grew from there. He became not only a great friend, but also a mentor in my walk with God, joining the ranks of the chaplains and teammates who were already nudging me along. Collectively, they all played a significant role in the making and shaping of my faith.

When I met Richie, I was twenty-four. I was a young kid with a lot to learn. My attitude toward born-again Christians reflected my immaturity to a certain extent, but to be honest, I think it's also just in my nature to be judgmental. I'd like to think that I have largely outgrown this over time, but the fact is, even though I'm a Christian, I'm still human and I still have my tendencies. It's not so much that

I am self-righteous—it's that I sort of naturally have what I call a "Prodigal Son" outlook.

If you've ever spent any time in a Sunday school classroom, odds are you are familiar with the parable of the Prodigal Son from Luke 15. It's a story about a father who has two sons. One day, the younger son asks his father to give him his half of his inheritance now. His father appeases him and splits his estate between his two sons. The eager, younger son promptly packs up, leaves town, and as the Bible puts it, "wastes all his money on wild living." Next thing you know, a famine spreads across the land. The younger son is forced to take a job as a swineherd and he eventually finds himself coveting the food that he's feeding the pigs. He decides to return home, repent of his sins to his father, and ask for his forgiveness. Upon his return, his father is so overjoyed that he throws a spur-of-the-moment party.

Meanwhile, the older son returns home from working in the fields all day. When he finds out all the attention is for his wayward brother, he refuses to join the celebration. His father has never slain his finest calf to recognize anything *he's* done and he's been here working hard and doing the right thing the whole time. He sulks outside while his father tries to explain his motives: "For your brother was dead and has come back to life. He was lost, but now he is found!"

At this point in my life I was that older brother. I didn't want to hear any of these lost-and-found stories. As far as I was concerned, if you did wrong, you deserved the judgment you received, not a party. Again, it's not that I thought I was better than anyone else, but I was just caught up in the seeming injustice of it all. I'm not proud of it, but that's just where I was back then: My own resentment kept me from rejoicing in some people's testimonies, especially the über-zealous born-again Christians. To me, it was as if some born-again Christians had this tendency to see themselves as hammers and other people as nails. And now, as newly minted hammers, their newfound purpose in life was to pound us sinners home, literally beating us over the head with their message: "I'm free now, I want to tell you why I'm free, and this is why you're living your life wrong."

In retrospect, my Prodigal Son attitude wasn't getting me any closer to God. It was actually distancing me from Him. But you couldn't have told me that back then because I wasn't ready to listen. I was too busy worrying about doing the right things and doing all the things that I thought were going to get me to heaven. I was constantly checking and double-checking that I was on the right path. Baseball chapel? *Check*. Prayer? *Check*. Be a good person. *Double check*. What I didn't know was that there were a few more things on the list. You know, things besides just having good intentions.

If there's one consistent trait I've had since childhood, it's that I have always been extremely well intentioned. I was fortunate to be raised by a great mom and dad who began lessons in moral training early and repeated them often. I'm sure I was still in diapers when I first started hearing about the Golden Rule. My mom and dad laid the framework for me, they taught me the moral principles, they taught me how to live with moral character, and they taught me right from wrong. I'm not convinced that this happens a lot in our society today, but it was the way things were in our house. Over time, it just became natural to me: I always wanted to do right. I never wanted to get into trouble.

So on one hand, there were my parents, guiding me along in my faith and helping me continually orient my life by my own moral compass. On the other hand, there was baseball and my dream to one day pitch in the major leagues. These were the two constants that defined my life, and therefore to a large extent my behavior, from the age of seven on. I avoided anything that might jeopardize my baseball ambitions or my morals. I never skipped school, I never drank, I never smoked. I was never caught up in doing things that would make me popular. I went to church, I went to Bible study, and I practiced my butt off. I always showed up on time and I never told a lie. I was a good kid. The ranking order in my life was God first, then family, school, and sports. It was a great way to be brought up and it helped form me into the man I am today. But my obsession with wanting to be good and do good didn't always pan out for me. It wasn't solidifying me, it wasn't giving me peace, and in certain scenarios it wasn't even turning out "right."

Everything I did for baseball and everything I did for people, the way I was living life—it wasn't for God. It was all about pleasing other people. I wanted people to like me. I wanted to do the right thing and do the right things for people. The way I was looking at things wasn't necessarily bad, but it was skewed. When you live your life like this—trying to please man and not God—I guarantee you will not find peace. And for that matter, you won't find your salvation either. You are far more likely to find frustration and confusion; at least that's how it was in my experience.

Prior to 1995, my misplaced intentions caused me not only heartache, but they cost me wins as well—I'm absolutely convinced of that fact. I just wasn't properly equipped to deal with success and failure yet. When things were going well, I'd feel good about myself. When things didn't go well, I felt like I let people down. It was always a roller coaster of emotions and mixed results. Take, for example, my relationship with my mom and dad at the time. My mom and dad were so important in my life that I wanted to make them proud every day. Everything that I did, the work that I put in, a lot of it was just to try to make them happy. I used to call my dad a lot, but I'd only call him if things were going well with baseball. If things weren't going well, if I was playing poorly, I didn't call. It wasn't right, but it was the way I was.

Honestly, I think that living a life in the public eye easily exacerbates this kind of thing. I'm sure there are a lot of people who can relate to some of the things I'm describing here, but the difference between me and most people is that my mistakes were often made in front of thousands of fans, if not broadcast on national TV as well. And when you're in that kind of spotlight, I think it becomes an almost monumental task to keep your own feelings of self-worth separated from your performance on the field. I know for me, before I truly became a Christian, a lot of times the way I performed was simply a measure of how well I was reacting to situations and controlling my thoughts. A lot of it basically boiled down to how I felt about myself at that moment. And, like I said, it was always a roller coaster.

Before that lunch with Walt Wiley at Bennigan's, all I was really doing was putting up a good Christian front. From the outside, everything looked and sounded really good. On the inside, when it came down to my motivations, my reasons for doing things, it wasn't adding up. I thought I was walking and living my life the way God wanted me to, but it really was the way *I* wanted to. What I was missing was the self-relying freedom and peace you get when you truly accept Jesus Christ as your personal savior. What I was missing was the knowledge that all I had to do was honor Him, please Him, and live for Him: Everything else was insignificant.

When I think about the things I really believed back then, I just have to shake my head at myself. Like I used to think about heaven as if there was a fence separating who was in and who was out. I *always* envisioned myself on the chosen side. But in reality, I was no different from anybody who claimed that God didn't exist at all, because I had not yet made a personal choice. I was more like a fish that was satisfied just to get pulled along by a current. What I hadn't yet considered was that maybe the current wouldn't take me where I wanted to go.

I think I knew on some level that I didn't have everything figured out when it came to my faith, but it was really people like Chaplain Walt Wiley who motivated me to do something about it. He made me realize that there's more to being a Christian than just harboring good intentions in your heart. Good intentions will certainly get you *somewhere* in life, just not always where you intended.

So back to Bennigan's. I can remember sitting there and asking Walt, "Why can't I live my life the way I want and then at forty years old turn it all over to God? You know, to that personal relationship you're talking about."

And Walt just said, "Well, the problem is you might not get to the age of forty, you might only get to thirty-nine. You don't know your expiration date."

It really was nothing more dramatic than that simple exchange of words. The lights just went on. It really was as simple as me sitting in Bennigan's going, "That's it." Things just finally clicked for me and it was at that point right there that I decided I didn't want to take chances with my life anymore. It was at that point that I basically said, "I hear you, God," and my life started to change radically. I finally understood the relationship that was possible with Jesus Christ.

Prior to that night, I was completely convinced that God put me here on earth and gave me a measure of talent, but everything else was up to me. I was always trying to bear the burdens of life myself, like a big backpack of junk. I'd wear that backpack every day and keep stuffing crud into it until it wore deep grooves into my shoulders. I'd empty it out sometimes, but the reality was that it always filled back up—whether it was my emotions on the field, or dealing with people, or getting ripped or wronged in the papers, I carried all of it around and tried to endure it all myself. The perspective that I gained at Bennigan's was really finally understanding and experiencing the freedom of giving everything—everything that I was trying so hard to handle on my own—to Him.

My life was completely different after that day. It was seriously like the difference between night and day. Pitching was different. Flying was different. The fear of things was gone; the fear of the unknown was gone. I had always wanted to control everything I could, but it finally just sank in to my brain that there are precious few things in life I could actually control. None of us has any control over those nightmarish, "what if?" scenarios in life, like a drunk driver crossing the center line, or a house fire caused by a lightning strike, or a tornado ripping through a town in the middle of the night. Nobody ever intends for these things to happen, but from time to time they do. That day at Bennigan's, I finally relinquished control over my life—something I had previously held on to with a kung fu grip. I finally surrendered myself to the power of God, and by doing so, I was finally able to know and experience the presence and peace of God that I had always heard about.

It is no coincidence that the very next year, 1996, would be the best year of my entire career. Nineteen ninety-six was truly a magical year. I remember even in spring training I just had this feeling in my heart, this newfound confidence. For some reason, I just knew that I was going to be a different pitcher on the mound. I'm really not a boastful guy at all, but I remember telling the guys at one point, "Okay, Maddux had a nice run, but it's my turn now." I didn't mean to say that I felt like I was suddenly better than Greg, but I just felt incredibly healthy and free. Around that same time I also told a group of reporters, "You're going to see a different guy." They really didn't know what I was talking about, but I told them, "I may lose my first one and win my next fourteen, but you're going to see a different guy out there." And that's what happened. I lost my first one and won my next fourteen. I went on to win twenty-four games and the National League's Cy Young Award.

Now, I'm not saying becoming a Christian armed me with some kind of supernatural prophetic abilities. And I'm certainly not saying I won the Cy Young because I accepted Christ. I won the Cy Young because I got freed up; I had given my big backpack of junk to God. Physically I was doing nothing different than what I had done in '91 or '92 or '93, and so on. The difference was all on the inside: in my heart, in my mind, in what I was feeling. If you look back on my career before '96, I had managed to string together a couple of good seasons, but it was always a constant struggle for me, thanks to my skewed perspective and my good old backpack of junk. Becoming a Christian allowed me to find peace and become the pitcher I always knew I could be. I'd always had a strong arm; now I finally had a strong faith to match.

Now, don't get the wrong impression here; it's not like I had this perfect peace in my heart and on the mound after that day at Bennigan's. It wasn't like that at all; I was tested. I faced the same sort of adversities I had always faced, but as a Christian, I was better able to keep my mind at peace. There were still times when I wasn't able to control my thoughts; I got mad; I got double-minded on occasion.

The Bible talks about being double-minded in the sense that you can't serve two masters at once: the world, man, money, God, you name it. It's the first commandment—"Thou shalt have no other Gods before me"—and it's expanded upon in other scriptures as well, such as Luke 16 in the parable of the Shrewd Manager. The gist of it is, you can't value your possessions, your money, your power, as you do God. When you do so, you're being double-minded and you're liable to be unstable in all your ways, as the Bible tell us in James 1:8.

When I was double-minded on the mound, thinking about other things I shouldn't have been thinking about, I didn't have a lot of good results. On the other hand, when I was clear in my objective that I was going to do the best I could, pour everything I had into it, and leave everything on the field, more often than not I was able to do exactly that. This to me was honoring God in a warrior's way, a way that said, "This is what He expects."

People sometimes ask me if I ever prayed on the mound, and if I did, what was I praying for? Now, I don't claim to have all the answers, or to have done all things the right way, but I always believed that when I needed to pray for something, I should pray for a chance to set a good example. I never felt myself on the mound going, *Okay, God, I really need this slider down and away.* I never did any of that. The only time I felt compelled to ask God for help when it came to baseball was on days when I didn't feel good, when I was physically hurting. On those days, I would pray something like *Lord, I just want to be able to do my best. Allow me to have peace in what I'm doing.*

I didn't pray for success; I didn't pray for failure for the other team. I didn't do any of that stuff. When it comes to athletes, I think God wants us be warriors. We are to train ourselves in such a way that there are no excuses and no alibis. And whatever happens, happens. You're trained in a way to glorify Him. He's not helping you pull a ball foul any more than he's helping you throw a strike. When I would step off the mound and try to refocus and clear my mind, I was doing exactly that—trying to refocus and clear my mind. It wasn't anything more than that.

Now, I'm not going to lie: I have prayed on roller coasters. You know like, *Please Lord, let me get through this because I don't think I'm going to make it*—those kind of prayers. But when it came to lacing up my shoes and buttoning up my uniform, my prayers were for peace and the concentration that I needed, the commitment to whatever I was doing. That's it.

My faith sustained me for the rest of my career in a way no other thing could have done. I don't make light at all of the fact that the one thing that allowed me to persevere through some of my toughest moments was my faith. When you consider the pressure of playing baseball, and then you add on everything else that I was always carrying in my backpack before that meal at Bennigan's, I'm telling you, there isn't a human alive who can withstand all that over time. Thankfully, I didn't have to anymore.

So that's the "drastic" change. How simple it was, yet how complex it can be at the same time. For a long time I used to think, *Gosh,*

I've got a boring testimony. Okay, so maybe it's not *boring,* but it is what it is. I think a lot of people have this perception that you've got to clean up to get God. I didn't have to clean up to go get God. I just had to keep searching until I found the answers that made sense to me and were consistent with what the Bible says. It was a wayward and, at times, prolonged journey, but I will always be thankful that I finally made it home.

Speaking of journeys, this would hardly be a complete accounting of my own journey if I didn't share a little bit about what it's like to be a born-again Christian on a pro baseball team. Well, the short answer is that it's not easy. I always felt like the Christian guys . . . well, we had to find our own niche. I didn't ever try to beat guys over the head about my beliefs; I just tried to be a quiet witness and example for God. Thankfully, I never felt the urge to attempt to convert the entire locker room—that would have been extremely ill-advised. But at the same time I tried hard never to shy away from openings to talk about what I believed. And let me tell you, one of the hardest things I ever had to do was to share in front of my team.

The most memorable time that I had a chance to witness was when I was asked to lead the chapel service during a West Coast road trip. It was some scheduling thing where the chaplain just couldn't make it. I was nervous about it. I wasn't sure what I was going to say or how I was going to say it. I was still kicking around ideas in the back of my mind during our flight to Denver, when the pilot came on the intercom and said, "Guys, we've got a problem here, I need everybody to buckle up. We're going to have to make an emergency landing. We don't know how bad it is, but we'll know when we land. You're going to see some emergency vehicles on the runway as we come in, just in case."

Now, let me tell you, flying on a charter flight with a pro baseball team isn't anything like "normal" air travel. Let's just say nobody makes us keep our seat belts fastened while we are seated, even though the captain has turned on the "fasten your seat belt" sign. It can get a little, shall we say, *festive* on occasion. Anyway, when the pilot came on and delivered the news, our entire plane sobered up in a hurry. The card playing, movie watching, and aisle skiing all abruptly ended. Guys were nervous, worried. You could see it in their faces as they looked out the windows in anticipation of landing.

Apparently there was a problem with the plane's rudder, and had it been a little windier, as it usually is in Denver, there could have been some issues with steering the plane down. But as it was, the winds were calm and we landed with no problem.

The next day, baseball chapel happened to be scheduled. Predictably, after that flight, a record crowd showed up. Maybe some guys were keeping hastily made promises after the pilot's announcement; I don't know. I just knew that by then I wasn't nervous about leading the service. When it came time to deliver the sermon, I just started talking about the plane ride:

> So when the pilot came on the air, what was the first thing you thought about? What is the first thing that came to your mind? Maybe, am I in good graces with my kids? My wife? Is everything in order? You know, all those things. Well, do you want to know the first thing that came to my mind? The first thing that came to my mind was "I'm all right. If this is my last flight—now, I sure hope it isn't— but if this is my last flight, everything's okay." I'm all right with God and I'm at peace with whatever happens. All of those other things are nice and I sure hope my stuff is in order, but the main thing is I'm all right with God.

I just shared what I honestly felt in my heart and guys were like, "Wow." My message seemed to resonate with the team.

I'm certainly proud of the things that I accomplished as a member of the Atlanta Braves. I'm proud that my legacy is a favorable one, and one associated with great games—both wins and losses. But, with that said, if I could pick one thing, one moment that the guys I played with remembered me for, I would pick this service over any of my so-called achievements on the field. Stats and win-loss records might matter for induction into the Hall of Fame, but they're pretty worthless for induction into heaven. If I encouraged just one of my teammates to keep walking along in his own journey of faith, that would mean way more to me.

My journey, my evolution in Christianity, if you will, was a process that really spanned from 1988, when I first entered the big leagues, to 1995. A lot of influential people had a hand in really getting me to that full understanding and commitment to Jesus Christ. First, there were my parents, who not only allowed me to pursue the career that I wanted to pursue, but also laid the foundation for my faith and were always there for me, encouraging me, but allowing me to experience things on my own.

In Atlanta, I was extremely fortunate to be surrounded by great teammates and chaplains who took this sort of caretaking mentality toward me. They saw the man I was and also the Christian that I could be. They led me and inspired me in such a way that I finally found my own path. It was a freeing experience and one for which I can only thank God.

My journey from becoming a Christian to today never ends. I'm a work in progress and it seems like with every year that goes by, I'm learning something new. (And sometimes it's stuff I think I should have learned a long time ago, to be quite honest.) People can speculate about whatever it is I'm trying to do, or who I am, or what I'm trying to be. It really still boils down to a few basic truths: Whatever I do, I'm passionate about. I'm a guy who doesn't just have opinions, but thinks very strongly about them. And everything that's happened to me in my life is real, authentic, and it is what it is. My hope today is that my ability on the baseball field takes a backseat to the man that I have become, which includes all the mistakes that I've made, that I know are paid for, and the mistakes I'll continue to make. (Hopefully, they at least won't be the same ones.)

I don't have all the answers, nor do I claim to. I can't tell you what to believe, where to look, or what questions to ask, but I can tell you this: Finding God is the most important thing you will ever do in your life. I encourage you to start your walk today if you haven't started already. Join a church, speak to a Christian you know, seek out a pastor or minister or priest that you feel comfortable with. Ask questions, discuss the things you think believe, find your answers. It will not be easy, but I promise you will not be alone. God will help you find your way; witness Jeremiah 29:13: "You will seek Me and find Me when you search for Me with all your heart."

I pitched in the major leagues for more than twenty years and I went through some really, really tough times, but even in the midst of those tough times, there's been nothing but peace in my heart since that day at Bennigan's when, for whatever reason, this unbelievable man, Walt Wiley, didn't beat me over the head with the things I should be doing. He didn't tell me what I wasn't doing. He just allowed me to process life in the way I was processing it. Fortunately, I had enough opportunities to get to that point.

And fortunately for me, I finally listened.

John at six months old. *Hank Gootee*

Carl L. Wienke

John at seven years old, playing accordion in Dad's band, the Sorrentos. On guitar is Eligio DiBerardo, on trumpet is Paul Bronchak, and on drums is Ben Peterson.

Grandpa, John Frank Smoltz; Dad, John Adam; John Andrew, Sr.; John Andrew; Walt Lipiec *(in back)*; and Uncle Tony Dannon *(at right)*.

Belland Photography

John's high school
graduation, with
Grandpa John
and Grandma
Theresa Smoltz.

John, Bernadette, Mike,
Mom, and Dad.

John with Grandma
and Grandpa Tersigni.

Three generations:
John Frank Smoltz,
John Andrew,
and John Adam.

Four generations:
John Frank Smoltz,
baby John Andrew,
John Andrew, and
John Adam.

Mike, Bernadette,
Mom, Dad, and John.

Seventh grade football. John was quarterback (*first row, red helmet*).

Eighth grade champions, St. Gerard's grade school (*fourth from left in the first row*).

Eighth grade suicide-squeeze bunt by John. This won the game and the championship.

Lansing Fire Fighters, summer baseball. John is fourteen years old (*second from right in the first row*).

Lansing Fire Fighters.
John is fifteen years old.

Lansing Catholic
Central Cougars,
John's sophomore year
(*#3, first row, third
from right*).

Detroit Tigers win the
1984 championship.

Tigers, '84 champs.

Waverly High School basketball.

John's senior year of high school
(*fifth from left, next to his cousin Michael Melfi in front of trophy*).

Pitched a no-hitter for Waverly.
Eileen Blass

John hit an extra-inning home run to win
the 1985 Diamond Classic in Lansing.
Greg DeRuiter

John is mobbed after hitting an extra-inning home run.

John with high school coach Phil Odlum after a dramatic home run. Every year John donates a $500 college scholarship to an athlete from this tournament.

North Team, National Sports Festival (U.S. Junior Olympic festival). John's team won a medal (#3, *top row*).

1985 National Sports Festival in Baton Rouge. John's team, North, won a medal. The Junior USA team was then selected from the four teams at the festival.

On the Junior USA team.

John was brought down and put in a Detroit Tigers uniform. He pitched for general manager Bill Lajoie and worked with Billy Muffett. He then stayed for the game and, in the middle, went to the GM office to discuss signing.

Original telegram received when John was drafted in the 22nd round by the Detroit Tigers.

First spring training, Lakeland, Florida. New car purchased with bonus money.

John (*second row, far right*).

First victory, with Dad at Lakeland.

This was taken in Toledo when John was with the Richmond Braves after being traded from the Tigers (Richmond Braves vs. Toledo Mud Hens). John's grandmother Bertha Tersigni is in the background.

Pitching for the Richmond Braves.

Original sheets from manager
of John's first major league game,
at Shea Stadium.

John's first MLB at-bat.

John with Warren Spahn, first year
with the Atlanta Braves. *SEBO*

SEBO

John's first MLB All-Star Game, 1989 *(seventh from right, top row)*.

John at the All-Star Game with President Reagan and Tom Lasorda.

John with Arnold Palmer.

Ed Gehringer, owner of Gehringer Jewelers; John Adam Smoltz; John Smoltz; and Charlie Gehringer, Hall of Fame second baseman for the Tigers. (John's grandmother's maiden name was Gehringer. He would be a fourth cousin.)

Surprise party when John won the Cy Young Award in 1996, with his many teammates and coaches: Javier Cavasos, Coach Carl Wagner (grade school and Fire Fighters), Rick Carrol (high school), Phil Odlum (Waverly baseball and basketball), and George Parkinson (football Athlete's Village).

In 2008, An Evening with Smoltz, Foxworthy and Friends, a charity fundraiser to benefit the John Smoltz Foundation. John was onstage with Jeff Foxworthy (MC), Chip Caray, Dennis Neagle, and Brett Butler *(not pictured)*.

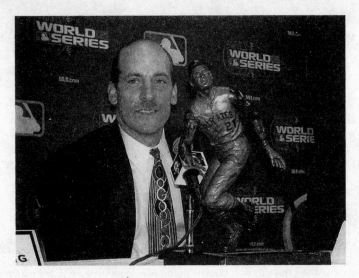

2005 Roberto Clemente Award.

Boston Red Sox

Boston Red Sox

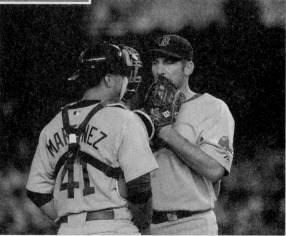

Chapter Ten

$$1 + 1 \neq 2$$

Ted Simmons had been in the big leagues for twenty years when we crossed paths for the first time in 1988 during my first spring training with the Atlanta Braves at West Palm Beach, Florida. I won't hazard a guess at what he was thinking when he sized up that year's crop of young pitchers angling for roster spots—myself included—but I can tell you whatever he saw prompted him to gather us all together in the loft above the bullpen one day and deliver a sermon on the art of pitching. He was preaching baseball like a Baptist preacher preaches the gospel, but instead of hellfire and damnation it was the gospel of chin music, down and away, and painting the black. It was awesome stuff, but unfortunately, I have to admit a lot of it went right over my head at the time.

Yet I'll always remember that he finished up his talk with some general advice about surviving as a major leaguer. "Listen," he said, "you guys have got to go get yourself an outlet from baseball. Find something you like to do and go do it. If you can't find a way to get away from the game, it'll eat you up. It will *consume* you."

Coming from a grizzled guy who had spent two decades crouching down behind home plate, knocking down wild pitches with his jaw on occasion, it seemed like advice worth taking, so I took it. Golf became the outlet that always propelled me through the mundane stretches and the mechanical grind (not to mention the pressure) of playing 162 games a year. It was the thing I could always count on to keep my competitive fire stoked year in and year out, from mid-February to October—if we were lucky enough to still be playing when the leaves were falling.

The more I got to know myself, through all my failures and regrettable outings, the more I realized what I needed to do, not only to enhance my strengths, but also to guard against my weaknesses and counterproductive habits. I learned that my high-energy personality could be both a blessing and a curse. On one hand, it always made me an intense competitor on the mound, but on the other hand, it was something that I had to learn to temper. See, I cared about pitching so much, it probably bordered on being unhealthy. I found out the hard way early on that I couldn't just sit around and think about pitching all the time. As Ted had warned, baseball easily consumed me. Golf proved to be the perfect antidote, something that, somehow, was always able to counteract all the pressure and lofty expectations I had a tendency to put on myself.

Through all the injuries, major surgeries, and just the monotony of doing the same thing for so many years, the two things I can point to that kept me persevering year after year *for so many* years were my faith in God and golf. There are, of course, lots of people who had a hand in encouraging me and taking care of me, not the least of whom were my manager, my doctors, and my family, but golf played a huge role in allowing me to pitch into my forties. Together with my faith, it helped me realize my full potential on the mound.

"Hey, let's go play golf."

Those were the five words that started it all. I don't recall the exact date, but it was sometime in 1985, after I had graduated high school and been drafted by the Detroit Tigers. I was hanging out at home in Lansing, Michigan, with Chuck Cascarilla, one of my best friends still to this day. It was Chuck who had the sudden urge to go play the public nine-hole course nearby.

I was like, "Golf? I've never played golf in my whole life."

I knew nothing, and I do mean *nothing,* about golf. The only thing I had ever thought about golf was that it must be a sport for nonathletes. Like most eighteen-year-olds, I thought I knew way more than I actually did.

But Chuck managed to talk me into it. Not that it was real a hard sell; I'm the type of guy who's always up for competing, but I can still remember teeing up the ball for the first time and thinking, *What in the heck am I doing?*

I was so clueless out on the course, it wasn't funny. You name it, I didn't know it. I remember looking at all the clubs in my bag and not even knowing where to start. Driver, iron, pitching wedge—it was like looking in a toolbox for the first time and seeing a bunch of tools that look really handy and useful, but having no idea or feel for how to use them to accomplish even the simplest repair. When I look in my bag today, after countless rounds of golf, instead of questions, I see answers. Once I know the lie, the yardage, and have taken note of potential hazards and other factors like wind, I usually know the right club for the job.

But back then, with no experience and barely any intuition, I did what I always do when I want to grow and learn: I started asking questions. Poor Chuck, who had some experience on a golf course, spent the entire round talking me through what to do on literally every shot.

Well, we finally got to the fifth hole. It was a long par five and I was still 160 yards away after my third shot. Chuck, my indentured caddy, recommended a five-iron. I figured the one thing I couldn't do, given the distance, was hit the ball too hard. So I took a couple practice swings and then proceeded to "grip it and rip it," as they say.

I definitely hit the snot out of that ball, but my technique left a lot to be desired. The leading edge of my club struck the middle of the ball and it took off like it was shot out of a bottle rocket, only parallel to the ground—and without the telltale sound effects. It seriously never got higher than ten feet in the air, but it was straight as an arrow, and flew right up the center of the fairway, hitting the ground about twenty yards from the hole.

Little blades of grass proved to be no match for the momentum on this ball; it rolled right up the fairway and onto the green. And it would have just kept on rolling if it didn't happen to be on a collision course . . . with the pin! Chuck and I watched as the ball crashed right into the stick and ricocheted into the hole.

"Man, Chuck," I said. "This game's *easy*."

Chuck just stood there in absolute disbelief, shaking his head. Then he looked over at me and the ear-to-ear grin on my face and said, "That's not even right. Your first birdie is a skulled five-iron."

My first birdie was like a slam dunk launched from the foul line—equal parts improbable and awesome—and it had left me smitten with the game.

Not long after, I reported to the Detroit Tigers Class A affiliate in Lakeland, Florida, where I had a gazillion hours of nothing but time, so I bought some clubs and started convincing guys to come out and play nearby courses with me. But it was actually the infamous Doyle Alexander trade that sent me to the Braves in 1987 that really started my evolution in golf.

In Atlanta, I was fortunate to have the late Rick Mahler, a veteran starting pitcher for the Braves, really take me under his wing and introduce me to golf in the big leagues. Every round with Rick raised my golf IQ. He took the time to teach me about the history and the etiquette of the game, as well as the fundamentals, while we played eighteen holes. I've never taken a golf lesson, but with Rick guiding me along, I soon realized that golf wasn't just something I enjoyed doing; I seemed to be blessed with a little natural ability for it as well. I just have a knack for it, even going back to that very first birdie. I've never shot a hundred in my life—and there honestly haven't been many rounds in the nineties either.

But besides basically having him teach me Golf 101, there was definitely another perk to hanging around Rick. You see, Rick had this famous little black book that all the guys wanted to borrow whenever we rolled into a new town. He always knew where to go to have a good time, and he was always gracious enough to bring me along and let me experience things I never would have experienced otherwise. Rick taught me how to appreciate the good things in life. You know, like Oakmont, Bay Hill, and Winged Foot. His little black book was a veritable *Farmers' Almanac* for pro baseball players who were addicted to golf. It had all the answers you needed for every city you visited: the closest courses to the stadium, the best courses within reasonable driving distance, and who you needed to call to get a tee time.

All of those years that I traveled to all those cities—Los Angeles, Denver, St. Louis, Cincinnati, Philadelphia—my first thought was always, *What great golf courses are near here?* I never went to a single museum. I guess that sounds bad, but the history of a city or some fancy artwork just wasn't anything that ever interested me.

A perpetual mix of baseball, golf, and downtime spent with my family proved to be the perfect formula for me. It kept me hungry and staved off the feelings of monotony that sometimes settle in midway through a season; I was always looking forward to my next day and whatever was up next in my own rotation: pitching or golfing.

Over the years I developed a routine that helped me balance the demands of playing baseball, the escape of playing golf, and my responsibilities as a husband and father. I tried to pare my life down to the bare essentials, and on any given day of the week I was basically following one of two schedules: one for days I pitched (when I didn't golf) and another for the four rest days in between (when I sometimes did). What I was doing on any given day always depended on a variety of factors: when I was scheduled to start next, if we were playing at home or away, and if the kids were in school. Perhaps it sounds complicated, but it really kept things simple for me. During the season, I didn't make time for much besides my family, baseball, and golf.

When we were playing at home, spending time with my family was always the priority. On rest days, I would get up, make the kids breakfast, and see them off to school. It was really the only way I was going to see them when the baseball season overlapped the school year. For the most part, I tried to fit in my golf on road trips—when my family wasn't able to come along—or during spring training when the kids were still in school.

Keeping things in balance was always a challenge, just as it is for all parents, I think. Most people work and have families. Most of us have things we like to do and quite often *need* to do in order to blow off steam and take a breather from the sources of stress in our life. The same dynamic that existed for me and my family during my baseball career still exists after my retirement from playing, and I thrive whenever I can effectively balance three things: family, baseball (now as a broadcaster), and golf.

I loved getting up in the morning and going to play a round of golf. I'd make it a point to get out on the course early so I'd be done by around noon, leaving me with several hours of downtime before it was time to go to the park.

I never felt worn out or tired after I finished a round. It was actually quite the opposite. As far as I was concerned, going out and playing eighteen holes was like plugging me into a wall charger: It always seemed to reenergize my inner battery. It also enhanced my focus, enabling me to go to the park and devote my complete attention to my off-day routines.

After I was done prepping for my next start—which could include watching video, meeting with the pitching coach, or throwing a bullpen, depending on what day it was—I'd go sit in the dugout and watch the game. I always tried to observe as much as possible from my perspective on the bench. Sometimes I was responsible for charting pitches, but even if I wasn't, I'd really try to pay careful attention as the game developed, pitch by pitch. I always figured if I was sitting there, I might as well try to learn something (and joke around a bit and share a few laughs with my teammates as well). And once the game was over, I was headed back home.

Professional baseball, by its very nature, lends itself to late nights and this sort of work-hard, play-hard mentality. For me, that was true, too, just in a different way than it was for some other players. At times, my passion for golf sort of made me this square guy in the round world of baseball, but I was okay with that. Even going back to my early years in the league, even as a young rookie, I was really comfortable with who I was and who I wasn't. I was always much more concerned with being able to perform for my team at my highest level whenever I was called upon than my relative popularity within the clubhouse.

If I wanted a reputation for anything, it was for being the guy who everyone wanted to have the ball when the stakes were the highest. *That* was my priority. And in order to do that, I learned early on that I needed to do certain things. For me, that included making time to play golf.

The game I stumbled upon thanks to Chuck turned out to be a tremendous blessing to my pitching career. Golf was such a release for me. In baseball you're always trying to perfect your mechanics, you're trying to perform. When I played golf, I didn't worry about my mechanics. I just let go and had fun. It's no coincidence that some of the greatest games in my career happened to follow rest days on which I had been able to play eighteen holes. The day after golf, I would just feel fresher on the mound, both mentally and physically. Golf freed up my mind in a way that nothing else ever seemed to be able to do.

As perfect an outlet as golf was for me, it's safe to say that a lot of people—even my own teammates at times—had a hard time understanding how golf helped make me a better pitcher. There seemed to always be this undercurrent of suspicion, this notion like "Wow, imagine how good he could be if he ever gave up golf and truly focused on baseball."

Whenever a position player had a problem with my golf, I'd say, "Buddy, you and I were both shortstops in high school. We were both the best players on our team. You chose the wrong position." In baseball, as in life, there are trade-offs. The shortstop *gets* to play every day. A starting pitcher *can't* pitch every day. As the old cliché goes, you can't have your cake and eat it, too.

The one person who always understood how golf benefitted me was my manager Bobby Cox. Bobby stood beside me all those years, in some ways acting as a buffer between me and the front office. The great thing about Bobby wasn't just that he allowed me to golf, which he did, it's that he had a completely different attitude about it. He *embraced* it. He was always one to encourage and even remind his players to do things like this, to find things they enjoyed doing away from the game. He knew it couldn't be all baseball, all the time.

When it came to the front office, though, it was a slightly different story. Now, it wasn't like they hemmed and hawed after every round of golf; they respected Bobby's decision to allow me and other pitchers to golf on our rest days. But it was always something you knew was liable to be used against you in the future. The tension surrounding my golf really cropped up every time anything was slightly off or wrong with me. Golf became the front-office guys' built-in excuse for everything.

It wasn't really until I became the closer for Atlanta that my golf habit really became a point of contention with them. Over the years they had grown to sort of tolerate my fondness for playing golf on rest days in between my starts. But for someone who was a closer, things were different.

I had a feeling that when I became a closer, my golf was going to do more than just raise a few eyebrows upstairs in the front office and in the media. There were no longer days prescribed for work and days prescribed for rest. I could pitch a couple nights in a row, every other day, or go three to four days between pitching just as I did as a starter. The problem, in the minds of the powers that be, at least, was where golf fit into this new schedule. But I resolved to continue golfing, even on days when I might have to pitch.

Now, it's not like I was running around doing whatever I wanted to do like an entitled veteran. It wasn't like that at all. First of all, I *knew* that playing a round of golf would not in any way affect my ability to pitch one inning a day. And second, I had already talked about it with Bobby and he agreed with me. He knew how important golf was to me and he also knew he could trust me to be smart about it. I always had such respect for the game of baseball that I never did anything in my career without first checking with my manager and/ or a doctor.

But predictably, when I started working out of the bullpen and I was playing golf as usual, I started hearing about comments being made upstairs. General Manager John Schuerholz talked to me about it directly in Colorado when we played golf at the same time on the same course—ironically, I set his round up for him!

He said, "Do you think golf will cause a problem with you closing now? I mean, look, I understand when you were a starter this was something you did on your off days, but with closing, it could be on the same day. Don't you think . . ."

I said, "No, John. It will not be a problem. I play golf at eight o'clock in the morning. I come back at noon. I've hit the ball probably thirty-five to forty times and putted the rest. I'm in a cart. If I can't get ready to put in one inning's work at nine or ten o'clock at night, something's really wrong here and it's not my golf."

Fifty-five saves later, no one said another word to me about it.

Winning baseball games is always the best way to prove your critics wrong. Right, wrong, or indifferent, I think that fact is just part of the nature of sports today. When you're winning, nobody questions you or your methods. But when you're struggling, or your team is losing, questions are asked. Everyone—the media, the fans, the team's front office—becomes hungry for answers. They examine and dissect every angle and try to come up with reasons why expectations are not being met.

Now look, this is not an unhealthy discussion, on the surface. Obviously this is how teams become successful, by knowing what adjustments to make over the course of the season. The problem is that too often the conversation strays from a topic like the lack of depth in the bullpen to players' habits away from the game. In the search for reasons why things have gone awry, possible distractions provide easy answers. In reality, though, most of the reasons they come up with just aren't valid. The way I see it, there are baseball things that cause you to win and lose and there are nonbaseball things that can be *blamed* for why you win or lose. And the two are not the same.

I've heard people make such ridiculous claims: that a team didn't win because the players played cards too often, or a team didn't win because they *didn't* play cards. If you ask me, a lot of time it's really much ado about nothing; it's just hauling out the same old excuses for explaining failure. The underlying logic isn't sound, but such talk has a powerful effect on some organizations today. Some teams have become so obsessed with what activities like golf or cards *seem* to imply about players that they just eliminate them from the get-go and ban players from engaging in them. It's certainly an easy way to avoid bad press, or the threat of news stories casting certain perceptions about a team's failures. But if you ask me, all the attention on these aspects of the game is counterproductive and, well, just plain distracting.

Think about it. We only read or hear these stories when things *aren't* going well. When a guy is overweight but he's hitting well, no one says a word. When he's not hitting well . . . he's overweight. With me, when things went wrong, or when I might have had an injury here or there, people had to come up with something. And golf was that something. If I was in a slump? It was because of golf. If my elbow was hurting? It was because of golf. If my shoulder hurt, it was surely because of all that golf. I really didn't have any other habits that they could point to, or pin on me (well, I did go to Bible study a lot, but that never came up). Golf was always the scapegoat, the magic answer for what was wrong with John Smoltz.

Had I not played golf, I'm not sure what they would have blamed.

The truth is, sometimes you just don't play well and it is counterproductive for others to pile on the blame while you're trying to work it out. A second truth is that I played almost all of my golf with other teammates, but because I was so up front about how much I enjoyed the game, I drew more attention—and occasionally more criticism—than anybody else.

At the end of the 2011 season, we all saw what happened in Boston after the Red Sox had one of the worst closing months in baseball history and fell out of the playoffs. What came next were stories from anonymous sources that some Red Sox pitchers were drinking beer in the clubhouse during games and perhaps even in the dugout. The media latched onto this story, using it to help paint this picture of a supertalented yet lackadaisical team that frittered away what looked like a sure-thing trip to the 2011 postseason.

Now look, I haven't talked to these guys; nor do I claim to know anything more about the situation than what we've all heard from the media, but I'm not buying it. I'm not condoning any players' behavior, but I'm not buying the stories either. I'm not buying that the Red Sox's hapless, 7–20 September record can be hung on the heads of pitchers drinking beer in the clubhouse on their off days—if they indeed were. This is just one of those situations where a team happened to have one of the worst months in baseball history and now everybody wants to know why. Something—other than poor performance and injuries—has to take the blame.

See, the thing that I hate about this story is that it makes it seem like these guys were lazy, that they weren't pitching well, and that they obviously didn't care. What I can say after playing with the Red Sox not too long ago is that I've seen how hard some of these guys get after it. So to me, that part of the story couldn't be more wrong. When it comes to being prepared to do their job, I guarantee these guys were as prepared and as focused as you can get. Whatever went on that might have caused team distraction or team dissension is what went on. Like I said before, it's not as simple as one plus one equals two.

Year in and year out, I battled the inherently flawed perception that playing golf somehow meant I wasn't taking baseball seriously. For me, nothing could be further from the truth. I have never put too much stock in my career stats, but if they are useful for one thing, it's for proving the following point: My golfing habit shouldn't have worried anyone.

Well, that is, anyone *besides* a guy trying to get the barrel of his bat on my cutter.

Chapter Eleven

FAIRWAY TALES

I was not only incredibly fortunate to find an outlet that really worked for me and a manager who allowed me to pursue it, but I was also lucky enough to be surrounded by guys who shared the desire to tee it up on their off days. It was really remarkable how this worked out, but almost to a man, everybody who came to Atlanta to pitch during this era either golfed already or was ready and willing to be indoctrinated into our culture. Steve Avery, Pete Smith, Tom Glavine, Greg Maddux, Charlie Leibrandt, Kevin Millwood, Denny Neagle—I could go on and on. We all went out and played golf together, and I'm telling you, we had the time of our lives.

For us, it was always golf served with ample sides of trash talking and practical jokes. When we got out on the golf course, we undoubtedly resembled a bunch of fraternity brothers more than a bunch of pitchers. We always kept score, but we also prided ourselves on inventing new and improved ways to startle, scare, or otherwise mess with each other during a round. We loved to draw a reaction out of somebody. When we weren't busy thinking up novel ways to screw with each other, Mother Nature certainly did her part, duly delivering some of the most hilarious moments. That reminds me, have I mentioned that Greg Maddux is scared to death of snakes? Words cannot do it justice, but trust me, whenever Greg spotted a snake, a scene of sheer, funky-chicken *panic* ensued. You'd be laughing for the next day and a half guaranteed.

One of our trademark maneuvers was to mess with someone who was legitimately trying like heck to bury an important putt. If this has never happened to you, take it from me, there's nothing like standing over your ball, completely focused down to your last exhale, then smoothly drawing back your putter only to have someone sneak up right behind you and whip the flagpole through the air right as you make contact with the ball. The noise that flag can make if you whip it fast enough—I'm telling you, it's enough to shock you into next week, not to mention make you inadvertently fire your ball eleven feet past the hole. But at least it was standard procedure to take a mulligan in those circumstances. That's when you know the guys care.

Typically, there was always a subplot underscoring the round and the main story line of who was winning or losing on any given day. The antics revolved around whoever happened to be sharing carts that day. We never stripped down to shirts and skins to differentiate between teams, but it was always understood that it was "every cart for itself." A cart left unattended and without proper surveillance was an open invitation for mischief. The occupants were liable to return and find the key missing, the scorecard pencil hopelessly lodged between the windshield and the dashboard, or the bag straps loosened to allow for a nice game of fourteen-club pickup the next time they punched it. We were really just a bunch of guys doing our best to *not* act our ages.

One of the best stories from golfing with the guys involves three main characters: Steve Avery, PGA Tour pro Billy Andrade, and a dead bass. On this day we were playing in two groups of four: Steve, Greg Maddux, and I were in the lead group, and Billy was in the trail group with Tom Glavine. So we're out playing the round at Keene's Pointe, an amazing course near Orlando, and Steve finds this big dead bass, like four or five pounds easy, washed up on the side of a pond. He promptly picks it up and stuffs it behind the gas pedal of Greg's golf cart when he isn't looking. (Standard procedure whenever you find a dead bass, right?)

Of course, the next time Greg gets in his cart and stomps down on the pedal, much to his consternation, neither the pedal nor the cart is going anywhere. He finally looks down to see what the heck the problem is and is predictably taken aback by the dead bass lying on the floorboard of the golf cart. But then he just starts laughing. You come to expect shenanigans like this when you golf with our crowd.

So Greg, inspired by the classic dead-bass-behind-the-gas-pedal trick, attempts to one-up Steve. After our group finishes out number nine, he retrieves the dead bass from the cart and promptly stuffs it, mouth first, into the hole. It was so big that half of its body and tail flopped over onto the green. We just stood there cracking up at the sight of a dead fish nestled up next to the flag. Nothing had even happened yet, but it was already *hilarious*.

So the next thing you know, Billy hits his tee shot into the water. He takes his drop, and then somehow manages to hit this epic iron shot out of the rough. We're all standing there, our eyes peeled on the arc of the ball, thinking, *Man, that's a nice shot. Look at thing carry . . . you don't think it's going to . . .* as the ball promptly landed on the green and started rolling toward the hole. *Wow, it looks like it's on a good line.* Still rolling. *You don't think?* Still rolling. *No, it's not going to . . . (Gulp.)* The ball disappeared into the hole!

Now, out of all the things that could have happened, *that* certainly wasn't what we were envisioning. Everyone in Billy's group was hooting and hollering about the birdie and they didn't even have a clue about what else was in the hole. With the dead bass and the flagpole, it was tight quarters in there. There was only one gap, just wide enough for the ball, remaining. And somehow, Billy's ball had found that precise spot like a heat-seeking missile. It was nothing short of a miraculous shot, and let me tell you, we never heard the end of it. That dead bass turned out to be a real pain in the . . . well, you know what I mean.

As much as we all loved playing golf together, it became pretty clear early on that if I wasn't the one organizing it, it wasn't happening. I think it's fair to say that I was the most avid and structured guy in the bunch, so I took care of all things golf. For lack of a better term, I became the *golf concierge* of the Atlanta Braves: I made all the phone calls, I got all the rental cars, and I lined up all the tee times. I told the guys the time and the place, and their only job was to show up. It was a lot of legwork, but I did it and it was always well worth the effort.

And thanks to Rick Mahler, I was already well on my way to authoring my own little black book. It actually came in really handy, because over the years we played at so many places that I would never have been able to remember all the people we had met and spoke to at various clubs. And things like people's names are no small matter when you are basically trying to talk your way onto a golf course. I learned that fact the hard way in '89 and '90 when I would call a place like Oakmont out of the blue. I'd finally get a clubhouse guy or a starter on the phone and I'd say, "Hey, this is John Smoltz with the Braves and I was just wondering . . ." *Click.* A lot of times I didn't even get to finish the sentence. Now, after 1991, I didn't always get to finish my sentences either, but at least I wasn't getting interrupted by a dial tone anymore. I was usually getting interrupted by an excited voice wanting to know who else I was bringing with me and when we'd like to play.

For Maddux, Glavine, and me especially, golf was our common bond. The three of us, we just had the perfect personalities for one another. I was the jokester, Maddux was the goofy son of a gun, and Glavine was the dry, stoic guy. I'd have to work on Tommy a little bit, get him to come out of his shell, but once he did, he could be really funny. We had such camaraderie together, we loved competing against each other, and it was really through all our rounds of golf that we became great friends and trusted allies. Some of my favorite memories of Greg and Tommy stem from the time we spent out on the golf course.

Take Greg Maddux, for example. Here's a guy they called "The Professor," and for good reason when it came to baseball. It was like his mind was an encyclopedia of his pitching career and he could thumb through the chapters at whim, recalling all kinds of details on hitters he had already faced, including what pitches he had thrown on what count and what it had led to—walk, hit, strikeout, etc. It was information he exploited ruthlessly on the mound. Here was a guy who never had a 98 mph fastball but could downright *baffle* a hitter. He had this almost photographic memory for pitching, but he was *horrible* at remembering people's names. I'm not much better, but seriously, he's the worst.

So there we were at the Houston Country Club one time and we introduce ourselves to our caddies. Greg's caddy is named M.C.

I almost lost it right there as they were shaking hands, but I managed to hold it together long enough until we had teed off and the caddies were out of earshot. Then I was like, "Man, Greg, this is *perfect*. You'll never forget this caddy's name. Just remember MC Hammer. You got this."

Greg's penchant for screwing up names was a running joke with all of us. It never failed that one of us would bring along some friends to play with us for the day and Greg would end up calling them all sorts of things, anything besides their actual names, before we were done. Say, for example, the two friends were named Mike and Eric. We'd all shake hands and introduce ourselves before we started the round, just as anyone would do. But the next thing you know, Greg's calling them Mark and Earl and he doesn't even realize what he's doing. He's just trying to make conversation and be friendly, as he is by nature, but meanwhile he's punting their names into the stands left and right. The rest of us would all be snickering and getting a kick out of it, when we weren't busy explaining to our buddies that Greg didn't mean anything by it. He was just really bad with names.

So, back to good ol' M.C. I remember standing there, thinking to myself, *There's just no way he can screw this name up.*

Well, as it turns out, during the round Greg came really close to hitting M.C. with one of his tee shots. It was just one of those things: a misfired shot, a total accident. Greg felt bad about it, even though his ball had missed M.C., and as we drove up the fairway we stopped so he could get out and apologize to him before we continued playing.

So Greg walks over to the caddy and says something like "Man, that's my bad, C.W."

I seriously fell out of the cart. I mean, my goodness. Here's a guy who can remember a changeup he threw on a 2–2 count to Mike Piazza in the fifth inning with one out and a guy on third in a game *four* years ago, and he can't remember a caddy's name. That's just ridiculous. We finally ended up just warning friends not to take it personally when—as opposed to if—Greg screwed up their names. If he couldn't remember M.C.'s name, there was no hope he'd remember theirs.

I don't know how apparent this was to all the fans, but Greg, Tommy, and I were genuinely friends who enjoyed each other's company. We really enjoyed a cohesive relationship, even though we were basically taking turns for the Cy Young (except when Greg hogged it for four years straight there) for five or six years. We competed against each other all the time in golf and in baseball, but we never let anything get too serious. It was always about giving a guy a hard time, not messing with him to the point that you really trounced on his confidence. We kept it fun and I think we all made each other better.

Without any hesitation, I readily admit that I would have been a completely different pitcher without the influence of Greg and Tommy. I learned so much from those two, and golf opened that door for me. Greg and I played together for eleven years; Tommy and I for fifteen. If you can just imagine the amount of time we spent in cars traveling to and from golf courses, let alone on the courses themselves, you start to get the idea. Golf became the medium through which we shared a lot of things, not the least of which was baseball.

When we were together, I tried to tap into things that made me better as a baseball player and I wasn't afraid to ask questions. I think we all felt like this, like there was something we could learn from each other. We all had our strengths and our weaknesses. We all brought a different perspective to the table. Like, for example, I had been trying for years to learn how to throw a changeup and was never really able to get the hang of it. Here I had access to two guys who could throw devastating changeups. So I asked them about it, and they tried to explain it to me. Now, I never did master the changeup, but I assure you it wasn't due to a lack of effort or asking questions on my part.

One of the most important things I learned from Tommy he didn't even have to communicate to me. I learned a lot just watching him pitch all those years: his mental toughness, his ability to always go out there and put himself in position to win baseball games. His stubbornness was a big part of how he was successful, and I tried to emulate him in that way.

When it came to Maddux, I think I was served an apprenticeship in pitching just sitting there in the dugout next to him during games. Even from the dugout, Greg just had this ability to pick up on little things that a hitter would do that would expose his flaws. I wouldn't see it, I couldn't pick it up like that during a game; I'd have to see it on video. But he could recognize it right there. What was also uncanny was some of the things he could predict. I can't tell you how many times we would be in the middle of a conversation and he would suddenly tap me on the shoulder and say, "Hey, heads up. If this pitch gets down and in, all he can do is pull it foul, and it's coming over our dugout." And sure enough, the next thing you know, the ball is whistling over the dugout and we're ducking out of the way. Stuff like this happened on more than one occasion and it always amazed me.

When it came down to it, we were always of the mind-set that it was "us against them." Not "Glavine vs. Smoltz" or "Maddux vs. Glavine" or so forth. Sure, we cared about our personal stats on some level, but really our desire to be able to pitch deep into games consistently and put together quality starts was a by-product of driving for our ultimate goal: helping our team win championships. Thankfully, we did get to accomplish that goal together in 1995.

Okay, so enough about Glavine and Maddux. Their heads are already big enough as it is. Let me pick on one of my other partners in crime for a moment: Steve Avery. As you might have guessed already from the dead-bass story, Steve is seriously one of the funniest guys I've ever been around. Just saying his name makes me want to laugh, especially when I start thinking about my favorite golf story starring him.

On this occasion we were playing at the Old Marsh Golf Club in Palm Beach Gardens, Florida. Now, I think most people know that Florida is one of those states where it pays to keep your eyes peeled for wildlife when you're spending time outdoors. The state harbors some reptiles that not only have a penchant for hanging out on golf courses, but let's just say they can ruin your day. What we all learned through this story is that it's not just the reptiles you need to be concerned about: You better keep your eye out for those baby cranes as well.

In this story, we had all made it to the general vicinity of the green on the eighteenth hole and things were serious. Scores were tight and bragging rights would depend on who could finish the hole with one putt or two. As we all went about our business and focused on our final shots, what we all failed to notice was a family of cranes, complete with little babies, meandering about in the adjacent marsh.

Steve's ball had landed on the back edge of the green, closest to the marsh. He walks up to the green, takes a quick look at his lie, and then starts backpedaling toward the marsh, attempting to read the break.

So there's Steve, backing up one step at a time, his attention completely focused on the pin and the distance that appears to be between it and his ball. And there are the cranes, just wandering about in the marsh, doing whatever it is cranes do. Steve was maybe fifteen yards from the hole at this point, which, as it turned out, was one step too close to one of the baby cranes.

Mayhem ensued, prompting both emotion and commotion. The mama crane, obviously fearing for her young, lets out this banshee-like scream. It was seriously like something out of a horror movie; it was just *deafening*. That alone was going to be enough to require a wardrobe change for Steve. At this point, though, his only concern was getting away from the mama crane and her precious brood. Quickly.

Meanwhile, the rest of us stood there doing what we do best: laughing our butts off. Well, that is, until we saw what was coming from the other direction: Big Daddy Crane.

Big Daddy Crane must have heard the mama's cry for help and he came swooping in from Steve's blind side. It seriously looked like the bird was going to land on his head! We're like, "Steve! Look out behind you!" He turns around and here's this ginormous bird coming right for him. I mean the wingspan on this thing is god-awful big; it looked like something straight out of *Jurassic Park*. Steve took one look at the talons closing in on him and took off running.

Once Steve had sprinted out of harm's way, the cranes wandered off. The rest of us laughed until we cried. And then we laughed some more. Steve just walked around shaking his head. So that'll teach you, beware when you backpedal, especially in Florida.

I'm convinced that it was things like this—you know, your typical run-of-the-mill crane brushups—that helped make our rotation better. All the time we spent together, all the ridiculous things that happened—they made us comfortable with each other. Golf was our collective escape from baseball, but it also became the avenue through which we shared a lot of good information. We were never out on the course breaking down baseball like it was rocket science, but we picked each other's brain. We'd talk about the next team we were facing, who was hot in their lineup, what made that guy vulnerable, etc. It wasn't all we talked about, but we did it enough that we all gained knowledge.

Now, don't get me wrong me here: I'm not saying golf is the answer for every starting rotation in baseball. I'm just saying it worked for us. It's like when people try to compare us to the Philadelphia Phillies of today. From what I know, I don't think their pitchers golf much. I don't know if they even hang out much. You'd have to go ask them what they do, but whatever it is, they obviously have a shared mindset of perfection. They may go after it in a different way than we did, but for the Phillies, it works. You can't argue with their numbers; and you can't argue with our numbers.

One thing is true, though. We enjoyed a luxury that hardly any other rotation enjoys today: Not only did we love to play golf; we were *allowed* to play golf. That fact is a reflection on both our manager and on the way we went about our business.

Each and every one of us took baseball seriously. We respected the game, we did our work, and we were responsible when it came to fitting in time to hit the golf course. We also respected Bobby Cox and his expectations, and we would never have done anything to make him think we were taking advantage of his leniency or letting golf become a distraction. If we had acted like a bunch of goofballs, I'm sure Bobby would have treated us as such and we probably wouldn't have been able to play golf.

My time on the golf course together with the guys in our rotation, Tommy Glavine and Greg Maddux especially, was an amazing gift to my game. I can't imagine baseball without them or without golf. And I suspect that might be the case for all us.

My golf story really doesn't end there, though—or at least I hope it doesn't. While it was a recreational outlet during my baseball career, I now actually have my sights set on playing professional golf in the future: My aspiration is to someday qualify to play on the PGA's Champions Tour.

You have to be at least fifty years old to be eligible to compete in events in this senior version of the PGA Tour, so this gives me roughly five years to try to get my game ready and learn how to play competitive golf. It's a daunting task, since I will be matching my will and experience against guys who are doing this for a living, but I truly believe that I have what it takes to compete at this level. And what may not be obvious is that I've been testing myself for years now in order to be able to make this jump.

I actually had the remarkable privilege of playing more than thirty rounds with Tiger Woods, back when he was in his prime. Watching Tiger play the game, the shots he took, the way he saw things—it was just unbelievable. Even high-definition TVs couldn't do it justice; you couldn't truly capture Tiger's greatness when he was at the top of his game except with your own eyes. To see him do what he could do in person, it was an incredible, incredible learning experience for me.

Once I got over the intimidation factor of playing golf with Tiger, I did, on occasion, give him a little run for his money. I never beat him, but there were several times when I *almost* beat him. But then again, that *almost* word is pretty popular when you talk about Tiger. I'm one of many guys who can say I almost beat Tiger.

Let me just say before I go any further that the events that unfolded with Tiger in November 2009 were as shocking and disappointing to me as they were to a lot of other people. We haven't spoken since, but I am rooting for him to rally and do incredible things; I am confident he will one day regain his form as one of the best golfers in the world.

I can't say that I ever beat Tiger, but I can say one year I beat Annika Sorenstam head-to-head. This was back in 2003 when Tiger and Annika were, respectively, the top-ranked men's and women's pro tour golfers in the world. I was really amped up for the round, but of course, it couldn't be enough for me to just go *play* with them. No, I've got to call Tiger up the night before and tell him: "Just between us, I'm willing to make a nice, friendly wager that I'm going to beat Annika tomorrow. But don't say anything about it during the match."

So we showed up the next day and Tiger and I are just playing it cool like nothing else is going on. Certainly, nobody has said a word about the bet. Then literally right before I am about to tee off the round, Tiger blurts out, "John, I'll bet you a hundred bucks that Annika beats you today."

Annika is standing right there and I'm like, *great*. But being a man with both pride and ego, I, of course, say, "All right, you're on."

Now, before I continue, it's only fair to point out that this was Annika's first time playing with Tiger, and when you're playing with Tiger for the first time, you're liable to do a few things you've *never* done before. We were also playing Isleworth Golf & Country Club near Orlando from the back tees, which back then probably covered 7,200 yards. That's a long way for anyone, let alone Annika, who was used to playing slightly shorter courses.

I played three under for the first eight holes before tapping in a triple bogey on eighteen, our ninth hole, since we had started on the back nine. Up until that point, I was playing really well and capitalizing on Annika's first-time-playing-with-Tiger nerves. I thought my miscue on eighteen might lead to my demise, but I managed to match Annika shot for shot down the front nine and finish the day a couple strokes under her score.

The round was great, beating Annika was obviously great, but I'll tell you what I truly cherished more than anything—the chance just to watch those two practice. There they were at the very top of their games and I got to stand there after the round and get an education not only on how hard they worked at their trade, but on the prowess they both clearly possessed. I would have taken the opportunity just to watch them practice over the chance to play any day, but thankfully, I didn't have to choose.

I never said a word about beating Annika, with the exception of a little "I told you so" when I snatched my new hundred-dollar bill out of Tiger's hands, but news about the round got out quickly. Everywhere I went for the next three or four days, people kept bringing it up. Michigan State was playing Florida that year in the men's NCAA Division I Basketball tournament and I had the chance to go to the game during spring training. I remember sitting down in my seat and a guy yelling at me, "Way to go, Smoltz! You beat Annika!"

The following year, Annika, Tiger, and I teed it up again, this time at Reunion Resort near Orlando. On this day, Annika shot in the sixties, beating me handily by five or six shots. She let me have it, serving up a round chock-full of both birdies and good-natured smack talk; she duly reminded me why she was getting paid well to play golf for a living.

Now, I'm not saying I think I am going to play professionally someday because I once beat Annika. Rather, I think I have a good chance at playing professionally because I am more than willing to get out of my comfort zone and force myself to stretch and grow. I wasn't afraid to fail in baseball and I am not afraid to do it now in golf.

While I'm convinced I can play with anybody, there's a critical piece I have yet to master: how to play tournament golf. You see, I like to play golf really, really fast. If I tee off at 8 A.M., I can actually play four rounds of golf—all seventy-two holes—in one day, finishing up around 6 P.M. A lightning-fast pace is great for me, but you just can't play like that within a tournament format. Learning how to deal with those idle minutes between shots has proven to be an enormous challenge for me.

Since I retired from baseball, I have played in two one-day U.S. Open qualifying tournaments, two Georgia Opens, and most notoriously, I accepted a sponsor's exemption to play one event on the Nationwide Tour, which is basically the Triple-A version of the PGA Tour. So far, I have made the cut twice, but it's safe to say those aren't the moments anyone remembers.

I always have this notion that I'm going to shock the world. Well, it's safe to say I shocked the world at my first Nationwide event—the South Georgia Classic at Kinderlou Forest Golf Club in Valdosta, Georgia—in late April 2011.

Coming into the event, I was concerned about three things: my patience, my technology, and my left shoulder. I knew the pace of play would be a challenge, but I also had a feeling that the clubs in my bag wouldn't match up well to the ones true golf pros use today. And then there's my shoulder. My left shoulder suffers from the same loose joints as my right, but I never had to really rely on it when I played baseball. Since I picked up golf in a serious way, it's been a different story.

While I had a read on my weaknesses and I knew enough to suspect these things *might* give me problems—I would have never imagined how all three of them would conspire to lead to one of my absolute worst performances on a golf course ever. And, conveniently, in front of all the cameras in my first time out playing with the "big boys." I should have known it was destined to be a monumental learning experience when the tournament actually began with a five-hour rain delay.

Surprisingly, I actually weathered the first delay in fairly decent form. I started the tournament with a good mind-set and my score reflected it: I notched my first birdie and I was one under through the first three holes. I was in a rhythm and rolling right along right up until my third shot on the fourth hole. That's when the sirens went off again and they suspended play for *another* five hours due to rain.

This was uncharted territory for me and I didn't know to handle the delay; I had no idea how to pass the time yet stay focused. I went back and forth from the driving range, the tee box, and the clubhouse. I was restless and unsettled, and when we finally resumed play, it showed. We played five more holes before darkness set in, and I shot bogey, bogey, *double bogey*, and bogey. I was completely out of my rhythm, and try as I might, I couldn't get it back again. I rallied slightly to finish with a par before play was suspended yet again. I ended the day four over, which isn't completely horrible, but certainly not where I had expected to be.

Despite the best of intentions, when I came back the next day to finish the last ten holes of my first round, I wasn't able to salvage my score. When I finally tapped in on the eighteenth hole, my score had gone from marginally bad to straight-up horrific: I had shot eighty-four over the two-day first round. I was dejected but determined to rally; I went out and found a local public course and played another eighteen holes before I went to bed to try to work out the kinks.

I tried to come back the next day, compose myself, and get after it again, but on Saturday it was a similar story line: I was plagued by tap-in bogeys and stupid little mistakes. Of all things, I shot even worse. In my first introduction to golf at the next level, I shot eighty-four in the first round and eighty-seven in the second. I was humiliated, I was furious with myself, and all I really wanted to do was get in my car and drive home. But regardless of how I felt, I knew what I had to do. I knew it was time to face the music and answer all the predictable questions that were coming after I had just missed the cut by twenty-seven strokes.

I didn't turn down a single interview after the round and I followed up with every media outlet that had asked me to do so before the event, including ESPN's *Pardon the Interruption*. To be honest, most people were genuinely surprised even to hear from me. More than one person told me, "John, what are you doing calling? I would *never* have called if I shot those numbers!" Well, I myself certainly didn't enjoy shooting those numbers, but I owned the moment as best I could and tried to explain to people why things had gone so poorly. I tried to explain why my scores were not indicative of what kind of golfer I really was.

I had a four-hour drive home after my final round, and when I got in the car, I was spun up. On my way home I struggled with the humiliation of what I just went through and I battled in my mind whether pursuing golf in this way was worth all the struggle and heartache. But the longer I drove, the more I started to cut myself some slack and give myself the credit I deserved for taking the chance to go out there in the first place. How many people would have just sat in the stands and said "no thanks." That would have been the safe thing to do, but in golf, as in baseball, I am patently uninterested in playing it safe.

There's no way to sugarcoat it: I bombed out at the Nationwide. For some people that would have been the end of the line, but to me it was actually the greatest thing that could have happened. The truth is, I would have learned much less if I had barely missed the cut or played great. After the Nationwide, I knew what I needed to do: I needed to upgrade the shafts in my clubs and I needed to pursue surgery on my left shoulder. Never would I have imagined that I would ever undergo major surgery again after I retired from baseball, but after the Nationwide tournament it was painfully apparent, in more ways than one, that for me to really attack golf like I needed to, it absolutely had to get done.

So here I am today, ironically enough, working through another round of rehab and up to my usual tricks of pushing myself and my body and keeping it fun. Just yesterday, about two weeks since surgery, the stupidly nice December weather here in Atlanta lulled me out onto the golf course. Now, I can't even stand to hold a club in my left hand yet, but that didn't stop me from playing an entire round one-handed. And no kidding, I actually birdied eighteen.

There's still a long, long way to go to get myself back to 100 percent, and there are certainly no guarantees that even with my new shoulder I will be able to accomplish my dream to make the Champions Tour, but I'm taking that one-handed birdie as my first good omen.

I probably have about as good a shot at actually making it as I did at age seven when I wanted to be a major leaguer, but I could care less about the odds. I just want to prove to myself that I can do it. It may not mean much to a whole lot of people, but it means a lot to me.

Chapter Twelve

STARTING OVER

I was in for a whole new world, quite literally, in this next chapter of my life with the Boston Red Sox. The irony of the situation was almost palpable: Here I was at age forty-one, after twenty years in the major leagues, about to basically relive another rookie year.

The enormous challenge of starting over again in my professional career was really only half the battle, as there was a whole other side of the story, namely my personal life, that we have yet to discuss. I was quite literally still picking up the pieces from 2007, and that added yet another layer of uncertainty and doubt amid everything else.

The year 2007 marked the end of my sixteen-year marriage to Dyan, the mother of my four children. I found myself in a circumstance I deeply regretted, and one that I honestly never thought I would contribute to: the staggering statistics of divorce in professional sports. But I could only start picking myself up and moving on and adjusting to a new way of life.

One of the most difficult parts was simply coming to grips with the time I had now lost with my kids. This new reality, compounded by the life of a pro baseball player, was the hardest pill to swallow. As any divorced parent who shares custody can attest, it's mighty hard to get used to the idea that you can no longer walk down the hall every night and make the rounds through your children's bedrooms, tucking in stray feet under blankets and securing closet doors to ward off monsters. I truly missed the everyday opportunities that come with just being a dad.

My life had turned in a direction I had never intended, and to be blunt, I had no idea where I was going and what was next for me. I had a ton of questions and a new void to fill in my life.

As they say, desperate times call for desperate measures, so I decided to take a year of solitude and I committed the next 365 days to just focusing on myself and forgoing any dating. During this time, I surrounded myself with eight people who would basically become my accountability team. These eight close friends served as my sounding boards, counselors, and guides. These were people who were committed to my best interests and were willing to level with me and tell me the hard truths that I needed to hear.

As the months wore on after my divorce, there was some pressure, especially from the guys in the clubhouse, to get back "out there" again. It seemed like everybody knew someone I just *had* to meet. The offers were flattering, but I knew there was still work for me to do, and throughout my time of solitude, I stuck to my plan and dedicated myself to finishing the walk through the aftermath of my divorce.

It certainly wasn't easy and I certainly wouldn't want to do it again, but my year of solitude ended up being a time of great growth and reflection. It's hard not to be emotional about the end of a relationship, especially within the context of my religion, but I was able finally to come to a quiet inner place that allowed me to process this great sadness and move forward again. This challenge allowed God to show me things about myself, and further reveal His plan to me. God took me on a journey I didn't think was possible, a journey of forgiveness that made it possible for me to trust again. On my own strength alone, there's no way I could have done this.

With God's help and with the help of my most trusted advisers, I was able to let go of the bitterness I once felt and somehow, someway, be at peace today. I found closure, and finding that has allowed me to forge ahead, together with Dyan, as the parents we still are, and put our children's best interests before anything else.

Speaking of my kids, they have been *incredible* at adapting to the ever-changing environment in which they now find themselves. I love them for that, I'm proud of them for that, and I can only thank God that we have all weathered this storm together.

Looking back now, I believe that by allowing myself to go through a journey of solitude and devoting myself to work on things I needed to work on, God rewarded me with a miracle. If you ask me, there's no other way to explain it. There's just no other way to explain meeting Kathryn Darden eighteen months later.

Kathryn and I were set up on a blind date by mutual acquaintances. She was extremely resistant to the idea at first and actually had to be persuaded over a period of time that I was not your stereotypical professional athlete. She was not a baseball fan at all and might have been one of the few people in Atlanta who didn't know the first thing about me and my career with the Braves. It wasn't until she watched a video of a speech I had given at a Fellowship of Christian Athletes event that she agreed to meet me for dinner at a Taco Mac in Atlanta.

Kathryn and I immediately connected in ways that didn't seem possible: in our faith, in our passion for life and for our kids, but most importantly of all, in our shared outlook on embarking on a new relationship that would never be just about us. The fact was, wherever things were headed, our decisions were going to impact a lot of other lives, as the start of our relationship also marked the start of the blending of two families from two previous marriages. This would prove to make life interesting and challenging all at the same time, but one thing was undeniable. At age forty-one, I had found something I thought I would never find again: love and happiness.

So as I began my new journey with the Boston Red Sox, I was really beginning a new journey with Kathryn and our families. Looking back, I don't know how I could have made it through 2009 without this new support system, because nothing about the road ahead proved to be easy.

When I signed with the Boston Red Sox, it's safe to say that there were more questions than answers. There was, of course, the obvious question about my shoulder and how it would perform for my new team, but that was really only the tip of the iceberg. The fact is, when you've played baseball in the same place for twenty years, you know everything about everything there is to know about your team and your surroundings. When you suddenly sign with a new team, there's absolutely *nothing* you know. Quite literally, I had to go back to the basics of organizing my new life in the context of my new team. Where would I live during spring training? Where would we live in Boston? And how would we get Kathryn and me, my four children, and her two children from Atlanta to there?

As I worked out and tried to get myself into the best shape I possibly could for spring training, eventually some of these not-so-minor administrative details started falling into place. I was offered a great place to stay during spring training with a friend of a friend, and Kathryn was going to stay in Atlanta for the moment while the kids finished the school year. We were still mapping out our plans for Boston after spring training, but I felt like we were over the first couple hurdles—things were working out and headed in the right direction.

As I counted down the final days to spring training, I really had a great mind-set; I felt ready to embrace everything this new journey had in store for me, and the newness, while disorienting at times, was really more exciting than anything else. I was anxious to just get started and face the task of proving that I was worth the investment the Red Sox had made in me. Despite my dogged attempt to embrace everything, I was unfortunately about to learn that even the simplest of activities with the Red Sox—such as *finding* spring training—was just not going to come easy.

When I left for spring training in Fort Myers, Florida, I *thought* I knew where I was going, but I really had no idea where I was headed—in more ways than one, as it turned out. I had plugged in the address for City of Palms Park into my GPS, but when it announced my arrival, there wasn't a stadium in sight. I remember sitting there in the car thinking, *There's no way there's a ballpark anywhere near here.* I mean, I looked around and all I could see were lines of palm trees, houses, and an apartment complex. At one point I stopped looking for the park and started looking for TV cameras because I was sure I was getting Punk'd.

As it turns out, the Red Sox conduct spring training at what might be the only complex in all of baseball that's practically hidden in a neighborhood. But since I had never been there before, it was just another item on the long list of things I had to learn.

When I walked into the Red Sox clubhouse the first time for camp, the whole organization, from the front office to the coaching staff to the players, welcomed me and helped me feel as comfortable as I think any new person can expect to feel. It was awesome to be joining a roster that was considered to be one of the best in the American

League and already projected to make the postseason, but the hardest part for me was coming in as a veteran and wanting to fit in right away. I came through the door with a pretty good career, one that people respected, but I also knew that everyone was counting on me for the future. I had to resign myself to the fact that I wouldn't be able to contribute right away. I wasn't going to fit in for quite some time.

I had expected to experience a spring training unlike any I'd had before—as every team obviously has their own methods of preparing for a season—and those expectations were duly met. I found myself doing exercises and drills I had never done before, but this part was more fun and challenging than anything else. The thing that really caught me off guard was the changes the Red Sox wanted to make to the rehab process for my shoulder.

I found out right away that the Boston Red Sox intended to be very cautious and calculated about getting me ready to pitch again, and understandably so, but their way of going about it just didn't really mesh well with the way I had been rehabbing my shoulder.

When I arrived at camp, it was basically like putting on the brakes, as for all intents and purposes I was basically shut down from actual throwing. The Red Sox's plan was to give my shoulder a break and work on building up strength during the standard six to eight weeks of spring training. Then they would bring me back down to Fort Myers after Opening Day for extended spring training. Essentially, my throwing preparation for the season would be stunted for a while and then would pick back up again in April. This was the part that gave me a little heartburn.

In theory, I understood what the Red Sox were trying to do and I understood why they felt they had to shut me down: Giving my shoulder more time to rehab without throwing would, according to the consensus view, give me a chance to have more strength in it later in the season. In theory, there was nothing wrong with this plan. It was probably a great plan for rebuilding the foundation of a shoulder over the long term. The problem was, I had a desire to get there *much* faster. I was concerned with this year and being able to contribute sooner than what I felt this program would really allow. These two philosophies would prove hard to blend into a perfect plan.

I felt like I came into spring training in the best shape I could possibly be in and my shoulder was completely acclimated to throwing every day, but after the calisthenics and conditioning portions of the day were completed, for the most part they had me just sit and watch as the pitching staff got to work throwing—which was really difficult for me. I wanted to continue doing the things Peter and I had been doing during our rehab and I didn't want to lose all the momentum I had going. My body was telling me that I needed to throw the ball a little more, if anything just to keep my shoulder moving and not lose the flexibility Peter and I had worked so hard to attain, but within the Red Sox program there were days when they didn't even want me to pick up a baseball.

My body was telling me what I should be doing, but at the time I was very reluctant to push back and risk coming across as the new guy who knew better than everyone else. Looking back now, I just wish I had been a little more stubborn right here. I knew what the Boston Red Sox couldn't possibly know. I knew that I had come back from countless injuries and five surgeries throughout the years, but always prided myself on using unconventional and innovative ways to recuperate.

I had done things the different way my entire career, but here I was with a new team and I suddenly got away from all of that. And the unfortunate reality was that it started to feel like I was staying in neutral. My shoulder wasn't getting a lot worse, but it also wasn't getting any better.

The one thing that made things easier for me amid all of this was Kathryn. I had asked her to marry me and the timing of our new relationship was crucial to everything I was going through in starting over with a new team and a new shoulder. Going through something like this on your own, whether you've had twenty years in baseball or not, is not something anyone wants to do. There was obviously some serious trepidation associated with it—which I was willing and ready to meet—but it would have been a whole lot harder if I'd been completely on my own.

When I proposed, it's safe to say we didn't know when and we didn't know how we would fit in a wedding, of all things, into the other logistical challenges involved in this transition from Atlanta to Boston. Kathryn and I wanted to get married sooner rather than later, but it probably goes without saying that it's difficult to plan an event like a wedding when you're starting a new season of baseball and having to spend time in several minor league cities over the course of several weeks. We finally identified an opportunity in May, but thanks to baseball, all we had really set was a wedding "window," not a wedding date.

The ceremony was planned around a simulated start I would make in Fort Myers on May 15. As long as the game went on as planned, without any kind of weather delay or postponement, I had permission to fly home after the game, get married on the sixteenth, and then keep right on trucking, picking back up with the team in Florida again on the seventeenth.

Thank goodness we really just wanted to have a low-key wedding with close family and friends, because everything was subject to the whims of the elements. If it rained, we were prepared to push everything to Sunday. If it didn't, Saturday would be the big day. It was an unusual circumstance for a wedding in Alpharetta, Georgia, to hinge on the weather in Fort Myers, Florida, but that was just the way things were, and thankfully our friends and family were willing to be flexible and go along with our plans.

For something that could have gone sideways quickly in so many ways, our wedding, amazingly, went off as planned, without any delays. Somehow I was able to step away from baseball for one magical day in order to marry an amazing woman. I still honestly shake my head over how we were able to shoehorn a wedding into everything else, but we did and it would prove to make all the difference in the world.

Kathryn's and my wedding proved to be an event that would really help bring our two families together and unite us all on the verge of what would be my final year in baseball. I didn't know it yet, but the happiness of this day and having Kathryn now at my side would be two things that would keep me going through the journey that lay ahead—a road that would be filled with more hiccups and setbacks than I ever imagined. I was really on the brink of failure, and I didn't know it. And the funny part is, Kathryn's not knowing much about my baseball past in a lot of ways helped me handle the new future that was unfolding.

Our wedding would prove to be the easy part in the grand scheme of things because shortly afterward, I began the process of basically feeling my way back into pitching shape with my now surgically repaired shoulder. Dr. Chandler had always warned me that whenever I finally had shoulder surgery, things would never be the same for me. *Before* surgery, the incredible flexibility and looseness in my joints was something that I used and abused all the time to my advantage. I was always able to make adjustments and tinker with my delivery so as to overcome whatever I needed to overcome; I always had mobility in places that other guys just didn't. When it came down it, I was about as good as anyone when it came to manipulating my own body in order to manipulate a baseball. Now, though, after surgery, I was very, very limited. It wasn't just that I lost a few degrees in my range of motion—which I had—it was that I had also lost flexibility *within* that range of motion, if that makes any sense. I was just always able to torque my shoulder in some pretty unique ways, and after this latest surgery I just couldn't do it anymore.

As I adjusted to life on the mound with nine anchors holding down the labrum in my shoulder, I visited three rungs of the Red Sox minor league system, with stops in South Carolina, Maine, and Rhode Island, starting all the way down in Class A, with the Greenville Drive. I worked my way up through Double-A with the Portland Sea Dogs, and finally to Triple-A with the Pawtucket Red Sox, along the way learning how to pitch effectively within my new limitations. I knew success was certainly possible, but it certainly wasn't going to be easy.

The best way I can think to describe this is to have you imagine what it would feel like if someone suddenly disengaged the power steering in your car while you were driving. You would still be able to steer your car and get to where you needed to go, but it would take a lot more work than you were used to. That's how pitching after shoulder surgery felt to me.

My quick tour of the minor leagues in 2009 gave me the chance to face some hitters and see how my shoulder would hold up during a game and then, just as importantly, recover afterward, but I really didn't put too much stock in the entire experience. Regardless of how things felt, or how promising some things appeared at times, I knew from experience that pitching in the minors was really more like just going through the motions. And going through the motions would not in any way simulate what it was going to be like, or how my shoulder was going to perform, under the pressure and the spotlight of the big leagues.

So all things considered, when I finished the minor league circuit in June and found myself headed to Boston, there was a certain sense of accomplishment in knowing that I had made it back to that point, but I wasn't kidding myself: I knew that in all reality, my journey had just begun.

I knew enough to expect that the road ahead wasn't going to be easy, but I never would have guessed how hard it would actually be.

Chapter Thirteen

HICCUPS

When I arrived in Boston, it's safe to say that I found myself disoriented and out of my comfort zone in so many ways, but firmly embedded in all the dizzying newness was the *excitement* of playing for the Red Sox. Fenway, the Green Monster, and "Sweet Caroline" in the middle of the eighth—those were all really cool things to get used to in my new environment. Really, it was hard not to be a little awestruck at joining one of the most storied clubs in baseball. I was a little swept away by their history, their traditions, and their disdain for all things associated with the Yankees; I have to admit, that part had me feeling like a little kid again, in love with the game for the very first time. It did nothing to diminish my loyal feelings for the Braves, but there was just something undeniably cool about playing for the Boston Red Sox, even if it was only for a glimmer of a season.

When it finally came time for me to pitch my first game for the Red Sox on June 25, we were on the road in Washington, D.C., facing the

Nationals. I wanted to do so well the first time out for my new team that all my emotions were whipped up and I was anxious. My mindset was one I had rarely experienced on the mound: I was *nervous*.

I had always felt this sense of comfort on the mound throughout my career, and yet here I was, in what would be my last season, alarmingly apprehensive. It was almost as if I had *never* pitched before. I was as nervous for this one start as I'd ever been in my entire life, including every World Series game I had ever pitched. I lost feeling in my legs, I had trouble catching my breath; it was just *bizarre*.

I can't explain it any better than to say that everything seemed to be happening too fast once the game began. I had been playing baseball for almost thirty-five years, yet at one point in the first inning I found myself gesturing for the catcher to come out to the mound. We didn't need to discuss signs or even the strategy for the next batter. Nope, the bases were loaded and I was so overwhelmed that I needed a moment to remember where to put my foot on the rubber. It was *that* bad.

As things unraveled more and more—in the game and in my mind—I started to think about all the people in my corner, rooting for me: my family, friends who had come to the game, and the Red Sox—who were obviously hoping that I was going to pitch well. I knew my mind was not where it should be, but I just couldn't seem to control it. By the time I was able to settle down, the game had already gotten away from me; by the bottom of the third, I had allowed five runs on seven hits.

I rallied toward the end, lasting two more innings without giving up another hit or run, and I had struck out all three batters I faced in the bottom of the fifth. Looking back on the game, I wasn't completely disheartened, but I was disappointed that I hadn't been able to control my anxiety. I had always prided myself on my ability to slow the game down in the biggest of moments and I just hadn't been able to do this early in that game.

As I said before, in many ways, it felt like I was a rookie all over again. My experience in Boston would prove to be filled with a lot of tiny moments like this, moments when I found myself making mistakes, and reverting to behaviors I had learned to avoid much earlier in my career. All of these things, in combination with adapting to my new shoulder, just didn't add up to a whole lot of success.

As I look back now, it's easy for me to see that I did an incredibly poor job at managing my own mind-set in Boston. I knew the rich history of my new team and what a gamble they had taken on me, and from the very beginning I started carrying around my old backpack of junk again. It's natural to want to do as well as you can, but in my case, this desire ended up hurting me. I got anxious. I wanted to do so well, so bad, and so fast, that I lost patience and started obsessing over the outcomes instead of having faith in the process. The Boston Red Sox actually had more patience with me than I had with myself.

In total, I made eight starts with the Red Sox, from June 25 through August 6, the date of my last appearance, and the numbers themselves tell the uneven and largely underwhelming story: I was 2–5 with an 8.32 ERA. I pitched forty innings, averaging only five innings per start. I had recorded thirty-three strikeouts, but also allowed fifty-nine hits and eight home runs. In the month of July alone, I allowed twenty-three earned runs.

No matter how I justify it or how well I pitched at times, things just didn't go well. I was bound and determined to make it work and make it happen on the mound, but this desire never materialized into success. The irony is that in twenty and two-thirds innings as a visitor at Fenway, I hadn't given up a single earned run. But as a home-team player, well . . . it's safe to say, in that market, I just didn't deliver.

Never would I have imagined it being the way it was, or ending the way it did, in Boston.

On August 6, on the road at Yankee Stadium, in what would prove to be my last start in a Red Sox uniform, I was absolutely shelled by the Yankees, giving up nine hits and eight earned runs in just over three innings. I went back to the hotel after the game and I'll never forget telling Kathryn, "I think that's it. I don't know what decision they are going to make, but just based on gut feeling, I think that's it." And a few hours later, I found out that it was: The Boston Red Sox were designating me for assignment, which for all intents and purposes meant I was being released; I had promptly arrived at the absolute lowest point of my professional career.

Even though I had sensed the impending doom, it certainly did not in any way soften the blow of hearing the news that I was being released from Boston. I was crushed. I was humiliated. And I was incredibly disappointed in myself. I had just been knocked down harder and farther than ever before, but in a lot of ways I felt like I had been down this road before.

Getting released in Boston felt eerily similar to the time when I failed miserably in my first real debut in the national arena of competitive amateur baseball in a little place called Johnstown, Pennsylvania. Remembering Johnstown helped remind me of a simple fact, one that always seemed to be painful but had always been true about me: The more I fail, the more I learn.

Johnstown, Pennsylvania, is home to the All-American Amateur Baseball Association national tournament, largely considered to be one of the best amateur baseball tournaments in the country. Each August it's a veritable showcase of some of the best age twenty and under talent in the country, all on display for scouts of major league clubs. My summer baseball team from Lansing had an every-other-year, automatic bid into the tournament back then, and I went to Johnstown for the first time when I was sixteen years old.

I was three to four years younger than most of the other kids at the tournament, but that was pretty status quo for me. I had been playing up, or playing with older kids, my entire life, and I was used not only to holding my own, but to being one of the standouts. But that was in Michigan. Johnstown was about to be an eye-opening experience for me.

Johnstown gave me my first taste of baseball on a national scale. It was the first time I had seen scouts, it was the first time I had seen radar guns, and it was the first time I was about to figure out that I wasn't as good as I thought I was.

To this day, I can remember pitching in a game against a team from Brooklyn, New York. The first three innings were promising; it was three up, three down, three times in a row. I remember sitting in the dugout waiting for the fourth inning thinking, *Wow!*

But then came the fourth inning, which would turn out to be the single worst inning of my entire baseball career. I'm not so sure if there's ever been a pitcher who's had an inning this bad. I can remember it like it was yesterday: I gave up a single, a home run, a walk, a home run, a double, a home run, another double, and a home run. *I gave up four two-run homers in one inning.*

As the inning wore on and the runners kept circling the bases in pairs, the Brooklyn team, which was largely Hispanic, had transformed into full-on rally mode. They were going crazy in the dugout, jumping up and down and beating on all these upturned pails they normally used for hauling around their equipment.

As the home runs continued to fly out of the park, they broke into this chant and they just kept repeating some phrase over and over again in Spanish. I could only imagine what they were saying, but it was safe to assume from all the finger-pointing that it had a little something to do with me.

My coach at the time, Javier Cavazos, who was very fluent in Spanish, came out to the mound after I had just given up the fourth home run of the inning, obviously to take me out of the game. When he arrived at the mound, Coach Cavazos didn't say anything about my pitching.

He just looked at me and said, "Do you want to know what they've been yelling?"

I said, "Yeah, why not."

He said, " '*¡Dale a ese tipo su Icy Hot!*'— which means 'Get that guy some Icy Hot!' "

After watching me jerk my neck back time and time again to see if the ball was going to stay in the park, the Brooklyn players were obviously concerned that I might be sore the next day. It was nice to know they cared.

To use a boxing analogy, that Johnstown tournament was like taking a sucker punch to the face. I had momentarily dropped my guard, I wasn't prepared, and my opponent had made me pay. The whole experience definitely left me reeling for a moment, but by the time we were packed up and headed back home, I was already planning how I would bounce back off the mat.

I didn't need anyone to tell me what I needed to do. My dad didn't have to push me; he really didn't even have to say a word. As far as I was concerned, it was my dream and it was on me.

I remember just telling my dad on the drive back home to Michigan in our old RV, "I'm not as good as I think I am. I need to be better and I need to be pushed a little bit."

I came back from Johnstown a little bloodied but more determined than ever. I had always worked hard, but now I rededicated myself to working harder than I ever had before. In retrospect, it was this tournament that inspired me to take my game to the next level.

It wasn't like I was cocky before Johnstown; I don't think I've ever been cocky really, I'm just naturally not that way. It was more like, before Johnstown, I didn't realize how far I had to go. Here I had been in my Michigan bubble, not fully realizing that there were other kids out there who were just as talented as I was, if not more talented, and working just as hard, too.

After playing professional baseball for so long, I can't tell you how thankful I am for experiences like Johnstown. I can't quote you any statistics because there's really no way to track something like this, but I'm convinced that it's true. I think the majority of the players who make the pros are so naturally talented that they have been dominating other people their entire lives and they've never experienced real failure. They get to the big leagues and they are in for a rude awakening. They get in a slump or are challenged in a way they've never been challenged before, and a lot of them don't know how to handle it.

That was simply never the case for me, and in a lot of ways it defined me as a pitcher. In many ways, I was used to being an underdog and I never played like any lead was safe. I didn't mind rallying and I didn't mind working my way back out of a tough spell. The bigger the odds, the more unlikely the outcome, the better, as far as I was concerned. When things got really tough and the moment got bigger and the pressure kept mounting, it just seemed to lock me in.

When I go back to those Johnstown days and consider what has happened in my career, it all seems to make sense, like pieces of a puzzle. Whenever I felt my life was going really fast as a major league baseball player, I always remained grounded to my roots and I made myself remember what got me to that point. I never forgot what I went through or how I went through it. At age forty-two or age sixteen, it was all the same. Sure, I had just gotten my teeth kicked in, but now it was time to rally.

When I look back on my time in Boston, what I see is a string of missed opportunities. The Boston Red Sox took such a big risk on me and I gave them every effort I possibly could, but when the moments where I was used to being really good arrived, I wasn't good. On top of basically learning a new arm and a new slot, mentally I had lost something. I couldn't go to that next level where I had always been able to go in order to override the pressure. I had been playing baseball and facing mental adversity on the mound for more than thirty years by this point, and somehow, amid everything, I had lost my edge.

And once things started going downhill, there was going to be a really short window of time in which I could control my fate and have a chance at redemption. It's just the nature of the job. When you're with an organization for a long time, you have a longer leash, if you will. There's generally more time granted to recover from a bad start or a slump. When you're the new guy, you just don't have the luxury of a lot of time to fix anything. There's no history, no statistics to show you're worth the money you are being paid. The discussion in the front office quickly dissolves into something like "Man, I thought he was going to be better, I can't believe . . ."

I don't regret going to Boston. I wouldn't want to live through it again, but I don't regret it and I don't sit here today and wish for things to have been different. Really the only thing I would say about Boston is that I wish I had been a little more stubborn about listening to my body.

As for the rest of it . . . well, of course, in a perfect world it would have gone better, but in the end it served a purpose. Here I was at the ripe old age of forty-two, out of my comfort zone, making rookie mistakes, and being pushed and challenged in ways that I hadn't been for quite some time. It wasn't comfortable, but it certainly was purposeful. The undeniable truth was that I was an old veteran who still had a lot to learn.

Chapter Fourteen

SUCCESS AND FAILURE

Pitching for the Boston Red Sox proved to be one of the few challenges in my career that I was unable to overcome. With almost every other challenge that had been presented to me, I had always found a way, within the given time frame, to make things work. In Boston, what I really ran out of was time. In the window I was allotted, I wasn't able to do what I was really hoping to do.

While I had experienced failure in Boston, I didn't view the *entire* experience, or even myself personally, as a failure. This might not sound like much, but when my life was turning upside down in the aftermath of being released, it was this perspective on success and failure—a perspective that had been honed through years and years of dealing with adversity—that really carried me through. I just had to remind myself to apply the very same principles I had been preaching to others for years and years at this point.

For the better part of my career as a player, I did motivational speaking, and it's something I still do today. When I first started speaking to groups, I realized that while I thought I had some compelling and inspiring stories, and of course my testimony, to share, if I wanted to have an impact, if I wanted to motivate people to make real changes in their lives, I was going to have to work a little harder. I had to think up a way to give the folks in the audience something— some kind of tool, if you will—that they could easily pick up and use in their own lives. My trick for doing this was devising two acronyms, one for success and one for failure. If people were going to remember anything I said, I figured this was my best shot. And to be honest, I always thought I sounded like a pretty smart baseball player whenever I used a word like *acronym* in a speech.

Now, don't judge me, you obviously have to stretch a little bit for some of this, but for *success,* I came up with "Striving Under Constant Challenges and Enduring Stressful Situations." For *failure,* I came up with "Fear And Insecurity Lead to Un Realistic Expectations." I use these acronyms, paired with stories from my career and my journey in faith, in an attempt to get people to think seriously about their own ideas about success and failure.

To me, there's a little irony in motivational speaking, or at least my style of motivational speaking anyway. When a group invites me to speak, more often than not they want me to come to inspire people to chase and achieve their dreams. They want me to talk about success, but in reality, I'm really going to talk more about failure. The truth is, one of the keys to my success has been how well I have handled failure. Embracing failure has helped me become the pitcher that I was and the man that I am today.

In my speeches, I naturally cycle back to some of the worst moments in my career, like starting a season 2–11, or giving up eight runs in two-thirds of an inning, and I tell people what I had to do to overcome those obstacles. I tell them about my mind-set and how I would have to tell myself, *I'm not going to give in, I'm not going to give up; I'm going to rally.* I really try to teach people a new way of looking at failure, not to look at it as a signal for quitting time, but to see it as a crucial stepping-stone to success.

I think it's pretty clear that my career wasn't all about natural talent; I wasn't sprinkled with any magic dust. I wasn't the fastest or the strongest or even the smartest, but I would argue that whatever I lacked in sheer talent, I made up for along the way with tenacity and perseverance; a lot of my success was achieved by constantly learning, adapting, and overcoming obstacles.

I'm convinced that these are traits that can be learned and applied by anyone at any stage of their life. It matters not how old you are, how talented you are, or how much money you make right now—these are not the determining factors in whether or not you can be successful. The determining factors will be your passion, your desire, and your ability to truly accept responsibility for where you are in life, to recognize and embrace your own God-given strengths and weaknesses as well as the outside factors that you cannot control. If you can step back and look at everything and say, "So be it," you've taken the first step toward realizing your dreams. The next step is putting forth an earnest effort to make the most out of whatever you have. I'm telling you, if you do this, you can achieve things you never thought possible.

While I certainly hope that a few of my words throughout the years have resonated with folks and made a positive difference in their lives, there aren't any convenient statistics, as there are in baseball, to help gauge my effectiveness. Regardless of that fact, I can tell you for certain that learning has definitely taken place. I know this because along the way *I've* been the one who has been constantly reminded that I still have a long way to go. Frankly, I never would have guessed how much I stood to learn from motivational speaking.

The first time I really faced this reality was at a Fellowship for Christian Athletes event in Tennessee. In the days leading up to the speech, I had thought up this great plan to share my testimony and talk about the transforming power of God in my life. I was convinced it was going to be amazing. Everything was going fine—until I actually got to the podium. As I stood there, I was distracted by the unmistakable twinge of hypocrisy in my heart. While everything I was about to say was true, I couldn't escape the fact that I didn't feel like I was truly living the best Christian example at that point. After standing there for a moment in the awkward silence, considering my options, I just looked at the crowd and confessed.

"I had something here on my notes that I wanted to tell you," I started, "but I'm just going to be gut-honest with you right now. I haven't read my Bible in a week. The truth is, I stand before you today guilty of becoming complacent. The truth is, I probably need this talk more today, than some of you."

I really didn't know how everybody was going to react, but from what I could tell, my words seemed to resonate with the crowd. I went on with my speech in a completely different direction than I had planned, but it seemed to be just as effective, if not more so. When I talked to people afterward, they told me it was really refreshing to hear a pro athlete just be honest and human. Ever since then, it's become my habit to open faith-based speeches with the following message: "The divine appointment that I have tonight is for me to hear what I am about to tell you, because I *need* to hear what I am about to tell you." It always comes out a little weird and people always have to sit there and think about it for a minute, but it helps me set the right tone both for me and for the audience. It's important for me to note that no matter what I've achieved in this life, it's always a constant process of two steps forward and one step back. And sometimes in the midst of that natural ebb and flow, I find myself drifting along and becoming complacent, despite my best intentions.

I never would have imagined the role that motivational speaking has had in my life. Beyond the fact that it has helped keep me from slipping into neutral at times, it has on occasion shown me the true power of God. In fact, the first time I ever felt the presence of God was actually during a speech I made in Atlanta.

I know that a lot people struggle to understand what it means when someone says something like I've just said. You know, "What do you mean, you *felt* God? What do you mean when you say He *spoke* to you?" To be honest, I didn't really understand it until it started happening to me. Through the years, as I grew in my faith, I started to feel God's little nudges from time to time, but it wasn't until after I truly accepted Christ that I truly felt the extraordinary experience of God literally lifting me up and carrying me through something that I knew I was not capable of doing on my own.

In 2007, I was scheduled to speak at one of Zig Ziglar's "Seize the Day!" motivational seminars. Zig's folks had contacted me an entire year before the event and asked me to participate. I remember looking at the date, then twelve months away, and thinking, *Yeah, that should be fine.* There was no way of knowing it then, but I had just scheduled a big-time speech during what would be one of the worst times of my life.

Mere days before the seminar, I had found out that my marriage was probably over. In those first few days as I adjusted to the news, it was like I was going through life in somewhat of a daze. I remember going to an all-day Christian school-board retreat and sitting through the meetings; I was going through the motions on the outside, but on the inside I was absolutely devastated. Nobody knew what was going on yet and we still had our four kids to tell. I really didn't think matters could get any worse until my agent, Lonnie Cooper, called me on the way home.

"Hey John," he said, "just wanted to give you a call and make sure you were all set for your speech tomorrow."

I'm like, "Lonnie, what are you talking about? *What* speech?"

I was so numb and entrenched in the upheaval of my entire life that I had completely forgotten all about my commitment. Just the thought of giving a speech the next day made my head ache, and the more I thought about it, the more I was filled with absolute dread. How was I going to give any speech, let alone a motivational speech, in the state I was in? I suppose I could have called and asked to be excused, given the circumstances, but I wasn't comfortable even asking the question, as much as I might have wanted to. As much as I wanted to just crawl under the covers of my bed and escape everything at the moment, I'm too principled to do it. When I say I'm going to do something, I'm going to *do* something.

So I showed up the next day and I can still remember sitting in the green room outside the auditorium and feeling so overwhelmed and so consumed by what was going on in my life that I just couldn't see how I was going to get through it. In a few moments I was supposed to walk out on this stage and speak to twenty-two thousand people, and I literally had nothing to say. On top of that, the organizers had just told me I had exactly twenty-five minutes to speak, not one second less or more. I hadn't realized this before, but they had an extremely tight schedule and lots of speakers to accommodate in one day. I had never even timed one of my speeches. How I could possibly pull this off was beyond me. I finally just ended up praying. I said, "Lord, I can't do this, but I know You can and I need help."

I remember walking out into the center of this boxing ring and standing there for a moment, staring at the clock and watching it tick. I remember telling myself, *Don't look at the clock or you're never going to get through it,* and then I just started talking. It's hard to describe what happened next, but it was really like this sort out-of-body experience. It was my voice, it was my words, it was my stories, but it felt like I was on autopilot. I wasn't the one pulling the strings. The only thing I was really doing was standing there and letting it happen. To me, it was the most amazing thing ever.

Somehow, what came out of me was flawless: I never stumbled over my words or found myself wandering off on tangents. I ended right on time *and* got a standing ovation. I walked off the stage and it was like I didn't even know what had just happened. I felt light. Numb, even. It was as if God had literally picked me up and carried me through it.

The next day I had to get up and speak at a church, and I tell you the same thing happened. These were two distinct moments in my life where I didn't have either the energy or the desire to accomplish the things I ended up accomplishing. I didn't even have anything I wanted to talk about, yet somehow, someway, He brought me through it.

Getting out of my comfort zone, pushing myself through adversity, and dealing with failure have been critical to my journey. But on the flip side of these truths, I think my attitude toward success, and what it means to me to be successful, have been just as important. To put it simply, I have tried never to let myself get too carried away with either one.

While I undeniably found a measure of success on the baseball field and certainly feel a sense of both pride and accomplishment for the things I was able to do in my playing career, these things do not define me, in *my own* mind, as a successful person. It would be disappointing to me if when I leave this earth, I am remembered only as a good pitcher, because to me there's a whole lot more to my story.

My ability to throw a baseball has given me an enormous opportunity in life. Baseball has given me a platform that I have tried to use to make a positive difference in the world around me. As I have grown up and come to understand my place in life, I don't see it as my duty or responsibility to do these things. I look at it instead as "I *get* to do these things."

From the beginning of my career, I have made time to support and be a part of things that I am genuinely passionate about. And what I have come to realize is that the satisfaction you get when you know you've made a difference, a true life-changing difference, far outweighs the excitement of throwing a baseball.

The credit for this attitude must go to my parents. My parents are incredibly down-to-earth and not materialistic at all. We were never rich, by any means, maybe middle class at best, but we always *felt like* we were rich. And my parents instilled in all of us a feeling of respect for what we had. As I moved up in the tax brackets throughout my career, I tried to remain as grounded as my parents had always raised me to be. I remember telling my best friend, Chuck Cascarilla, a long time ago, when I signed my first big contract in baseball, "If I ever change, hit me over the head with a shovel. I'm serious." And to this day, I try to live with an attitude of service rather than a feeling of entitlement.

When I look back on my life and the various things that I have accomplished, it's safe to say that some of the things I am the most proud of have nothing to do with baseball. It was always my intention to live with this attitude of service, but along the way I realized that God had bigger plans for me than I could ever have imagined. Along the way I have learned that when you get that nudge, when you feel God is asking you to do something far greater than you could do by yourself—*that's* something worth following and doing. I learned this lesson for the first time in 2000.

Back then one of my neighbors was Jeff Foxworthy. I had met Jeff a long time before, but it wasn't until this year, when our kids were all going to the same Christian school, that we really became good friends. Jeff was serving on the school's board of directors and the minister wanted me to be part of the board as well. When Jeff asked me about it, I really felt inclined to take a pass. With my baseball schedule, I just didn't see how I could possibly fit in board meetings and actually serve *in person* and not just in name. I don't know what came over me, but for some reason I ended up saying yes.

The next thing you know, a couple weeks after I leave for spring training, I end up having Tommy John surgery. I soon found myself at home with nothing *but* time. Since I had accepted the school-board position, I now felt obligated to do my part. I didn't know what a baseball player could possibly contribute, but I started showing up to these meetings and God started showing *me*. I would soon find myself in the most faith-challenging situation I've ever been in in my life.

I became a regular attendee at three-hour board meetings focused on the church's plans to build a new high school. I knew nothing about school boards or policies or even meeting etiquette, but even I could tell from the very first meeting that things weren't exactly right. There seemed to be a lot of tension in the room at all these meetings and I was trying to understand why.

I sat through months and months of board meetings focused on building this new high school and I finally started to piece things together. There were legitimate questions that were not being addressed—things that just could not be ignored. The entire board was struggling to get to the bottom of it, but we needed some answers from the leadership and we weren't getting any.

To be blunt, the minister had grown used to controlling and manipulating the board members. He had worked himself up into such a position that he was deemed to be beyond reproach—until I came along, that is. I was fresh, new, abrasive, and unafraid; challenging this minister was not going to be an issue for me. So one day I did. I stood up in the middle of this board meeting and confronted the minister with the truth.

It did not go over well, to say the least, but I don't think I or any of the other board members had any idea what events would transpire in the next few weeks. We were called before the church's charge conference and all promptly removed from our positions. Here we had been hired by the church to help them build a school, and in the very next moment we had all been fired. The charge conference never talked to us, or engaged us to find out what had really happened. We could only assume that the minister had basically lobbied for our removal because we weren't willing to simply agree and conform to his ways.

This ignited a firestorm on the church board. Jeff was so distraught that he took his kids out of the school, which eventually led to most of us taking our kids elsewhere as well. As things were unfolding, you can imagine all the rumors and speculations that were flying around about what happened, but there was not a lot of truth in any of them, and I felt a genuine desire to set the record straight. I just wanted the chance to explain what had really happened, so I got the bright idea of holding a meeting.

Jeff thought I was crazy. In some ways I had to agree with him, because frankly, I didn't know the first thing about running a meeting, but there I was renting a venue and making sure there were at least twenty chairs available—I didn't have high expectations for a big crowd.

Well, it turned out to be a standing-room-only affair. There must have been 150 to 200 people jam-packed into this room: parents, teachers, administrators, and board members. The minister sent a representative with a camcorder and a message: He was going to sue us if we did anything damaging to his reputation. The stage was thus set for a good, old-fashioned spectacle.

The goal for the meeting was just to tell the interested parents what had really happened and what it meant for the education of their children. Things started off civilly enough, but soon there were some tempers flaring and things were starting to get a little out of hand. It was right about this time that a woman walked in the room and the entire crowd literally gasped.

At the time, I had no idea who this lady was, but as it turns out, she had been one of the very first teachers at this school when it first opened. Years ago, the minister had accused her of doing things she didn't do, but she never stood up for herself and was eventually fired. It was a real sour deal and she ended up moving out of the neighborhood because of it. Those who knew her story assumed that she had come to the meeting in order to finally spill the beans on the minister—but she didn't.

She stood and delivered a message that still gives me chills when I think about it today. She simply said, "A long time ago, I didn't listen to God and it cost me dearly. This afternoon, I was sitting on my porch and I knew this meeting was happening. The first time I felt a nudge to go, I just picked up my paper and started reading it. The second time I had this incredible nudge to go, I pulled my paper even closer to my eyes and was determined not to go. The third time I finally put the paper down, and here I am. I am here to deliver a message. I want to tell all of you that when God speaks, *listen*."

By the time she was finished, the hair on the back of my neck was standing up. Her message was obviously meant for everyone, but her words pierced my heart like an arrow. What started out as this worldly "I'll show you" moment instantaneously transformed into something higher, a moment when God told me, "No, I'll show *you*." In that moment it just hit me. I suddenly knew what I was supposed to do. I was supposed to start a Christian school.

It was the first time in my life that I felt God using me in such a way that I didn't even know what I was saying at the time. Unlike what I said during the Zig Ziglar speech, the words I was about to speak were *not* my own. I found myself telling this crowd, "Look, this group is going to go on and build their school the way they want, and I'm sure they'll be fine. Let's go build our own school somewhere else." I somehow persuaded people with my passion and desire to build a new school of our own, and I asked them to join me. I didn't know what I was going to do, how I was going to do it, or who I was going to do it with, but I was filled with ambition and good intentions. And for some reason, I was sure I would find my way.

The ultracondensed version of the rest of the story is that we founded a board called the Advancement for Christian Education with thirteen brave people. Nothing went as planned, nothing was easy, we ended up in court fighting to build a school on property we had bought, but we persevered through it at all. We went from humble beginnings in a refurbished Bruno's Grocery Store (not kidding, the meat department was our school's cafeteria) to a seventy-acre campus at the corner of Bethany Bend and Cogburn Road in Alpharetta; this campus is now called King's Ridge Christian School. Today, we have more than 700 kids from kindergarten up to high school and we are about to embark upon another project to build a separate facility on the campus for grades nine through twelve.

Almost every free moment that I had that year, I spent working on the school, and the work has continued since. I served on the board for ten years and was chairman for five of them. I was always able to devote more of my time and attention during the off-season, but when baseball season rolled around, we found a way to make it work, scheduling the weekly board meetings around days I pitched and road trips. Some years, I think I spent more time at the school than my own kids, who are now enrolled there, did. I recently rotated off the board and have taken a bit of a backseat in the day-to-day running of the school, but you can rest assured, this school will be something that I will look after for the rest of my life.

I could never have known that the thing I dreaded the most, baseballwise—Tommy John surgery—would lead to one of the most unbelievable appointments of my life. Building a Christian school was unlike any other challenge I've ever faced in my life. It was a painstaking process and one that I never imagined I would engage in. There were so many roadblocks and so many challenges, but I learned that when you do something that is not of yourself, you will have the desire to see it through.

Beyond the school, I have been involved in many different charitable causes, but there are two that I have been fortunate enough to be involved with for really the better part of my life: Children's Healthcare of Atlanta and the Atlanta Community Food Bank. I have been fortunate in not having a major disease or chronic illness touch my family, so I have never really had much of a deeply personal cause to fight for in that sense. Fighting hunger just seemed like a logical place to start. Without food, you can't even attack diabetes or cancer or other chronic diseases that affect a lot of people.

I was introduced to food banks in my hometown of Lansing, where I got involved in the annual Lansing Can-A-Thon. When I got traded to Atlanta, of all things, a guy I had worked with at the Greater Lansing Food Bank ended up transferring to the Atlanta Community Food Bank. It was crazy how it worked out, but it was really a seamless transition from a food bank in one community to a food bank in another. I've participated in countless events to raise funds, solicit food donations, and bring awareness to the issue of hunger in our community. The Atlanta Community Food Bank is a phenomenal organization and I have been proud to lend my name and efforts to its causes for many, many years.

My relationship with Children's Healthcare of Atlanta, and most specifically, Children's at Scottish Rite, was actually inspired by an experience I had during a winter caravan for the Atlanta Braves.

Back then in my earliest years of pro ball, winter caravans were pretty extensive affairs. We would drive to all these cities in a big bus, meeting with fans and signing autographs. It was something of an exhausting process, as we'd literally hit fifteen cities in about five days, drumming up support for the team. One thing we always did was visit the hospitals, and I've just got to be honest here, I didn't like it. I didn't like it because it made me uncomfortable; I saw things as a young player that I wasn't prepared to see. I'll never forget the first time I saw a child who was so stricken by cancer that you couldn't tell if it was a boy or a girl. Memories like that stick with you.

Once I opened my eyes and stopped focusing on myself, I saw the joy we were giving these kids and their families, who were basically living at these hospitals struggling to fight these chronic diseases. I knew then that visiting a hospital was something I needed to make time to do. It was the least I could do for these kids and their families.

So when I got to Atlanta, I got hooked up with Scottish Rite Children's Medical Center, which later merged with Children's Healthcare of Atlanta to became Children's at Scottish Rite, and I began a relationship with them. I tried to make it part of my routine to stop by the hospital whenever I could. Sometimes I would bring in a bunch of toys; other times I'd just go hang out and talk with the kids and their parents.

I remember one time I had gotten home at 4 A.M. from a road trip and had gone straight to bed. A few hours later, my wife came in and woke me up. I knew it had to be important and she just handed me the phone. It was the hospital. They were calling me to see if I could come right away to visit a kid named Andrew McLeroy. He was suffering from a brain tumor and I was his favorite player. His parents were hoping I could see him before he had to undergo major surgery. Of course, this was an easy decision to make. I got up and I got in the car.

I remember not knowing what to be prepared for on the ride over, but when I saw a priest standing outside the room, I knew it must not be looking good for the poor kid.

I spoke with the parents first. This was always tough because you never knew exactly what to say or what to expect; sometimes the parents were angry, bitter, and mad—and understandably so. Andrew's parents were unbelievable. I remember talking to them, trying to give some hope when I didn't know if there was any. Then I went in and talked to Andrew, and he was just a normal kid with a terrible disease. We talked baseball and he told me he was hoping to get back out and play again after surgery. I was there to inspire Andrew, but it was Andrew who inspired me.

When I left the hospital, I said some prayers on the way home and hoped for the best, but from what I could tell, things didn't look good. I was shocked when I got a phone call later from Andrew himself, after nine hours of brain surgery. It was unbelievable; this kid was one of the bravest kids I've ever seen in my life.

Andrew wasn't with us for very long, but he and his family made a lasting impact on me. It was Andrew who inspired me to start a golf tournament to raise money in his honor for Scottish Rite. Together with his dad, Loy, we did it every year for almost fifteen years, before I turned things over to Tim Hudson and Kevin Millwood.

Andrew is one of many kids who I had the honor of meeting and hopefully inspiring through all the years that I have been visiting the hospital. But in terms of giving and receiving, I can honestly say I have been on the receiving end of the inspiration more often than not.

In all the years of going to Children's at Scottish Rite, I never truly knew what it was like to be on the other side of things until my youngest daughter, Kelly, was born. Dyan, my wife at that time, had a tough labor, and the nurses had offered to keep Kelly in the nursery during the wee hours of the night so she could rest and recuperate. Dyan was adamantly against it, but I talked her into it. That's how Kelly ended up in the nursery that first night of her life.

Later that same night, one of the labor and delivery nurses was passing through the nursery on her way home. She wasn't even on duty at the time, but as she walked out the door she swore she'd heard something. It was a noise that she knew all too well, and it stopped her in her tracks. Off duty or not, she promptly started investigating and realized that one little baby was ever so audibly struggling to breathe. That little baby was our Kelly. In an instant Kelly was whisked into the intensive care unit, where it was discovered that her lungs were not yet fully developed. Dyan and I spent the next two and a half weeks learning for ourselves what it was like to be concerned parents living at a hospital.

Kelly made a complete recovery and I am proud to report that she's a normal, healthy kid today. It probably goes without saying, but whenever I hear her laugh, I am reminded of what I owe to others. This keeps things in perspective and it keeps me involved with Children's Healthcare of Atlanta.

People have asked me time and time again throughout my career to talk about the awards I have received during my playing days or to talk about what it would mean to me to be inducted into the Baseball Hall of Fame someday. I always told people then, as I tell people now, that I never played baseball to set records or attain personal fame. The personal milestones, the trophies, the awards—sure, they're nice. It is always nice to be recognized for doing something you love to do, but those things do not fulfill or define me—at least in my own mind.

One time I was actually playing catch with my son Andrew and I noticed some writing on the ball as he threw it back to me. Curious, I stopped for a moment to take a closer look, and I realized we were playing catch with my two-hundredth-win game ball. I jogged inside real quick and swapped it out with another one, but the new grass stains on it didn't really bother me. The memories I have of that day (have I mentioned that the losing pitcher was Tommy Glavine?) mean more to me than any of the souvenirs.

The one baseball award that really does mean a lot, and that I was truly humbled to receive, is MLB's Roberto Clemente Award, "given annually to a player who demonstrates the values Clemente displayed in his commitment to community and understanding the value of helping others." It is an honor even to be in the running for an award like this, especially since each team gets to nominate only one player every year to be considered. I'm sure many past recipients of the award have done way more than I have ever done, and many future recipients will do way more than I will ever do, and I certainly don't claim to be in the same league as a man like Roberto Clemente, but it is very rewarding to be considered a player who represents the game as he did.

At the end of the day, an award like this means the most to me because it has more to do with John Smoltz the person than John Smoltz the pitcher. I didn't win the award in 2005 because I had a low ERA or because I had won twenty games that season. This award had more to do with the physical sweat and effort that I have put into my community and the various charitable causes I support. And that's what makes me proud. That's what makes me *feel* successful.

I will continue to support and bring awareness to all of these causes for the rest of my life because it's the least I can do in the time I have left.

Chapter Fifteen

CHASING RINGS, PART I

My baseball career had always been full of calamities and misfortunes—bleak moments when my future in the sport appeared legitimately doubtful—but in mid-August 2009, things had just plummeted to an all-time low, even for me. My career had basically suffered a major heart attack: I was in the process of being released. *Released.* Not on the DL, not traded, and not even sent down to the minors, but *released.*

It was as if I was being sent home in a coffin with a toe tag, all ready for the mortuary. All that was seemingly left to do was make arrangements for a viewing of my body when I returned to Atlanta, so my friends and family could stand around eating tuna casserole and Jell-O salad, sadly mourning what once had been and what was no more.

Things had never been this depressing and it was hard to explain everything I was going through to Kathryn. She just didn't have the context. Kathryn had never experienced the good times—the four-teen consecutive division titles, the deep playoff runs, the trips to the World Series, or even winning it all in 1995. You name it, she had missed it. Her knowledge of my baseball career began with my reluctant decision to become a free agent and my signing with Boston, and, as of this moment in time, ended with me pitching myself right out of a job.

I decided to forgo the "funeral proceedings" when I got back to Atlanta, but I still had a lot to do and a short amount of time to do it in. All told, I had about ten days until I would officially become a free agent and could start talking to other teams and entertaining various scenarios, but there were a lot of questions left to be answered. Did I still want to pitch in the major leagues? Was I still capable of pitching in the major leagues? There was only one thing I really knew for certain: I wasn't interested in mediocrity. I wasn't going to come back just for the sake of coming back. I wanted to compete. I wanted to stand on the mound, stare down the best hitter in baseball, and fire a fastball right past him. *That's* what I wanted. My mind was ready and willing. It was my body that was suspect.

At age forty-two, I couldn't escape the knowledge that I was basically becoming a geriatric major leaguer. I was now paying for all the years I had pitched on layaway, if you will, pushing through pain and just making it work. Now all the bills were coming due for the 3,642 innings I had thrown during twenty-plus seasons. Thoughts that I had delayed and postponed for so long were steadily creeping into my mind, lingering around like dinner guests who just won't go home. Should I just retire? Was I crazy to even consider another comeback? I honestly didn't know what to do.

We've all had these moments in our lives—times when the "right" answer just doesn't seem readily apparent. We worry, we second-guess ourselves, and we lie awake at night wondering "what if?" It's just human nature. But I've got to be honest here—times like this became easier for me after I truly became a Christian and developed a relationship with Jesus Christ. When I came home from Boston, as much as I didn't know exactly what I needed to do, I knew there was one thing I *had* to do. First, I needed to devote some time to trying to figure out what God wanted me to do, which is really easier said than done.

Whenever I find myself in situations like this, what seems to work for me is to find a quiet place where I can sit and be still and try to quiet my inner thoughts. Honestly, it's not really something I excel at—being still for any length of time has always been a challenge for me—but it's the best way I know to sort things out in my head and in my heart. I don't know if you would call what I do meditation, I just do what feels natural.

On this occasion, I spent several nights sitting out back around our fire pit, trying to put my worries and anxieties aside. I tried to let go and ask earnestly for God's will to be done in my life. As I sat there, night after night, breathing and listening and sifting through the quietness, one thought—one feeling, really—began to rise to the surface. I hadn't felt it before, but now there it was as plain as day. I doubted it at first, but after more prayer and reflection, I felt that what it was, was unmistakable. A feeling of peace passed over me. My mind, once filled with the noisy clamor of uncertainty, was quieted and united again in purpose and desire. I went back into the house. Kathryn saw the look on my face and started to smile. I just told her, "I don't think I'm done yet."

Significant progress had been made by the fire pit, but in reality I had solved only half of the equation. Now there was the not-so-little matter of "Could I still pitch effectively?" to attend to. I had certainly made mental mistakes in Boston, but I was also convinced that there was something mechanical that was plaguing my delivery. Something felt off and I didn't know what it was. I didn't know what was wrong, but I wasn't about to try to come back this season if I couldn't figure this part out. It was time to get back to work.

First, I called my godson, Dylan Kelly, who happens to be a great catcher. He was in high school at the time and I enlisted him to come out to the local high school field and catch for me. From the first pitch I threw with anything on it, I could feel it—something was still off. For more than a week, we spent anywhere from an hour to ninety minutes a day in hundred-degree heat trying to figure out what exactly it was. I threw more pitches than I care to admit as I broke down my whole motion piece by piece, attempting to analyze every phase of my delivery. I cycled through all the different technical drills I had used throughout my career. I tried every little trick I knew, but the problem was eluding me and I was frustrated.

I knew it was time to recruit more help; I needed more eyes. I reached out to the people who had been working with me my entire career, who knew my motion and had been watching me pitch all those years. My agents, some local coaches, a couple buddies: anyone who I thought might be willing to come and help me figure it out. And thanks to the graciousness of Danny Hall, the baseball coach at Georgia Tech, I moved my sessions to their indoor facility nearby.

It seemed like it took every day I had to figure out the problem. It was one of my longtime agents, Myles Shoda, who finally picked up on it. He just said, "John, look at your heel, look at what it's doing when you release the ball." I threw another pitch, focusing on my heel for the first time, and that's when it finally hit me. I don't know when or how I had started doing it, but somehow my right heel had gotten into the habit of sliding away from the rubber as I planted my left leg and followed through. That little two- or three-inch movement was keeping my hips from opening up properly and effectively blocking me off as I attempted to finish my pitches.

With that one small adjustment, I could immediately see the difference. With one small adjustment I could, most importantly, *feel* the difference. It was a watershed moment. With one almost annoyingly trivial change to my mechanics, my stuff *and* my confidence were restored. I finally had my answers and I knew, really knew, it was time to get back in the arena.

That's when I started talking to St. Louis. Now, it wasn't as if they were the only team shopping around for a veteran pitcher for the stretch. Several teams had expressed interest since I had been released and some had even offered some nice one-year deals to start. But this wasn't just about finding a spot in another rotation this season. I wasn't interested in just coming back to pitch. I was talking to St. Louis for the same reasons I had signed with Boston: I was still relentlessly pursuing another trip to the postseason.

Being a member of the Atlanta Braves throughout their historic run of fourteen consecutive division titles had made me accustomed to frequent postseason trips. I was quite literally addicted to it. But the streak ended in 2005 and it had been almost four years since my last taste of the playoffs. I was on the hunt for one last chance to pitch in October, to feel the magic of the playoffs and the intensity of the matchups.

Both St. Louis and I happened to be in the right place at the right time. I knew Adam Wainwright a little bit and I had the chance to talk to him before I signed. It was a little odd really, but from everything Adam told me, the 2009 Cardinals sounded a lot like the Braves of the nineties. Besides that, I respected their manager, Tony La Russa, and their pitching coach, Dave Duncan, in the same way I had always respected Bobby Cox and Leo Mazzone. In some weird way, it felt like I was almost going home again. It wasn't Atlanta, but it did seem uniquely familiar.

The most important thing about the Cardinals, though, was the undeniable fact that they were running away with their division that season. They hadn't mathematically clinched the NL Central yet, but they were far and away the best team that year. In St. Louis, I had found everything I was looking for; it seemed like the feeling was mutual.

The negotiations were simple, earnest, and straightforward. They basically just said, "We've been watching you, we know what happened in Boston, but we still think you can help us out of the bullpen down the stretch."

I said, "Great. The only thing I ask is for you guys to just give me a start or two. It's going to be two weeks now that I haven't thrown and I need to get reacclimated."

The Cardinals, currently enjoying the luxury of a practically insurmountable lead in the Central, didn't bat an eye about giving me a chance to get my feet wet. Their response to my lone request? "No problem." And with that, it was official. I was the newest member of the St. Louis Cardinals, and most importantly, I was back in the hunt.

It was a surreal moment for me. I had begun the month with my pitching career dead in the water, and now, approximately two weeks later, I was a member of a championship-caliber team. I had clawed my way back from baseball limbo land and landed on my feet again; I was stoked and ready to go. But I can't say everyone around me, most especially the media, shared my optimism and enthusiasm for giving it another go.

To a lot of people it looked like I was about to commit career suicide. Signing with St. Louis meant taking the risk of failing again and experiencing double jeopardy. The consensus seemed to be that the chance to pitch again wasn't worth potentially marring all my career statistics and the legacy and reputation that I had worked for so many years to achieve.

I've never been one to care too much about what the media thought I should be doing, and I didn't feel at all inclined to listen to their pleas to invoke some common sense. But the fact is, I knew what they didn't know and couldn't possibly have known. I knew that what happened in Boston was not destined to happen in St. Louis and I was willing to accept any of the aforementioned risks for the opportunity to prove to myself that I wasn't done yet—*especially* when another trip to the postseason was basically guaranteed.

It wasn't like I was going into this deal with blinders on and I just assumed everything was going to go my way. I had my eyes wide open. I knew the risks were great, but on the other hand, I knew the potential reward was even greater: I had the *chance* to pitch in another postseason and compete for another championship.

I had been to the postseason a lot—an awful lot, frankly—with the Braves. But I had been to the World Series five times and only won it all once. It was a fact that still stuck with me all these years.

Chapter Sixteen

CHASING RINGS, PART II

When you Google "World Series champions" between 1991 and 1999, the name "Atlanta Braves" appears only once, listed as the 1995 champion. There's no little asterisk next to our name reminding people, "Hey, the Braves went to the Fall Classic *five* times during that time span." There is no small print at the bottom that explains, "Atlanta duked it out to the bitter end in some epic games that could have gone either way." When it comes to the record books, you're either a winner or you're not. And the record books will tell you, we were losers more often than not. What they won't tell you is *why*.

It's something I'm asked about a lot honestly, and I'd be lying if I said it didn't bother me sometimes. When you play baseball professionally, dedicate your life to it, and come *insanely* close to achieving your ultimate goal so many times only to watch the Commissioner's Trophy be handed to another team, it hurts. It sticks with you. It becomes more than just a game.

I lived and breathed our entire run of fourteen consecutive division titles and I still can't quite understand it, to be honest. I still look back on all those years in the playoffs and wonder. I mean, it is almost *nonsensical* how we didn't win a whole handful of rings. Whether you're a Braves' fan or not, you can't deny the odds; we should have won more than one championship, no doubt about it. But last time I checked, baseball could care less about random odds, or who is supposed to win or lose on paper.

This whole issue of our team winning only one championship becomes especially frustrating when people try to compare us to the New York Yankees or the Florida Marlins of that era—teams whose names you'll find listed more than ours on the roster of World Series champions during our streak. What's even more annoying is this feeling I can't shake that our team somehow helped turn the Yankees into the powerhouse they became after 1996. To me, Tuesday, October 22, 1996, serves as the starting point for their dynasty—and, conversely, our demise.

On that fateful night, Game Three of the World Series, it was as if the baseball gods consecrated the Yankees and cursed the Braves. After that night, the Yankees would go on not only to win that World Series after being down two games to none, but to dominate the next few years, winning the Series three out of the next four. (And that's not even counting a runner-up finish in 2001.) On the other hand, since that date, the Braves have yet to win another World Series *game*. Despite stringing together nine more division titles, we would make it back to the World Series only one more time. That was in 1999, when we were swept in four games by—wait for it—the Yankees.

And then there's the Florida Marlins: an expansion team that had existed for only four years in 1997 when they won it all. When they clinched the wild card that year, they were little more than a nice, feel-good story for baseball. That is, until they swept the San Francisco Giants 3–0 in the National League Division Series and then beat us 4–2 in the National League Championship Series. The next thing you know, the Marlins are popping open bottles of champagne on national TV after defeating the Cleveland Indians in the World Series in seven games. And not only did they win it all in '97, but they pulled off another improbable wild-card World Series win, over the Yankees no less, in 2003. If the Florida Marlins can win two World Series without ever winning their division, it's safe to assume that anything is possible.

When it comes down to it, I'll admit I do have a few regrets, but it's not like I would go back and change everything if I could. I certainly don't look back and wish that I could have been a Yankee or a Marlin instead of a Brave. Not at all. And even if you offered me a choice, even if you told me, "John, you could either have two world championships or fourteen straight division titles"—I'm taking the fourteen straight every time. *Every time.* I seriously wouldn't trade any part of my experience for one more championship.

As a player, I wanted nothing more than a chance to compete in October; it's the most exciting thing that can happen to a player. As a member of the Braves during that magical run, I reached the postseason for almost a decade and a half straight. That's just unreal, especially when you consider that some guys spend their entire career toiling away on teams that never even get a whiff of the playoffs. The closest some guys have ever come to the World Series is a nice pair of seats along the first-base line. Looking back, I was really spoiled: I played almost every year knowing we had a *chance.*

Our record is a proud one and one that stands alone. Nobody had ever done it before and it's likely nobody will ever do it again. We had the time of our lives. We sacrificed for each other on the field, and for the most part, we were genuinely friends in the clubhouse. Despite having a roster stuffed with exceptionally talented athletes, we were never really bogged down by a bunch of big egos. Take Greg Maddux and Tommy Glavine for example.

Without a doubt, Maddux and Glavine are the best right-hander and left-hander to ever be in the same rotation at the same time. Beyond that, they are two of the best pitchers ever. We're talking about guys who routinely posted nineteen to twenty wins a season in their prime, who won three-hundred-plus games, and who have six Cy Young Awards between them. Both of them had the stats to have an attitude, demand special treatment, or otherwise cause a rift in the clubhouse. It never happened. They never displayed any animosity toward each other or anyone else. It was actually quite the opposite.

Our entire rotation enjoyed a special camaraderie. We took things seriously, but we were always having fun, too. From the mound to the golf course, everything was a competition. We kept track of who lasted longer in their last game, who had laid down a bunt—and who didn't—and who had hit the last RBI. Remember that triple Glavine hit in Game Seven of the National League Championship Series against the Cardinals in 1996? You know, the one where he knocked in three runs all by himself? Yeah, Maddux and I are still hearing about that one.

Anyway, my point is, sure the championship issue is a sore one. Undoubtedly. But I think our team has earned its own distinction in baseball history, never mind the lack of an asterisk by our name. We were dominant, but we were also a team. We had poise. We had class. And I think you could say that by and large we were good to each other and to our fans. Looking back, I hope it's those kinds of things that define our legacy. We were a bunch of guys getting paid to play a game we loved and we kept coming back, year after year, and competing, despite the odds. Rings or not, we played like champions. And I wouldn't have it any other way.

Do I think we should have won more than one? Absolutely. And do I think that had we gotten a little more timely execution, it would have been more? Absolutely again. We would definitely have had a few. But one of the things that bothers me most about the conversation is the oversimplified attempt to find a single answer or two for why fourteen *different* teams didn't win the ultimate prize. The truth is that during a number of those years we were fortunate to make the postseason at all and had no chance of winning the World Series, yet because those seasons fell within the fourteen-consecutive-division title streak, they add to this sense of world-class futility.

The best way to get your arms around what we faced is to look at each year individually, and as I take you through this quickly, I think you will agree that the picture takes on a new look.

Humor me for a second as we ever so briefly walk through the streak.

1991—We shocked the world, including ourselves, by making it to the Series. We lost Game Seven by one run, but what you need to remember is that we were not picked to do anything.

1992—Another year, another one-run loss, this time in Game Six. In our first two World Series appearances, nine games were decided by one run, and we were on the losing end of seven of them. These weren't blowouts; we just weren't as good.

1993—This is the first time I think you can say we had a better team and we should have beaten the Phillies in the NLCS. But it's the same story, again just one run, and what a difference it might have made.

1994—No postseason due to the strike.

1995—We were so lucky to get by the first round this year. Colorado had us beat, period, but then we proceeded

to shut down the three best offenses playoff baseball
had seen in a long time in the Rockies, the Reds, and
the loaded Indians. We were finally champions.

So after five years we were 1–2 in the World Series.

1996—Now comes a year we would all like to forget, and
I would say it was the last time we were truly domi-
nant. This year we were beaten by the Yankees in the
World Series, which still hurts to write.

1997—We had a really good team again, and if you
remember, the Marlins went out and spent a ton of
money to try to knock us off and win the division. We
still took the division, but played poorly early in the
NLCS and the Marlins beat us with the help of great
pitching by Liván Hernández and a strike zone that a
forty-inch bat could not have helped. (I know we had
a generous one as well, but you know I had to throw
this in.) The Marlins went on to win it all.

*So that's 1–3 in the years I felt that we were better. Now, here is
where lumping in all of the next years is unrealistic, I believe, because
these next few years we started to lose players both to injuries—key
ones, I might add—and free agency.*

1998—Whether or not the Padres should have beaten us,
the Yankees were a very good team.

1999—We had no business making it to the NLCS, not
to mention the World Series. This team lost players
at the end of the season, but just knew how to fight.
We did get swept by the Yankees in the World Series,

but I maintain it was the closest sweep ever. In Games One and Three we took a lead into the eighth inning, but allowed the Yankees to come back and win both games.

The remaining years we did not get out of the first round of the playoffs. We truly were probably in a rebuilding era, but because of our continued success at finding ways to win the division every year, the frustration mounted and we were somehow viewed as failures.

The fact that John Schuerholz and Bobby Cox gave us a *chance* to win it all every year—remember, to win it all, you HAVE to make the playoffs first—was amazing. We won when the team was rebuilding, while most teams don't go to the playoffs when they are in transition. We won because our manager could take a variety of different teams with certain weaknesses and win, teams that had a lot of injuries, and still make it.

And finally, I would suggest that even the most widely accepted baseball theories and philosophies, although good on paper, don't always neatly sum up the final results. When a team has that special mojo, or whatever you want to call it, sometimes the game and its history can be turned upside down and things happen that you really can't explain.

We were provided with one of the most amazing and blatant exceptions to all the supposed rules with the 2011 World Champions, the St. Louis Cardinals. What the Cardinals did transcends any theory or philosophy of anything that *could* or *should* happen in the game. They weren't supposed to be in the playoffs, but they got there. They weren't supposed to win, but they kept winning. And they won in miraculous ways. I mean, you can't even describe Game Six of the 2011 Series. It's *unfathomable* to think that at two different times, down to their very last strike, they could come back and go on to win the World Series.

The St. Louis Cardinals arguably won with a weaker team than the teams that were supposed to win it all. And that can't be explained other than to say they took advantage of their moment in ways most, including some of our Braves teams, couldn't manage.

As has been proved time and time again, baseball's champion is not always determined by the most wins in the regular season—I think we won more games over those fourteen years than any other franchise—the biggest budgets, or the strongest starting pitching. Championships can come in very weird and complicated ways, ways that not even Cardinals manager Tony La Russa can truly explain.

It's hard to describe in a few broad generalizations what happened and why on the whole we only managed to win it all once, because like I said, it's really hard to generalize fourteen years of baseball. The truth is, there isn't one reason. There might be one reason for each year, but there's not one reason for all fourteen. All I am offering here are a few opinions that might help make sense of something that is, generally speaking, hard to understand.

And honestly, while I may have strung together a few nuggets of wisdom here, at the end of the day, I'm also almost convinced that there may be no better or more complete answer than this: Baseball is a beautiful game, but it can also be brutally heartbreaking sometimes.

With those thoughts in mind, I offer you four observations about the futility that overtook us during our streak: (1) It's not Bobby Cox's fault. (2) Superior pitching wins baseball games, but power pitching is a bonus in the postseason. (3) Starting pitching is great, but timely hitting is better. And (4) Sometimes fate just kicks your butt.

1. It's not Bobby Cox's fault.

Bobby Cox has taken more bullets about this than almost anyone else, and it's high time that credit is given where credit is due. If you aren't a die-hard Braves fan, you might not realize how influential Bobby was in building the team that would start our historic run. He was actually the Braves' general manager from 1985 to 1990, back when the only thing the Braves were competing for every year was the basement of the NL West. Bobby was the man responsible for righting our ship and turning things around. He made big, sweeping changes: revamping Atlanta's minor league system; stocking a stable of young arms, including myself, Glavine, and Steve Avery; and acquiring or drafting young talent, including David Justice and some guy named Chipper Jones. Bobby Cox had put together a talented young team, but it would take a few years to translate this into tangible wins on the field.

When June 1990 rolled around, Bobby moved to the dugout to serve as our manager and general manager until October, when John Schuerholz was brought in to be the new GM. It was the very next year, 1991, that our team notoriously went from worst to first and took the World Series into the tenth inning of Game Seven, before eventually losing 1–0 to the Twins in what is widely regarded as one of the best Series of all time. Bobby had helped build the nucleus of that team.

While Bobby helped lay the framework for our run, he also deserves a ton of recognition for *sustaining* our run. You don't win *any* division for fourteen years straight without finding ways to win games that you have no business winning, statistically speaking.

You can always second-guess a manager's moves: "Why pull the starter now? Hit and run here . . . are you kidding me?" Believe me, every player plays manager in his mind sometimes and you wonder what the real manager is up to. It's easy to do. But trust me: Bobby's moves were always calculated, made with the intention of preserving a lead, preserving his athletes, or generating some offense when the run-support well had run dry. He knew things the rest of us didn't know, saw things even the best in the game didn't see. This is what good managers do—they know the odds, they know the percentages, and they are always looking for opportunities to exploit another team's weakness and put their own players in position to crack open games. And Bobby did that better than anybody, if you ask me.

2. Superior pitching wins baseball games, but power pitching is a bonus in the postseason.

During our historic run, we enjoyed the best rotation in all of baseball, maybe even the all-time best. When you face a 162-game schedule with Greg Maddux, Tommy Glavine, myself, and Steve Avery on the mound, there's no denying that you are going to have a better chance to win more games than any other team. The best rotation can get you to the postseason, as we proved year after year, but things change when you get to the postseason.

Playoff baseball is so different from the regular season. Everything becomes condensed and magnified at the same time. In a postseason game, every hit and every pitch matters. In playoff baseball, a man on first is a rally and the crowd knows it. Everyone is dialed in, on task and sharp, and there are no free rides. Pitchers don't throw away pitches and hitters don't give away at-bats. This laserlike focus is only heightened by the fact that you never know when a moment might win or lose a game. When it comes to elimination games, there literally is no tomorrow.

What all this boils down to is that everybody makes adjustments to their strategies to survive and increase their odds of winning. Good hitters know that if they are facing finesse pitchers like Tom Glavine or Greg Maddux, a higher-percentage strategy is to take away part of the plate and settle for making contact. To put it simply, the more contact generated, the more chances a team has to be successful in the shorter format of the postseason. I, personally, am convinced that it's harder to be successful with a staff full of finesse pitchers in the postseason because you have to be that much more perfect. I'm convinced that if you live on contact and throwing strikes out of the zone, you don't always reap the benefit of it in the playoffs.

Hitters facing finesse pitchers during the regular season are much more likely to try to do more with the ball, like pull it down the line. This is precisely how Maddux and Glavine made their living; during the regular season, they won this battle more times than not.

Now, theories are nice and all, but the other thing I know is that when Tommy and Greg were on the top of their game, it didn't matter what approach the hitters took; the pitchers were going to win.

It's a different story for a power, or fastball, pitcher like me. The postseason gave me the opportunity to use other gears that would make it tougher on hitters. These extra gears allowed me to increase the velocity of my pitches and the sharpness of my breaking balls.

Now, I know what you're thinking. Why wasn't I doing this over the course of the thirty-five-odd starts I would get in the regular season? The short answer is that there's no way to do it. There's no way to sustain this type of effort. This is reserved for the games that look like they could be your last.

I think that in theory, the fastball pitcher has a better chance to be successful in the postseason because he can be aggressive and challenge hitters and feed off the intensity of the postseason. It doesn't do much good for finesse pitchers to try to feed off the intensity because they aren't going to benefit from throwing the ball harder; their finesse pitches and their command are their weapons.

So what do you do? Who do you start and when? Our manager, Bobby Cox, had the daunting task of trying to crack this code and figure out the order of his rotation every year. Every year there were some very tough choices—choices the likes of which other managers were surely jealous of—like which twenty-game-win starter goes first? And which future Hall of Famer goes second? In 1996, I made the decision easier for Bobby with the way I was pitching that year, and I got a chance to start Game One of the postseason for Atlanta. But in other years, maybe it wasn't so clear. What I can say is that wherever I pitched, I was very fortunate to be in positions to pitch some incredible games, and ones that would ultimately bring home a championship in 1995.

Now, I used to think the more power pitching you had, the better chance you had to be successful, but that has obviously been disproved on more than a couple occasions. But with that said, in theory, I still believe it's a great formula to have that go-to power guy, that guy who can strike out ten or eleven guys in a game when you need it, because it *could* lead to more wins when they count the most.

3. Starting pitching is great, but timely hitting is better.

Strong starting pitching often delivers you to the postseason, but in the playoffs you are all but destined to go up against other great starting pitching. I think our run all but proves that a lack of timely hitting can hurt you way more than a starter who can't get you safely into the sixth inning.

The one thing I think you can say about our World Series appearances is that rarely did we get outpitched. Now that may seem a little nonsensical because we lost way more times than we won, but the fact is, when you talk about getting outpitched, you have to look at the number of games that were decided by one run. We went to the World Series five times: 1991, 1992, 1995, 1996, and 1999. Over those five Series we played a total of twenty-nine games. More than half of those games—seventeen to be exact—were decided by one run and we lost twelve of those. That means we lost roughly 70 percent of the time in extremely close games that could have gone either way. The year we won, 1995, was the lone year when we won more close games than we lost.

Our pitching kept us in games, but it clearly wasn't always enough to deliver championships. What we really lacked almost across the board was some timely hitting. The fact is, when you lose World Series games by one run, you fall victim to that clutch hit, that one play coming in and costing you a game, and eventually the whole Series.

As starting pitching goes, so goes your organization, but to win it all you've got to have a combination of a team that's hot and is capable of timely hitting. There were years when we just didn't get that timely hitting, in 1991 and 1992 especially, and one year that we did, in 1995.

I'm telling you, sometimes all you need is that one run.

4. Sometimes fate just kicks your butt.

I'm going to warn you in advance that I realize what follows is subjective. Surely there's a more scientific way to explain our shortcomings, but I'm a simple man: I'll leave the equations and acronyms to those with a proclivity for math and for the use of calculators. What I do know is that a few things about baseball can't be explained *Moneyball*-style. You can't define momentum any more than you can predict impetus. Things happen—things that don't get recorded in the record books or official box scores—that can tip a game one way or the other. Call it a curse, call it fate, call it bad karma; it just seemed like more often than not, we were on the losing end of all of it, with the glaring exception, of course, being 1995. There are many, many examples that I can point to, but for the sake of brevity, I'm going to limit myself only to the 1996 World Series.

Now remember, it's 1996 not 2006. The Yankees have really done *nothing* for years; the last time they were in the Series was in 1981 when they lost to the L.A. Dodgers. Meanwhile, we came into the World Series in 1996 not only as the defending champions, after beating the Indians the previous year, but we had also been to the Series in '91 *and* '92. If anybody looked like the Team of Nineties at this point, it was us.

That year we had swept the wild-card Dodgers in the National League Division Series, but then somehow found ourselves down three games to one in the NL Championship Series against the St. Louis Cardinals. We proved to be down but not out, roaring back to win three games in a row in dramatic fashion and earn another trip to the World Series. We were returning to the Fall Classic for the second year in a row *and* we had momentum. We came in heavily favored to win another championship.

The Series opened in New York on Sunday, October 20, after the original opener was scratched due to rain. The delayed start did little to extinguish our bats, and two short days later the record stood at 2–0. We had manhandled the Yankees—in Yankee Stadium, no less—blowing them out and winning both games with a collective score of 16–1. We were headed back to Atlanta with what appeared to be an insurmountable lead.

But this is where things started to get a little screwy. We certainly had a nice lead, but everyone knows you never walk around like you've already won the thing. Well, someone should have told that to our local paper, the *Atlanta Journal-Constitution*, which ran an article that basically claimed, "The Series is over, why even play the games?" Seriously. I still remember picking up the paper and just groaning. It was such a bad omen. I couldn't believe they would run something like that. What were they thinking? Now, I'm not saying the *AJC* is entirely to blame for our downfall, but I certainly am pointing out that their fate-tempting article seemed to be the first omen that the tables were about to turn.

After the article, it seemed like we were fighting everything imaginable. The rest of the Series was one big train wreck for us. If it could go the Yankees' way, it did. We couldn't catch a break, let alone a foul ball, to save our lives. Here is a short—and incomplete—list of "random" occurrences that conspired against us in the next five days:

> **Accidental umpire interference:** Through five innings of Game Four, we're up 6–0. In the sixth, right field umpire Tim Welke inexplicably impedes right fielder Jermaine Dye as he charges in to snatch what appears to be an otherwise routine foul ball popped up beyond the first-base line. The ball hits the deck. The batter, a certain Derek Jeter, gets a second chance at the plate and singles, touching off a three-run Yankee rally. The score after the sixth: Braves 6, Yankees 3.
>
> **Some guy named Leyritz:** Later in the eighth, Rafael Belliard muffs what appears to be a routine double-play ball, only managing to get the runner out at second. With one out and two on, the stage is set for a rally, but the next batter due up, Jim Leyritz, a *defensive* sub brought in for Yankee catcher Joe Girardi in the sixth, doesn't seem to be a likely hero. Leyritz improbably delivers with a three-run home run, tying the game at 6–6, and bringing the Yankees back to life in the game and in the Series. It was later reported

that Leyritz, not expecting to play, had spent most of
the game in the Yankee weight room.

No earned runs allowed, we still lose: Game Five. I pitch
eight innings, strike out ten, throw 135 pitches, allow
one unearned run, and still get the loss. The Yankees
score their one and only run in the fourth, assisted
by an error by center fielder Marquis Grissom. What
should have been out number one results in Charlie
Hayes on second, in scoring position. Two batters
later, he scores. It was another error that would lead
to yet another Yankee win.

Win one for ~~The Gipper~~ Frank Torre: In between Games
Five and Six, Frank Torre, big brother of Yankees
manager Joe Torre, suddenly undergoes successful
heart-transplant surgery, after waiting three months
for a donor. He recovers enough to be able to watch
Game Six from his hospital bed. The Yankees, obviously supportive of their manager and his family, are
supplied with yet another reason to play hard.

On October 21, we appeared to be on a collision course with destiny in the form of repeat titles. Five days later, we had somehow lost
the World Series and destiny belonged to the Yankees. Their incredible win was our incredible loss. Not only did we lose another championship, we lost the foundation of the team that had gotten us to
the World Series four out of the last six years. If we had won, would
our general manager have gone in another direction and been able to
keep the likes of David Justice, Marquis Grissom, Terry Pendleton,
Jermaine Dye, and Steve Avery? That's the kind of thing we'll never
know. What we do know is what did happen. The Yankees went on
to dominate, even today. Meanwhile, the Braves are still chasing their
first World Series win since 1996.

Maybe to some people it sounds like we Atlanta Braves fans are crying in our spilled milk, but the fact is we were so close, it's so hard to explain. It doesn't make any sense, but the reality is a hit here, a pitch here, a run here, and I'm not writing a chapter about why there was only one ring. It's like I said earlier: Baseball is a beautiful game, but it can also be brutally heartbreaking.

Chapter Seventeen

VINDICATION

As I walked out to the mound for the first time for the St. Louis Cardinals on August 23, 2009, I was in a mind-set unlike anything I had experienced the entire time in Boston: I was comfortable, I was relaxed, and I was confident.

On paper, there was really no reason to be confident or to truly believe that I could suddenly turn things around and resurrect my season. With the way I had pitched in Boston at times, there really wouldn't have been any reason for my new team, the media, or anyone else to expect a win, even if they had sent me all the way down to Double-A ball. But that wasn't how I saw things and that wasn't how I felt about things either.

Fresh off two weeks away from the game, I felt completely recharged and in a good place mentally. I knew I had the luxury of a little time, in the form of two starts, to just kind of get back in the swing of things. The expectations were pretty low and I was under zero pressure to come out and pitch lights-out. The Cardinals were well into first place, and even if I stank it up both times out, I was not going to be the reason why they missed the postseason. St. Louis had a great pitching staff led by Chris Carpenter, Adam Wainwright, and Joel Piñeiro, and I was there to just give them that little extra boost at the end, if they needed it. My attitude was "Here we go, let's finish strong."

My relaxed outlook was only one part of my recent surge in confidence. It's really weird how this worked out, but it seemed like all the things that had been unknown and disorienting about Boston were now comfortable to me in St. Louis. It's no fault of Boston's; it's just the way it worked out. I have family in St. Louis, so I got to stay with my uncle while I was there. The city seemed easier to navigate, the clubhouse seemed similar to Atlanta's, and the philosophies were similar as well. I could go on and on. St. Louis was just a good fit for me all around.

On top all of this, there were still other reasons why I was feeling more comfortable on the mound than I had felt in a long time. In addition to discovering the mechanical problem—that little heel movement—that had been plaguing my delivery at times in Boston, the Cardinals had helped me figure out that I had also been tipping my pitches.

In St. Louis, all the starting pitchers made a point to come watch each other pitch side sessions in the bullpen. There was this great team mentality going on within their rotation, and they had created an open atmosphere where they were all sharing ideas and helping each other improve. Like I said before, St. Louis always reminded me of Atlanta.

The first time Chris Carpenter saw me throw a bullpen, he came up to me afterward and said, "Hey, you mind me telling you something?"

I didn't know what he was about to say, but I've always been really receptive to feedback. Even if it was bad news, I wanted to hear it. So I said, "Not at all. Go ahead."

He said, "I know every pitch you're going to throw before you throw it."

I was like, "Really?!"

Chris and I stood there talking for a moment and things started to click in my mind. It was one of those "Aha!" moments that I still remember today. There I had been struggling the whole time in Boston and I had somehow neglected even to consider the possibility that I could have been tipping pitches.

Tipping pitches is something that all pitchers have to guard against, and this can be hard to do, considering that pitching is basically an art of effective repetition. The problem crops up when you develop noticeable habits specific to each pitch you throw. We're talking about subtle things—like the way you grip or regrip the ball, change your arm angle, or the way you hold your glove as you get ready to throw—that telegraph what's coming next. If you're not consciously thinking about being deceptive, you can start giving off hints and be none the wiser for it.

For me, it was always my glove. If you watched me pitch long enough, you could start to detect by the angle I held my glove what was coming next—fastball, slider, change—to a fairly reasonable degree. I figured if Chris could tell what was coming after one bullpen session, he probably wasn't the only one.

I was eventually able to confirm that at least a couple of teams had cracked the code on my glove. It was disappointing news, but really a blessing at the same time. It was such a relief to know I had discovered two things that I could actually fix—just knowing this did wonders for me. Initially I had felt confident that the outcome *could* be different in St. Louis; now I had reason to believe that it *should* be. In my mind, it was time to get back to business as usual.

For my first start, we were on the road against the San Diego

Padres, so I began the game in the dugout, watching my new teammates come up to bat for me for the very first time.

The Cardinals got things going early as Skip Schumaker and Brendan Ryan came out swinging and hit back-to-back singles. Cesar Carrillo, the starting pitcher for the Padres, then issued a four-ball walk to Albert Pujols. Before you knew it, it was bases loaded, *no* outs.

I couldn't have scripted a better start for us, and I was thinking, surely, with no outs, we were going to strike first. It all proved too good to be true, though, as the next three batters went three up, three down, and Carrillo pitched himself out of an early jam. I knew that stranding three base runners in the first inning was an ominous way to start a game, but as I strode to the mound, I wasn't dwelling on the missed opportunity. I was anxious to just get out there and pitch.

As I launched into my warm-up, things just felt right, they felt familiar. Here I was back in the National League, in a park that I had pitched in many, many times before, about to face hitters who not only had names and faces I recognized, but also had habits I knew. On top of that, my parents had been able to fly in for the game, and I knew they were there with me in the stands. It really felt like things were clicking into place, right up until I threw my first ten pitches.

When the dust settled after my tenth pitch, I had runners on first and second with no outs. I had gotten ahead of both hitters actually, but the Padres leadoff man, Everth Cabrera, had hit a weak grounder to shortstop Brendan Ryan and beat the throw to first for a single. Tony Gwynn Jr. then hit what appeared to be a routine double-play ball to second baseman Skip Schumaker, but Ryan, covering second, bobbled the throw and both runners were safe on the play. Ryan got tagged with an error and I got tagged with two runners on and no outs—when it could easily have been *nobody* on and *two* outs.

Right here at this point, ten pitches into my first start in St. Louis, there was a legitimate chance for the Padres to post a four-spot in the first inning. Or in other words, there was a chance that I was about to pick up right where I had left off in Boston.

It might have seemed like it was time to panic, but I wasn't panicking. I really didn't feel anything but a lot of patience and a lot of peace. I was able to do something on the mound here in the very first inning with the Cardinals that I hadn't able to do very well the entire time I was with Boston: slow the game down and control my own thoughts. As I stood on the mound, staring down one of the most dangerous hitters in the Padres' lineup, Adrián González, I didn't let myself feel defeated. I didn't start counting how many runs were likely to cross the plate if I hung a fastball right now. I just took a deep breath, banished any negative thoughts from my mind, and reassured myself that I still had what it took to stop the damage right here, right now.

I faced the same moment that had owned me to a certain extent in Boston and had owned me way back in 1991, when I had pitched myself into the worst slump of my entire career and started a season 2–11.

In 1991, I was actually pitching pretty darn well, but what I couldn't do in '91 was pitch out of a jam. I would start a game and things would be going fine, but anytime things started to get a little hairy, I would begin to unravel. I would find myself up against the wall at some point in every game, and it was like *Oh, here we go again*. It became a foregone conclusion in my mind that once runners were on, they were going to score. And it seemed like more often than not, they did.

I started to convince myself that if it *could* happen, it was going to happen. I wasn't suffering from a lapse in fundamentals; I was suffering from a complete collapse of confidence.

As the season wore on and the losses mounted, I spiraled further and further away from my old mind-set, a mind-set that had always given me this edge, this supreme confidence that I would outcompete any hitter in any situation. Now the tables had turned in my mind and that confidence was replaced with doubt. I was no longer convinced that I could get out of my own way when the trouble mounted.

I lost game after game after game, but my manager, Bobby Cox, never stopped believing in me the entire time. I don't remember that he ever really pulled me aside or sat me down and gave me any special words of wisdom. It's hard to describe this, I guess, but Bobby just had this ability to believe in people and he had this gentleness about him. As a pitcher, you can tell when your manager loses faith in you: You can tell by the way he comes out to get you, you can tell by a lot of things he says and does. Bobby never lost confidence in me, and I can only assume he believed in something that other people didn't seem to see: my potential.

It was really right here, at this specific point, that my manager changed the course of my career. No, that's not accurate. He *saved* my career. I mean, you can just imagine the kind of flak Bobby Cox was taking for continuing to hand me the ball every five days. The critics were clamoring for the hook, for anything. The sentiment became "Send him down. Or send him to the bullpen. Do *something*, Bobby! The kid has obviously lost it." Who knows what would have happened to either of us had I not eventually turned things around; I could easily have cost both of us a job. If I have said it once, I have said it a thousand times: I will always be grateful for Bobby Cox.

This is one point in my career where both Bobby and John Schuerholz deserve credit, though, because it was John who came to me and asked if I would be open to seeing a sports psychologist. Without hesitation, I said, "Sure, absolutely."

I had already admitted to my wife that I probably needed to see someone and I was really open to it. I wasn't afraid to talk about the thoughts that were running rampant in my mind; I was just interested in getting better. I mean, at this point I was 2–11; I knew exactly what was going on. The truth was that at this rate, I was not going to be in the rotation much longer.

John made the arrangements and I met with sports psychologist Jack Llewellyn a couple times during the All-Star break. It was such a simple process. I went over to his house and we shot pool in his basement and talked. We didn't even talk much about baseball. We talked about how I was feeling in general about my life and my recent marriage. After a couple of visits, Jack had an idea that he thought might help. He asked me to go have the video guys put together a highlight reel for me, so I did.

It ended up being nothing more than an old VHS tape with two minutes of my best moments from the mound up to that point. He told me to watch it several times before the next game, paying particular attention to how I had been able to throw all my best pitches in situations where one bad pitch could mean the difference between an out and several runs. I didn't know if it was going to work, but obviously it was worth a shot.

The very next game after the tape was made, I faced that same moment on the mound that had owned me all season. Runners were in scoring position and things were on the verge of getting ugly. But this time, I thought about the tape: I saw myself overcoming adversity in the past and I didn't let myself think I couldn't do it. I stood there on the mound and dug in deep. I made the adjustment in my mind and I faced the adversity in front of me. And not only did I *face* it my first time out, but I *nailed* it my first time out, pitching my way out of a jam and keeping runs off the scoreboard for the first time in what seemed like all year.

Now, the adjustment wasn't physical, but what I was doing mentally was affecting me physically—if that makes any sense. Before I saw Jack, I was basically the victim of some warped thinking. Remembering my little highlight reel helped me break out of it and banish the negative thoughts from my head; it freed me up and allowed me to make the pitches I needed to make and had been capable of making all along.

And that's what happened. It was as simple as just a couple times shooting pool at Jack's house, putting the video together, and done. That was it for me. We've kind of touched on this already, but if I can feel it or see it, the way my mind works, I can apply things really, really quickly. Once my confidence was restored, I was back on track. The story should have ended right there, but as most of you probably know, it didn't.

I really turned things around in the second half and started winning games on a pretty regular basis. The problem was, as the wins started to add up, the media keyed in on the story. Some articles suggested that because Jack had started to make it a habit to sit in the stands wearing a red shirt on days I pitched, his presence was somehow an integral part of my resurgence in the win-loss category. The silly thing is that I didn't have any idea that Jack was sitting in the stands at all.

I was simply focused on pitching, and I wasn't even aware that the issue was snowballing into its own story. To compound matters, no one ever asked me for my side of the story and I didn't step in and address it either. It wasn't until it carried over into the '92 season that I finally had to say "time out" and take the time to set the record straight. I was by no means embarrassed by my association with a sports psychologist, nor was I afraid to admit I had needed some help. I remain grateful to Jack for helping me regain my confidence. What I didn't appreciate was how the story got twisted and made out to be more than it really was. And if I had to do it all over again, I'd have stepped in and put an end to it much sooner.

Perhaps part of what fueled the story was that this was one of the first times that it had become public knowledge that a pro athlete was seeing a sports psychologist. There were other guys doing it, even guys on my own team, but it had never made the papers. I had no problem being seen as some kind of trailblazer in this arena (even though I really wasn't); I just wish it had been more accurately portrayed.

If you'd have told me at the break, when I was 2–11, "John, you are going to not only go 12–2 and earn two wins in the National League Championship Series against the Pittsburgh Pirates, but go on to pitch fourteen innings in the World Series against the Minnesota Twins and only allow two runs," I wouldn't have believed it. In fact, I would have probably checked you into drug rehab. But that's what happened. I watched my little highlight reel whenever I needed to (at some point I didn't even need to put the tape into the VCR anymore; I could just close my eyes and see it) and I fought my way out of the worst slump of my career all the way to the opposite end of the spectrum—almost winning Game Seven of the World Series. The whole experience is a clear testament to how important your own thoughts are to your own success: Sometimes you just have to get out of your own way.

Fast-forwarding back to 2009, with runners on first and second and no outs in the bottom of the first, I just needed to remind myself of the facts: I knew what I had fixed and I believed in what I could still do. All I needed to do was pitch.

I was fortunate to get González to hit into a 4-6-3 double play, and just like that, the inning was reset with two outs and a runner on third. I threw three more pitches to left fielder Chase Headley, struck him out swinging, and the inning was over. Thankfully, on this occasion I not only avoided a four-spot in the first, I kept the score tied at 0–0. I walked back to the dugout already in and out of my first jam, unscathed. I hadn't really accomplished anything yet, but I remember telling myself, *Okay, I got over that tiny, little hurdle.*

In the second inning, Mark DeRosa led us off with a deep fly ball to center field for out number one. Yadier Molina, the second batter, walked, bringing me up to bat for the first time all year.

Before I stepped into the batter's box, I paused for a moment, taking a practice swing as I watched José Oquendo, the third-base coach, cycle through his signs. As I half expected, with Molina on first and only one out, Tony La Russa was calling for a sacrifice bunt to move the runner to second. I hadn't laid down a bunt in a game in I don't know how long, but when Carrillo wound up, I squared around like old times.

I made contact, but the ball ended up rolling foul. Carrillo then threw over to first twice, before picking up the battle with me again. The sacrifice was off now and I took the next three pitches for balls. With the count at 3–1, José signaled that the sacrifice was back on, and I fouled off another bunt. With the count now full, José gave me the green light to swing away. The next three pitches were good, all close enough that I had to swing, and I was lucky enough to get wood on all of them, fouling them away without harm.

At this point I was already pretty proud of myself. Here I was, the pitcher for the opposing team, and I was making Carrillo *work*. I had seen eight pitches already. The next pitch—the ninth of the at-bat—looked like it could easily be my third strike if I let it go, so I took a cut.

I made contact, dinking a weak ground ball to the shortstop. It was a fielder's choice and the Padres threw out Molina at second, but I escaped the double play and arrived safely at first. I hadn't advanced the runner, I hadn't been credited with a hit, but I had reached first base safely in my first at-bat and I felt an usual amount of satisfaction about it. It might have seemed like a minor moment to a twenty-one-year veteran, but I hadn't even taken batting practice in over a year.

It was a unique thing to find myself on first base in the second inning, and I felt the first twinge of magic that day. I had already pitched myself out a jam in the first inning and now here I was on first. I remember tilting my face up toward the sun for a second and just taking in a deep breath of warm Southern California air. It was a picture-perfect day weatherwise—mid-seventies with a slight breeze and a brilliant blue sky—and a *perfect* day to be being playing baseball.

As I settled into a modest lead off first base, Skip Schumaker hit a ground ball into center and I advanced to second. Now it was two on, two outs, and there I was striding out a lead on second, figuring any second I'd be exchanging my helmet for my hat and glove.

Brendan Ryan was up next and all he did was improbably extend this improbable inning by ripping a two-out grounder up the middle. I broke for third as soon as I saw him connect with the ball, but I figured it would just be a short sprint. But when I saw José windmilling his arms toward home, I took a good line, rounded third, and started digging it out for home as fast as I could.

The next thing I know, I see Albert Pujols waving me in like a 747—calling for a slide! It must have been *years* since I had slid into any base, much less home, but I promptly launched my aging body feetfirst and executed a hook slide. I slid away from the tag of Padres catcher Nick Hundley, and when I swiped home plate with my right hand, I was pretty sure I was . . .

"Safe!"

I was absolutely *gassed* by this point, but hearing home-plate umpire Todd Tichenor's call propelled me up and onto my feet again.

I could only shake my head and smile as I walked back to the dugout, knocking the dirt off my pants. As I slapped some high fives through the dugout and sat down to catch my breath, I definitely felt forty-two years old in my body, but in my heart and mind I felt the joy of a nine-year-old who had just scored from second for the very first time.

For me, things had come full circle in that trip around the bases. I had literally and figuratively come back home, back to my roots in the National League. I had been a little tense in the first inning after giving up a hit that was immediately followed by an error. You always want better results than that, especially in the first, but once I got through it, I felt like all those years of experience had kicked right back in and I was right where I needed to be.

I enjoyed a nice break catching my breath as my new team continued our unlikely two-out rally, eventually scoring three *more* runs. It was an absolute gift to my game, walking out to start the bottom half of the second with a four-run lead, and I promptly settled in on the mound and got into a groove. Twelve pitches later I had sewn up another inning, three up and three down, all strikeouts—two swinging and one looking. I had started the game with confidence, but now I had momentum.

In the third, Carrillo walked DeRosa, our first batter up. When he then threw two consecutive balls to our second batter, Molina, Padres manager Buddy Black came out of the dugout. Carrillo was done and we were into the Padres' bullpen in the top of the third— always a good sign. Edward Mujica came in in relief and didn't fare any better against Molina; Molina drew a walk, bringing me up to the plate again.

With runners on first and second and no outs, the sacrifice was on from the first pitch. I took a deep breath and steadied myself in the batter's box for a moment before squaring around. This time I laid down a beauty of a bunt toward third. I scampered down the line and somehow beat the throw. Bases loaded, no outs. I had not only advanced the runners, as my manager had intended, but the Padres hadn't managed an out. I stretched my legs, half expecting another trip around the bases.

But this time, it wasn't to be. Schumaker came up next and hit into a double play and then Ryan hit a deep fly ball to right field for the third out. It's always disappointing not to score *any* runs after you load the bases with no outs, but at least we still had a four-run lead.

I picked things up in the bottom of the third right where I had left off in the second, only this time I only threw ten pitches. Nine strikes, one ball, and it was three up, three down, all strikeouts again—one looking, two swinging.

I didn't know it at the time, but I had just fired off seven strikeouts in a row, something I had never done in my entire career and something that had never been done in Cardinals-franchise history. What I did know was that I was making all my pitches and that whenever I got to two strikes, things almost felt automatic to me. I'd get two strikes and I'd be thinking, *He's out.* And for two and a third innings straight, they were.

Albert Pujols hit a solo homer in the top of the fourth, so when I came out for the bottom half of the inning, we had a 5–0 lead. The first batter up was Tony Gwynn Jr. I should have known my crazy strikeout streak was destined to end because the son of Tony Gwynn had my number. I don't know what his career batting average was against me, but I wouldn't be surprised if it was up over .500. Tony Jr. had been a pesky thorn in my side for many years and he would prove to be again on this occasion, coming through with a single to left field on a 2–2 count. The single broke up my streak, but thankfully mattered little overall, because I retired the next three batters, including one more strikeout, and stranded Tony at first.

I ended up pitching one more inning, allowing one more hit, but no runs, and adding yet another strikeout. In total, I had pitched a five-inning shutout and would be credited with a win. I had given up just three hits, struck out nine, and allowed no runs or walks. Just seventeen days earlier, it had been a completely different story: three and a third innings, nine hits, eight runs—all earned, four walks, two home runs, and three strikeouts. In one game, in one magical debut with the Cardinals, I had resurrected myself. I felt more than satisfied after the game; I felt vindicated.

Despite my performance, there were questions and comments after the game that I still had to deal with. They varied from the obvious ("Well, how come you didn't do this in Boston?") to the unfortunate

("Well, he beat the Padres, big deal, they were struggling") but it really didn't bother me. For me, it was more than just that one performance. And at the end of this day, despite anyone's comments, I didn't feel like I had to justify anything to anyone.

I mean think about it: I had been released from Boston, I was completely out of baseball for two weeks throwing at a stinking high school field, and the next thing you know I'm back in the big leagues. I hadn't started a game in seventeen days (which for pitchers is an *eternity*) and I struck out seven batters in a row—something I had never done in my entire career. No way. There's just no way that could have happened. I mean, you couldn't write that in a book.

Well, I guess I just did.

Chapter Eighteen

A SWEEP WORTH SAVORING

Prior to my five-inning shutout debut in San Diego, the expectations St. Louis had for me could best be described as limited and calculated. It was all but a foregone conclusion that after my previously agreed-upon two-start test drive, I was headed to the bullpen. I was really acquired not to be their fourth starter, but as another weapon in manager Tony La Russa's bullpen arsenal.

For those who aren't up on pro baseball managerial trends, Tony is widely credited with transforming the way today's managers use their bullpens. He was famous for using relievers in situational roles, like bringing in a lefty pitcher to face a lefty hitter, to create matchups that tilted the odds in his direction—to the point of switching pitchers one batter at a time on occasion. I was certainly capable of being the right-handed specialist Tony intended me to be in the bullpen, but

I was also hoping to prove that despite my recent performances in Boston, I was really the ultimate utility pitcher at this point, capable of starting, closing, and everything in between.

I think it's safe to say my debut against the Padres kicked open the door of possibility for me with the Cardinals. It was probably the first time they seriously entertained the idea of expanding my role and considered keeping me in the rotation after all. I was ready to fill in wherever they thought they needed me, but certainly the ambitious competitor in me was hoping to contribute more than just a few innings here and there. For me, the thrill of knowing what *might* happen if I could pitch strongly down the stretch helped me focus on the one thing I could control between now and then: how I pitched.

My next start, against the Washington Nationals on August 28, would be another memorable debut with the Cardinals—my home debut, my first time pitching in Busch Stadium as a member of the home team. The fans in St. Louis are widely considered to be the Best Fans in Baseball, and after August 28, I can understand why. I had built up some equity with the fans in Atlanta over the course of twenty years: I played there, I lived there, and I loved it there, but in three short months St. Louis made me feel like I had been there twenty years as well. I received not one, but *two* standing ovations, one when I walked out to the mound for the first time and then again when I came up to bat to lead off the bottom of the third. I had never experienced *anything* like it in my life and it was all the more humbling because I really hadn't done *anything* for them yet and here they were making me feel like I was about to do something incredible. The fans understood my career, they understood that this was probably the tail end for me, and they acknowledged it. It's one thing to be a fan of a player; I would argue that the folks in St. Louis are fans of the *game*.

I didn't follow up with another shut-out, but I got the job done in my second start. I went six innings, allowing four hits, one walk, and one earned run, while striking out six. I didn't get the win, since the game was tied 1–1 when I left in the sixth, but I didn't need the tick in the win column to prove I had been effective. An ERA under 1.0 for my first two games said it all.

It seemed like with every start with the Cardinals I gained confidence, even though I wasn't getting wins. Really, when you look at it, my record didn't reflect how well I was pitching. What did reflect my performance was the Cardinals' decision to keep me in the rotation for the foreseeable future. It was still hard to predict how I would fit into the team's postseason strategy, but I was working on building a résumé that I hoped would prove me worthy of my ultimate goal: another postseason start.

Under the circumstances, my shoulder was holding up well, but I did have one setback. In early September, in between a start in Milwaukee and a start back home in St. Louis against the Cubs, it flared up a little bit. The Cardinals were obviously more than a little concerned, but I was able to convince them not to make any hasty decisions with regard to me and the disabled list. I had been down this road before and I knew *exactly* what I needed to do. I told them not to worry, to just give me a few days to treat it, and I'd be back. I wouldn't miss a beat and I would pitch well in my next start.

This was really a critical moment for me in St. Louis, the fact that this shoulder inflammation would be a nonstory. Had I not already traveled down all these roads of injuries and surgery and rehabs, and spent so much time with medical professionals dissecting, so to speak, my body and learning my own limits and tendencies, this could have really been it for me right there and then. But as it turned out, my shoulder needed nothing more than a few extra days of rest between starts. Ten days after my last start I would take the mound in St. Louis against the Cubs and it was business as usual: six innings pitched with six hits, two runs, and four strikeouts.

This was really one thing that made a tangible difference in my performance in St. Louis—I enjoyed the ability to do whatever I thought I needed to do for my shoulder, whether it was throwing between starts, not throwing between starts, or whatever. They simply left it up to me and it helped me thrive.

I continued to pitch well down the stretch until it came to my last start at Cincinnati on September 30. That game proved to be my only hiccup with the Cardinals and it was unfortunate because it kind of tainted the nice little half season I was having with them. I only lasted four innings that evening against the Reds, and I gave up not only six hits but *six* earned runs. It was really frustrating to end on that note, especially because I felt I was battling against more than just your run-of-the-mill challenges, like trying to establish the outside corner with the home-plate umpire. I'm not trying to grab for excuses here, but when I got my hands on my first game ball, I *knew* I was in trouble.

I'd been pitching now for more than twenty years in the pros and these were the worst baseballs I'd ever pitched with in my life. It's perhaps a little-known piece of baseball trivia that all game balls are required to be "properly rubbed so that the gloss is removed," according to MLB rule 3.01(c). The balls are rubbed with a special mud that takes the shiny, fresh-out-of-the box sheen off them, without scratching them or altering their aerodynamic properties, so pitchers can actually grip the ball. The balls in Cincinnati that day were so slick that I had no feel for the baseball—it literally felt like a cue ball in my hand—and that's about the worst thing you can have as a pitcher. The obvious lack of mud on the balls coupled with the crisp game-time temperature proved to be a nightmare combination for me.

Now the Reds' starter, Bronson Arroyo, obviously had to pitch under the same conditions and use the same balls, and he did a nice job. I tried to go out and battle, too, but it did not pan out well for me. I lasted only four innings, the low point coming in the third when

I gave up four runs on one swing from Laynce Nix—a grand-slam home run.

That game was one of many that didn't go our way in the final month of the season. We would lose six of our last seven after clinching our division on September 26, ending our season on a particularly sour note by getting swept at home in a three-game series with the Milwaukee Brewers. We were not roaring into the postseason; we were plodding. And plodding never bodes well for deep October runs.

In the first round of the playoffs, we were matched up against the Los Angeles Dodgers, the Western Division champions, in the best-of-five National League Division Series. Games One and Two would be played in L.A., since the Dodgers had posted a slightly better regular-season record. When you considered the strength of our starting pitching, with Chris Carpenter scheduled to start Game One and Adam Wainwright Game Two, I think all of us thought we had more than a good chance to take both games, even though we would be playing on the road.

Going into the series, I was in a little bit of limbo between the bullpen and the rotation. It was hard to tell where I would fit into the puzzle of the postseason from the outset. With Carpenter and Wainwright opening the series, Tony understandably slid me to the bullpen for the first two games. There was at least a possibility that I might get the nod to start Game Four, but we didn't even know if there would be a Game Four at this point. I understood all of Tony's decisions and I understood my role, but it didn't make it any easier to go sit and wait and watch as our postseason unfolded from the bullpen. Even now, at forty-two, with a surgically repaired shoulder, I still felt I could go out there and deliver. And I ached for the chance.

To say things got off on the wrong foot for us in the NLDS is a mighty understatement. Three pitches into Game One, Chris Carpenter had already surrendered a single and a two-run home run.

He would go on to last five innings, but the Dodgers roughed him up for nine hits and four runs. On the offensive side, we had plenty of opportunities, but we weren't able to capitalize on them, leaving fourteen runners stranded on base and going three-for-thirteen with runners in scoring position. Tony La Russa reached into the bullpen five times over the last four innings of the game, but none of the calls were for me, and I watched Game One from start to finish from the visitors' bullpen in right field. Final score: Cardinals 3, Dodgers 5.

Everyone's expectation of dominating starting pitching came to fruition in Game Two as Adam Wainwright faced off against Dodgers' starter Clayton Kershaw. Adam was cruising early, retiring the first eleven batters he faced before giving up a solo home run to Andre Ethier in the bottom of the fourth. He would go on to pitch eight innings, allowing only three hits, and the one run. Thanks to a solo home run in the top of the second by Matt Holliday and an RBI double in the top of the seventh by Colby Rasmus, we had established a one-run lead over the Dodgers going into the eighth. With the way Adam was pitching, it looked like it might be enough.

Adam had the game so well in hand that Tony La Russa was already contemplating his pitching strategy for Games Three and Four. Joel Piñeiro was already penciled in for Game Three, but it appeared Tony might be leaning my way for Game Four when he called down and instructed bullpen coach Marty Mason to have me get up and start throwing a side session during the eighth inning.

I knew throwing a side session that night boded well for me to be tapped as a starter later in the series, but the timing seemed a little off. Never in my life had I thrown a side session in the middle of a playoff game with a one-run lead, but Tony had called for a side session, so that's what I did.

Everything appeared to be going just as planned right up until we were a strike away from closing the game. With two outs in the bottom of the ninth, on a 2–2 count, on the very verge of the series going back to St. Louis all tied up at 1–1, Dodgers' first baseman James Loney hit a line drive right at left fielder Matt Holliday. Cardinals' fans everywhere rejoiced, anticipating the final out. It would be Dodgers' fan rejoicing seconds later, though, as Holliday infamously caught the ball with his body, not his glove, and the ball fell to the ground. Loney advanced to second on the error, and the door had swung wide open for the ensuing two-out Dodger rally. Two batters later, the tying run would cross the plate.

With the game now tied up at 2–2, Tony made another call to the bullpen. Conditions had changed and thus my assignment had changed. If the game stayed tied through the ninth, Tony was going to bring me in for the tenth. I was so shocked by the news, I didn't think my heart could take it.

You see, throwing a bullpen session and throwing to get ready to enter a game are two very different things. I hadn't been throwing hard, maybe 70, 75 percent, but I had been up throwing for a while. Now I had to switch gears, and switch gears fast.

I couldn't believe what was happening and I had an adrenaline rush I hadn't experienced in a long time. I loved moments like this, but I wasn't prepared in any way to hear the words *you're in* midway through my side session.

I got ready and I probably would have been okay to go for the tenth, but on this day there would be no tenth. The Dodgers kept their implausible two-out, ninth-inning rally going, eventually knocking in the go-ahead run on a walk-off single to end the game. In a blink we had gone from taking the series back to St. Louis all tied up at one game apiece to taking the series back entrenched in a two-game deficit. It was hard to wrap your head around the final outcome after we had basically dominated the game nearly wire to wire.

As expected, Tony La Russa went with Joel Piñeiro in Game Three. I had held out hope that I might get the nod, mostly because I had a pretty good track record in elimination games. I had lost only one such game in my career, Game Four of the World Series against the Yankees in 1999. At the same time I completely understood and respected Tony's decision. Joel was their guy, he'd rung up fifteen wins in the regular season, and there was no reason to believe he wouldn't do the same in Game Three.

As it was, Piñeiro struggled, allowing four runs on seven hits through only four innings of work. When the scoreboard read 4–0 in the bottom of the fourth, Tony La Russa decided it was time for a change. He called down to the bullpen and had both me and Dennys Reyes get up and start warming up. Dennys would get the nod first, in the fifth, coming in and retiring all three batters he faced. Right after he recorded the third out, the bullpen phone rang again: Tony wanted me to come out for the sixth.

My blood was definitely pumping as I cycled through my customary fifteen pitches and prepared myself mentally and physically to enter the game. On the verge of pitching in my first postseason game in four years, I remember thinking, *All right, this is what you wanted to do. This is what you worked so hard to get back to.* When Skip Schumaker hit a fly ball to left field for the final out of the fifth, after a year of wondering if the moment would ever happen again, I was headed to the mound in the postseason one more time.

I had made the journey from the bullpen to the mound so many times before, but never did it seem longer than it did that day. For the first time I could feel my heart racing, almost like I was having an out-of-body experience. I couldn't believe what I was feeling: I couldn't swallow and I had absolutely no saliva. It was an anxiousness I had never felt before. It wasn't fear; it was wanting the moment almost too intensely.

My racing emotions were accompanied by a sudden flash of memories before my eyes, like a thirty-second movie of everything that I had gone through in that last year. The day I went under the knife, the rehab, Boston, the widespread belief that I wasn't even supposed to be able to come back. It wasn't like I was dying, but it's like I sensed that this could be it: This could be my last trip to the mound.

In some ways I wished it all could be different, that I wasn't coming out of the bullpen in the sixth with my team already down 4–0 in an elimination game. In so many ways, the past year had not been the path that I wanted or the journey I thought it could have been even now, but rising above that bittersweet brew of emotion was something else entirely: a sense of amazing accomplishment. The fact was, when I finished my walk, I looked down and found myself exactly where I always wanted to be: on the mound in the playoffs. Just by being *there,* in that moment, I had accomplished something.

I knew enough from my years of closing that I couldn't come into the game and focus on the score. So I ignored the scoreboard and came in pitching as if we were locked in a tight game. I had always pitched playoff games like there was no tomorrow, but this time it was more than just a mantra to get myself locked in. It was the absolute truth.

The first batter I faced was Casey Blake. After working him to a 2–2 count, I got him to hit a ground ball to our shortstop, Brendan Ryan. When I saw the ball coming off the bat, I thought it was an out, but Brendan didn't play the ball cleanly and Blake ended up being safe at first. Man, what a frustrating way to start.

When I look back now, though, it was completely in keeping with the theme of things rarely starting off on a good note for me.

I shrugged off the reality of the base runner and focused in on the next order of business: Ronnie Belliard. And I reminded myself that the five pitches I had thrown to Blake had been promising ones. You usually get a sense pretty quickly of how good your stuff is, and by all indications, my stuff seemed solid. After five more pitches, I *knew* it was solid. Belliard went down swinging and he would prove to be the first of many on this day, with Russell Martin and Vicente Padilla following suit in the inning. After giving up that first weak hit to Blake,

I had struck out three guys in a row, all swinging, and I had to smile to myself as I walked back to the dugout. I was in a familiar groove.

Unfortunately for us, Padilla, the Dodgers' starter, was also in a groove this day and was still dominating our lineup in the bottom of the sixth. It was three up, three down, and I was quickly walking back out to the mound for the seventh.

I picked up right where I left off in the sixth, striking out Rafael Furcal and Matt Kemp to start the inning. I had just struck out five batters in a row, as many as I ever had in the postseason.

I had a healthy respect for the next batter up, Andre Ethier, the Dodgers slugger who had hit thirty-one homers in the regular season and who had already hit a two-run homer earlier in the game off Piñeiro, but I was still plenty confident with the way I was throwing the ball. Two pitches later the count stood at 0–2 and I was one pitch away from striking out six hitters in a row, which I had never done in the postseason.

I should have been suspicious that the story line was getting a little *too* good at this point, because it was. After fouling off two pitches, Ethier would get all of my next one, launching it to center for a triple. In a heartbeat I went from an 0–2 count with two outs and nobody on to a runner on third and Manny Ramirez up. Perfect.

Manny would be the Manny who delivered in this case, promptly driving a ground-ball single into left field, scoring Ethier. I would give up another single to James Loney before eventually getting Casey Blake out on a fly ball to left field to end the inning. As I walked off the mound, I didn't know if that was it for me or not, but when I got to the dugout, Tony confirmed it. He was bringing in Jason Motte for the eighth. My day was done after two innings in which I had allowed four hits, gave up one run, but recorded five consecutive strikeouts. *Almost* six . . .

I sat down on the bench with the rest of my teammates, hoping and wishing for a rally that would never happen. Albert Pujols drove in a run in the bottom of the eighth, making the score 5–1, but it would prove to be the last run of the day. When Rick Ankiel struck out with two outs in the bottom of the ninth, we could only sit and watch the Dodgers celebrate before a hushed crowd at Busch Stadium.

For all the postseasons that I had been a part of, to lose three games in a row like the Cardinals had just done—it was brutal. Just unreal. I think we all had this feeling like everything had happened too fast, that it wasn't supposed to go this way. It was hard even to process that our season was already over.

In my perfect world, things would have ended differently. In my perfect world, we would have gone to another World Series and I would have started Game Seven, but that wasn't to be. Sure, we were swept out early, but in the end, it was a sweep worth savoring for me. When I walked out of the game, regardless of the scoreboard, I felt a sense of accomplishment beyond what anybody could ever have known.

Losing was certainly a bummer, but there was enormous satisfaction in simply proving I still had it. I had been able to deliver in the moment again, and not only had I delivered, I was a click away from starting and ending my career with St. Louis on two improbable strikeout streaks. I was so proud of all the work that had gone into just getting back to that moment, and that alone was enough for me.

After the game, I remember trying to put everything into perspective for Kathryn, all the sadness and all the joy that I was feeling at that same moment. I remember telling her, "Despite all that you witnessed in this last year, despite all the pain, all the struggle in Boston, all the heartbreak with how things ended with the Braves, I somehow managed to also have the time of my life."

No matter how many times I had done it before, no matter how successful my résumé was in the postseason, this was different. This was a point where I was vulnerable and I wasn't quite at my best, but I got another chance to prove to myself that I could do it. To me, those two innings of postseason work solidified everything, and despite what anyone might say, everyone needs that sense of accomplishment to be able to say to yourself, *I did it.*

I did it. It might not mean much to anyone else, but it does to me.

Chapter Nineteen

A HAMBURGER, A HOT DOG, AND A FRENCH FRY WALK INTO A BAR . . .

When I walked off the mound for the last time in 2009, there was a part of me that thought this might be it for me, as in The End. But *that* thought at *that* moment was really nothing more than a premonition, or maybe even an acknowledgment that there were no guarantees at this stage of my career. If you had interviewed me after the game, I would have told you (and I remember telling some people), "I hope to be back again with the Cardinals in 2010." Really, my mind-set at the end of 2009 was the same as it had been at the end of 2008, coming off of shoulder surgery: I still thought I could pitch and I still had the *desire* to pitch. And in my mind, I didn't see any reason why I couldn't pitch for another year or two.

The way my contract was written, I became a free agent again after the World Series, but the Cardinals seemed genuinely interested in the possibility of bringing me back for another year. In my mind, I was really thinking it could be the start of a nice little run in St. Louis. They had such a strong team, I knew they would have more chances to represent the National League in the playoffs, and I was hoping to have a role in that journey. So with that said, I went into the off-season fully dedicated to preparing to play what would have been my twenty-second season in the major leagues. I knew the work ahead, but the thrill of chasing yet another postseason drove me on.

That off-season, though, was not as seamless and pain-free as I would have liked. I struggled a little bit at times, more than I had expected to, but even with my shoulder not being quite 100 percent, I knew I could still do what St. Louis was looking for me to do. I could still be the perfect insurance for them out of the bullpen. I'm telling you, I could still go pitch in a major league game today. I'd have to throw all sliders, but I could still get people out.

As February and spring training inched closer and closer, the Cardinals and I were still talking, but they hadn't offered me a contract yet and I was starting to get that feeling that it might not work out. Five other teams had conveyed interest in me, but at this point in my career I was going to be pretty picky. I wasn't just trying to make a roster for the sake of making a roster. Really, at this point, it was going to come down to whether St. Louis wanted me or not.

In the midst of waiting and seeing how things were going to play out contractwise with St. Louis, my agent Lonnie Cooper and I started talking with Turner Broadcasting System about joining their broadcast team.

Pursuing broadcasting was not really out of the blue per se, as later in my career I had dabbled with it a little bit, but my experience was limited to a handful of spots I did from the dugout in Atlanta and from working one series of the playoffs in 2008 for TBS. That year

I was out with shoulder surgery and they invited me to come broadcast alongside Brian Anderson and Joe Simpson. It was an amazing experience, but when I look back, what's even more amazing is that everything went as well as it did. I never really went through a whole regimen of preparation, like I didn't attend rookie broadcaster spring training or anything. I just sat down in the booth and started talking into the mike. I was completely clueless about some aspects of it, especially the production side of things, but I really felt comfortable in the booth from day one. In my mind, I was just sitting there talking about a game I loved.

Looking back, my performance during the playoffs in some ways served as an audition. All things told, I had one week to make a decision either way. What would be my occupation for 2010: player or broadcaster?

All throughout the negotiations with TBS, I was still negotiating with the Cardinals. As intrigued as I was about the opportunity to broadcast, my number one desire was to play in 2010. Realistically, I only had a few playing years left, whereas I liked to think I still had many years to get into broadcasting. I was really prepared to fill in for St. Louis wherever they might need me, whether it was pitching out of the 'pen, or spot-starting on occasion, and I still felt like I could deliver for them in either of those roles. But in the end, the Cardinals decided to go in another direction.

I'm sure there was a lot of concern about my shoulder and doubts as to whether or not it could hold up for yet another season. And in retrospect, they may have been right; I don't know. There's no way for anyone to predict what that next year in baseball would have looked like for me.

When the Cardinals decided not to re-sign me, I was really fine with it. The one thing I always appreciated about St. Louis was that they treated me with unbelievable respect and dignity, even down to our very last conversation when they delivered the news that I didn't really want to hear. In the end, St. Louis was the greatest place I could have gone and it was really a fitting end to my career. I will always be thankful for the opportunity they gave me in 2009.

It's a little crazy how everything came together in this one-week period: I ended my baseball career and I went right into this transition into the next phase of my life in the space of seven days. From the outside, it might have looked like I never missed a beat, but I was incredibly fortunate to have everything work out as if it had been planned along, because it really wasn't.

As I look back, maybe it shouldn't surprise me so much that I am a broadcaster today. When you consider that ever since I was first able to operate a radio, my life has been filled with a steady diet of play-by-play and color commentary, I guess it starts to make sense. I can't deny it: I love to *listen* to baseball games. In Michigan, I had the pleasure of growing up listening to the legendary Ernie Harwell, the voice of the Detroit Tigers, and I soaked up his love and enthusiasm for the game every chance I could get. Later on, when we started to get the games on TV, I would turn the volume down and watch the game, but still listen to Ernie. I loved the way he broadcast a game; he could captivate your attention like nobody else.

Tiger baseball games dictated a large part of my schedule. If the game came on at 7 P.M., all my homework, all my chores, everything that needed to get done was done by 6:59. If the team was on the West Coast and the game was late, I'd set my alarm clock for school in the morning and I would fall asleep listening to the game. I could usually get in three innings before I nodded off.

I never set out to be a broadcaster; it's just the kind of the way things worked out for me. But when I look back now, I wonder if it wasn't all a part of my master plan—just a plan that I wasn't aware of myself. I look back to times in my career and certain things I did, and it just amazes me, like all the times I impersonated broadcasters. Early in my career, I used to have a lot of fun with fellow pitcher

Mark Grant whenever we played in San Francisco. When we played the Giants on the road, all the starting pitchers would watch the game in the clubhouse because the dugouts were too small to fit the whole team. Left to our own devices, Mark and I began to do these elaborate mock broadcasts of the game. We'd watch the game with the sound off and call it for all the other guys. We'd get into it like it was a playoff game and every hit was high drama. Mark would be like, "And here's a line drive to left field!" and then I'd hit two bats together to make the sound effect. It was goofy stuff, but we had a blast. And the funny thing is that here we are today and both Mark and I are broadcasters.

One great part of my original contract with TBS in 2010 was the opportunity it afforded me to broadcast Braves' games for Peachtree TV here in Atlanta, which TBS owned back then. When they first approached me and asked me to do twenty-five home games, I warned them what they were in for. I said, "If you get me, you get the whole package. You're going to get the goofiness, the jokes, you're going to get it all. I'm going to call the game, but I'm going to bring some silly humor to it, too."

They were all for it and I had an absolute blast calling the games for Peachtree that year. For one, it was my team, it was the Braves, but then there was the opportunity to work at the local level. The local broadcasts afforded me a great chance to practice and make mistakes and learn in between calling the national games on TBS and the MLB Network, whom I also signed a contract with, and, at the same time, have some fun and let my hair down. (Even if I don't have as much of it as I used to.) I got into this routine of telling one funny joke a game, and people seemed to love it. When people ran into me at the store or somewhere out in town, I was amazed by how many could do nothing but talk about my stupid joke. One time I was hitting a urinal at a movie theater, and I'll never forget an older man in his seventies walks by and says to me, "Three-legged dog, I get it, I get it." It was so cool.

I was really looking forward to coming back in 2011; I had this funny gig planned out to wear a different toupee for each game—it was going to great. Only it didn't happen. TBS sold Peachtree TV to Fox Sports South and it was a real bummer; I missed out on covering the Braves and I missed that little irreverence you can't get away with as much on national TV as you can on local. Plus I still haven't figured out what I am going to do with all these toupees.

My penchant for having a little fun in the booth actually predates my first contract and my short time with Peachtree TV. You can actually trace it back to the very first time someone entrusted me with a mike in 2004, back when I was the Braves closer. TBS had approached me and asked if I would be willing to broadcast from the dugout during a game sometime, and I was really intrigued. I knew the guys were going to give me a hard time about it (which they did), but I thought it would be fun. At the same time it was obviously going to have to be a special situation. I talked it over with Bobby and we eventually worked it out so that I could have an off day during the final weekend of the season. So as we faced the Chicago Cubs in our last three-game series of the year, for one night I swapped my spikes for a set of headphones and dived in as the third man.

It was my first time out and I was determined to make it a memorable one. So the very first thing I did was set up a practical joke with the late Skip Caray and Joe Simpson, the broadcasters I would be joining, not so literally, in the booth. As a pitcher who had spent a lot of off time in the clubhouse, I had been listening to Skip and Joe go back and forth during broadcasts, and rag each other through the years, so I knew they would be up for it. The joke was going to be on Glenn Diamond, their producer, who of all things is now *my* producer. So anyway, I told Skip and Joe, "Listen, let's just get Glenn right out of the box. Whatever question you ask me, I'm going to pretend like I can't hear it, like there's some kind of a connection problem."

So the first time Skip brings me into the broadcast, he says, "So, Smoltzy. What are the Braves' chances this year for the playoffs?"

Though I had clearly heard his question in my headset, I immediately acted like I hadn't quite made it out. I started fumbling with my headset and I let some awkward dead air go by. About this time I knew Glenn must be starting to switch into panic mode. So I said, "Hey Skip, I'm having a hard time hearing you down here. I think you were asking me about the ivy? Something about what do I think about the ivy here at Wrigley Field?"

And with that, I launched into this elaborate answer about the ivy. I found out later that Glenn, all the while, was in the truck lighting up the tech guys: "What's going on, what's the problem?!"

When I had finished my soliloquy on the finer points of creeping vines and the lack of padding they truly provide outfielders gunning for balls at the wall, Joe Simpson, as only a good straight man would do, asked me, "John, what do you think about the ivy here at Wrigley Field?"

I said, "Joe, I'm really having a hard time hearing you. I don't know what the deal is, but I think you asked me about our playoff chances and the run we're about to go on?"

Before it was all said and done, Glenn finally figured it out and I then explained to the audience what was going on, because I'm sure they had no clue what was happening. But that's how I started my first gig behind the mike.

I think this is a side of my personality that didn't come across as much during my baseball career, but I love to mess with people. In order to understand this, though, you've got to understand a little about my dad and how I was really genetically predisposed to be a good-natured prankster from the beginning.

My dad is the kind of dad who would routinely dress up in a gorilla suit at Halloween and then sit stock-still in a chair on the porch. As kids came up to trick or treat and my mom handed out the candy, they would be looking at him, wondering if the thing in the chair was just a stuffed gorilla. And my dad would just sit there waiting for the right moment to do something. He might have been guilty of scaring the pants off a few kids, but nobody ever went home crying. It was all in good fun; he'd scare the older kids, but just surprise the younger ones.

I guess the other thing you could say about my dad is he's a tad eccentric. One of the best ways I can think to define eccentric in this case is to describe a car he once drove. My dad worked primarily in electronics sales while I was a kid. At one point he was working for Sony and they had just started selling one of the very first electronic display calculators, which were made by Ricoh. This was back when calculators were selling for like $1,250 bucks. Anyway, nobody back then seemed to know Sony was selling calculators, so he took it upon himself to clear up that little oversight in the Lansing area.

My dad bought a 1970 Ford Maverick and basically transformed it to resemble a calculator. He had the front end of the car—which was conveniently very boxy—and the hood painted with the keys and the display. Then he fabricated a life-size roll of paper that he mounted to the roof, replaced the gas cap on the back of the car with an industrial three-prong electric cord that sort of hung down on the bumper, and had big letters stenciled down the side panels that read FOR FREE TRIAL, CALL SONY. Then he topped it all off by adding a bunch of speakers so that he could broadcast this sound track of advertising about the new calculators mixed with crazy animal noises like dogs barking or windows breaking, as if people were throwing out their old rotary adding machines. His car, which he named "Ricoh," drummed up both attention and calculator sales, but it's safe to say that as kids, my brother and sister and I didn't always think it was the coolest car to be seen in around town.

When my dad would take me to school, I always told him, "Okay, Dad, the basketball coach wanted me to get some exercise in this morning, so if you could drop me off a mile from school, I think that would be a great start." I can laugh about it now, but through all these things he did, my dad really taught me a great lesson in life: He was never ashamed of who he was or what he did. As a kid, I didn't always understand it, but it's definitely something that I appreciate today. In my family, we embrace things like playing the accordion, dressing up in gorilla suits, and driving around in cars that look like calculators. We may be a little quirky, but we're proud of who we are, we're proud of our last name, and I guarantee we *never* run out of things to laugh about.

I think it's safe to say that these parts of my dad's personality rubbed off on me in their own way. I never broke out a gorilla suit in the major leagues, but there was one pretty famous hairy mask dating back to my instructional league days. And whenever I sensed that there was a moment when I could get someone, I took full advantage. One of my favorite stories happened just like that; I saw an opportunity and I ran with it.

This story unfolded on one of our many late nights on the road. We had played an evening game on the West Coast and then promptly flown back to Chicago right after the game, so we didn't get in to the hotel until like three or four in the morning. So our whole team shows up at the hotel at once and the lobby was quickly overflowing with bags and luggage.

I happened to be standing nearby when the phone rang at the bellman's desk, so I looked over and I noticed that the phone had caller ID. And then I noticed the name: It was a player calling for his bags. The lone bellman on duty was already busy ferrying bags to rooms, so I did what any good guy would do—I started fielding all of his calls for him in his obvious time of need. And, I might have taken the opportunity to say a few things that pro baseball players aren't used to hearing from a hotel bellman.

The first guy calling was adamant about needing his bags right away, so I told him, in a disguised voice so he didn't know it was me, "Look, I'm sorry, sir, I know how important you are and every-thing, but we're swamped. If you want your bag right now, you're just going to have to come get it yourself." And then I hung up on him. I could tell already that this was going to be good.

The phone just kept ringing and I just kept laying it on thicker and thicker. The next guy who wanted his bag all snappylike got the following response: "I'm sorry, sir, it appears your bag has been dam-aged. We're going to need you to come down and take a look at it."

I used every line I could think of, promptly ticking off one team-mate after another. I remember one of the guys called and said, "Hey, when you bring up my bag, can you bring change for a hundred?" I promptly told him, "Look, man, if I had change for a hundred, I wouldn't be doing this job."

By the end, I think I jacked with almost every guy on our team and I'm sure I had some folks spinning upstairs. You can just imagine what they thought about this bellman treating them like some punk.

I was having a good time already, but it was the very last call that night that was the best. One of the guys wanted to know if a certain place was open and if it was within walking distance of the hotel or did he need a cab. Initially, I was like, "Look, I'm so overwhelmed down here I don't have time for this. Find out yourself." *Click.*

Then I promptly called him right back and said, "Hey sir, look, I feel bad about that little outburst. I just don't have enough help down here. I didn't mean to take it out on you. Would you like me to call you a cab?"

He said, "Nah, don't worry about it. I can do it."

I said, "Sir, I really feel compelled to call you a cab. Do you want me to call you a cab?"

He kept refusing, but after we went back and forth three or four times, he finally said, "Okay, sure."

So I said, "You're a cab!" And I hung up the phone and immedi-ately exited the area. My work there was done.

Those are the kinds of things that I loved to do. Even today, if you are around me long enough, I'm going to getcha.

My dad taught me a little something about messing with people, but he also taught me a little something about *engaging* people. From a young age, I was always organizing games and getting the other kids in the neighborhood to come play. I always loved stirring the pot and challenging other people, and in turn challenging myself. I loved the camaraderie and bonding that could take place. When I was a kid, I didn't play it safe just to be liked or to fit in, or be cool. As a matter of fact, I took grave risks of not being popular and not fitting in. I mean, how uncool is it to try to get your entire varsity basketball team to go bowling? But it was always just who I was and what I thought was important. And it always seemed to help the various teams I played on gel and play better together.

This tendency to engage people and to play practical jokes has been a mainstay of my personality from the beginning, and it really permeates everything that I do and everything that I am involved in. By far the most elaborate way I have engaged a group of guys was the Bible Bowl.

But let me preface this by saying that I have been fortunate to be a member of one of the greatest Bible studies *ever* for more than fifteen years. I started attending way back in 1995 and it has had the most unbelievable impact on my faith. This Bible study was first led by Tim Cash, who later became one of our baseball chaplains. Tim has been one of the most powerful mentors for me in my faith. He has walked with me through some of the toughest times in my life, and both he and his wife, Barb, have helped me stay focused on the journey and helped me handle things that were way beyond my own abilities. I was always able to do things in the athletic world that amazed some people, but when it came to the philosophical world, I have always been amazed by the Cashes.

So this Bible study, which I attend on Thursday mornings to this day, is really a unique thing. It's a wide variety of guys, former NFL players, former baseball players, some businessmen, and then guys like Jeff Foxworthy and Ernie Johnson Jr., who I get the pleasure of broadcasting with today. We meet in a back room at this hole-in-the-wall barbecue joint here in Atlanta and we have this sign we hang on the door that says DROP YOUR FIG LEAF BEFORE ENTERING. That phrase has a lot of meaning and truth behind it in so many ways. There's the whole "we're all naked before God" part, but then there's also the fact that our Bible study is really a roomful of résumés: people who have accomplished a lot of great things in this life. But in this crowd, trust me, nobody is impressed or intimidated by anybody else. This is our chance to be raw and "organic" and transparent with each other as God-fearing men in this world who struggle with real issues, as we all do in life. We hold each other accountable in our faith, and at times, you know, not to get too corny, we hold each other. We are truly a band of brothers before God, and I am so fortunate to have a great leader in Tim and so many partners in faith who have helped keep me on this journey of doing whatever I can for the kingdom of God.

So now back to the fun part. Well, anyone who knows me knows that I am going to figure out a way to engage this group of guys and tap into their competitiveness, and thus was born the Bible Bowl. Now, let me tell you, this was no run-of-the-mill version of flag football. We had a draft, we had referees, we had announcers, *and* we had a video production crew. I mean, we're talking the works.

I was, of course, the quarterback of my team, and Don Majkowski, the former Green Bay Packers quarterback who will unfortunately forever be remembered as the guy who Brett Favre replaced, was the QB for the other team. In Bible Bowl I, the score was all tied up at 11–11 and I was consulting my wristband to select the next play. I opted for the Foxworthy Fake on two, and it ended up being the play of the game. Jeff, playing wide receiver, took off once we snapped the ball and started down the field like he was going deep. Then he pulled up suddenly and faked a hamstring injury. All the defenders bought it and then he just started running again. I threw one up for him and he came down with it in the end zone. It was seriously at least a fifty-yard pass. We really should have sent the tape in to *SportsCenter* because it easily could have made their Top Ten Plays of the Day deal. But as it was, the play would seal our victory and Jeff's selection as team MVP. And what a steal, to think that I had drafted him late in the seventh round. Who could have known all the talent that was hidden in that incredibly funny guy?

I'm sad to say we had to retire the Bible Bowl after the fifth or sixth edition because we would take it so seriously we had guys blowing up their bodies. We had a few guys mess up their ankles, a couple guys tore their ACLs, and the very last time we played, on the second play of the game, Ernie tore his hamstring. He had a basketball doubleheader that night for TBS, and there we were carting him off the field and taking him to the hospital first. That's about the time we realized, *Hmm, maybe we're too old for this.* So these days we've downshifted into bowling. Thankfully, we have been able to keep that up without any major medical issues.

But things like this—these are the types of things I have been doing my entire life: bringing a bunch of guys, or people, together and preying off their competitiveness. The bottom line is, I love to issue a challenge or do something to flat-out bring out the very best in someone. And when I win, you better turn off your Miracle-Ear, because you are going to hear about it.

When I look back, the way things worked out for me in broadcasting is truly remarkable, because I just happened to be in the right place at the right time, and I was somehow able to bypass a lot of the things that you normally have to do to get this job. I mean, the first game I did on the MLB Network was with Bob Costas. That was pretty wild. People have asked me if I was ever scared and I always tell them, "Look, it's no different than anything I did in life. I'm not afraid to fail, be human, and make fun of myself. I only know one way: I'm going to have fun."

What's interesting is that while people sometimes tell me that they've learned something by listening to me call a game, I'm not making a point to actually teach anything. I'm just talking about what I know and I am just doing what comes naturally. I've been watching baseball almost my entire life, and while I certainly don't have all the answers, I know enough and have been through enough scenarios to be able to predict or forecast what *might* happen next. That's the essence of broadcasting for me right now, reacting to situations and being able to forecast. And also bringing up what should be happening even if it doesn't happen. I'm trying to bring the game to life for the person sitting at home—why a pitcher did this or why a player did that under a certain circumstance. I'm basically trying to explain the game to the casual fan so they can go, "Oh, I get it now."

For me, I want to make my criticism positive criticism, and I want to talk to the fans in a way that always acknowledges that baseball is hard. I never want to be sitting up there in the booth coming across like the game is easy. And beyond that, along the way I also hope to explain that the only way you can play this game at a high level is to understand and embrace the fact that failure is always right there at your fingertips, and you've got to be quick, you've got to be able to respond, and you've got to be able to overcome. And all those things are not easy to do either.

I just finished up broadcasting the 2011 playoffs for TBS, and it was really a wild twenty-day ride of baseball. I put together a few strong games that I am proud of, but of course I also have a list of lessons I learned for next time. But the one thing I realized for the first time is that I think when it comes down to sitting in the booth, watching a game that I love, and being able to call it at its peak in big, nationally televised games—it almost feels like I am playing.

Back in 2010, when I turned the page to broadcasting, I made sure that every contract was written with an option that said if I wanted to go pitch in the second half, they would let me out so I could pursue an opportunity if it presented itself. I just didn't know if I was truly done with baseball or not yet. I really didn't know I was done with baseball until God told me. Sometime in February, after I signed my contract with TBS, I put the baseball down. I sensed that my desire, that flame that had burned so hot for so long, was waning, but I left it up to God. I said, "Lord, please take away my desire or fill me back up. Please let me know what you would have me do." And it was shortly after this that I noticed my desire had ended and I was in a place where I wasn't wondering if I had done the right thing anymore.

I faded away from baseball after 2009. I was at peace with where I was and I was grateful for my journey. And that's really where I remain today.

And I haven't picked up a ball since.

Epilogue

More than two years have passed since I last picked up a baseball, yet the peace that existed in my heart then still exists there today.

Mostly this stems from the great personal satisfaction I take in knowing I pursued my dream as long as I possibly could, but I can't deny that broadcasting has really helped ease the transition from my playing days to my post-playing days, because in a lot of ways I feel like I haven't left yet.

At the same time there are a few whimsical notions that pop into my head from time to time. Like for a while there I was hoping the Braves would offer me a one-day contract so I could just *say* that I retired in Atlanta. And, I still wish I had gotten the opportunity to play center field for just one inning in a big-league game. (If I had been able to retire in Atlanta, I might have gotten the chance. I shagged batting practice and pestered Bobby Cox shamelessly about it for years.) Besides these idle daydreams, though, I truly look back and cherish the opportunities that I did have.

As much as I love the game of baseball and plan on broadcasting for the foreseeable future, one place I can't imagine I'll ever be is back in the game as a pitching coach or manager.

Now, don't get me wrong; it's not because I don't think I could do the job. In a lot of ways, I would relish the challenge—I *love* the idea of working with a group of guys to try to accomplish a team goal, and I *love* working one-on-one with people to try to make them better. The side I don't like, the part that would probably make me chew my fingers off my own hands, has to do with all the New Age philosophies that now permeate the game, especially when it comes to pitching.

I just don't buy into all this emphasis on pitch counts and pitch limits, and I couldn't imagine trying to work with a pitcher who has bought into the theory that five innings is good enough, or God forbid, his arm might fall off if he throws 230 innings in a year. In my opinion, today's pitchers are being coddled. And despite all the good intentions behind reducing a pitcher's workload, it doesn't seem to be reducing injuries or lengthening careers.

I also don't put much stock in the theory of Moneyball and all these computer-generated models designed to wade through a bunch of statistics and tell organizations which players represent the best investment. I couldn't imagine being tied to an organizational philosophy that's based on a bunch of numbers, or having a computer telling me what my own eyes should be seeing, and I would probably lose my job over the tug-of-war between technology and my gut instincts.

But remember, I said I would never write a book either . . .

For right now, life after baseball for me represents an opportunity to pursue the things I have been passionate about throughout my career: spending time with my children and family, continuing to be a caretaker of King's Ridge Christian School, and devoting my time to the other charitable causes that are important to me. But beyond these aspirations, I view retirement as the chance to do some things I have been waiting more than twenty years to do.

When I retired from baseball, I started my quest to play golf on the Champions Tour someday, I started playing recreational basketball every Monday night, and I'm making the time to play tennis and racquetball—things I'd always wanted to do, but never could do while playing baseball. And I'm having the time of my life. Well, actually, it would be more accurate to say I'm having the time of my life within reason.

Perhaps it's easy to look at someone who played a professional sport for more than twenty years and think, *That guy's set. He shouldn't have to work another day in his life if he doesn't want to.* Well, I'm here to tell you, as often is the case in life, that perception is not reality for me.

While I grant you that I did play enough years to support my family for a long while, it's safe to say that things happened that I never planned for—you know, like life. And life in this time and economy for me—like it is for so many others—has been a real challenge. I suppose there might be some people who are immune to these lean economic times, but I am not one of them. Like many Americans, I'm downsizing and reassessing. Just like when I started a season 2–11, just like when I was coming back from my first shoulder surgery, and just like when I had just been released by the Boston Red Sox, it's rally time.

Just because it's rally time doesn't mean that I have given up on my dreams. It just means that right now I'm dealing with the economic realities in which those dreams arise. The reality for me is as it is for most people right now: I'll be working for the foreseeable future. And I am happy to do it. It's important to be flexible and adjust your goals as life goes on. I'm adjusting, but at the same time I'm still pursuing. Just because life isn't turning out quite as I expected, or I'm in a bit of a slump, I see no reason to forfeit my dreams. If you ask me, this is one of most important parts of rallying: being able to reinforce your dreams and aspirations.

Maybe my most ambitious retirement dream—playing golf professionally—won't unfold at the pace I once had hoped, but rest assured, I'll be out there testing myself whenever I can.

It's ironic that here I am at the end of a book about persevering through my final year in baseball and I find myself in need of perseverance again today. But it doesn't scare me or intimidate me, or make me just throw my hands up in the air and say, "Enough!" It's like I have said before, you can choose to be bitter, or you can choose to better. That's a one-vowel difference that changes everything. It really is a choice. A lot of people are bitter, but I choose to be better.

I am just going to do what I always do. I'm going to go back to the core of who I am and continue surrounding myself with people who can help keep me accountable, but also be supportive and honest. I'm going to make a plan and get moving, and I'm going to find ways to get it done. And while I'm not sure where it's going to lead me, I'm pretty confident that I'm going to come out on the other side.

And through it all, through the ups and the downs, the slumps and the victories, and the wins and losses, while I may at times be disappointed and frustrated, I have learned enough to know and trust that at the end of every day, God's love is enough. As I said in the beginning, joy is central. The rest of it is peripheral. You can have joy in the midst of some of your worst suffering.

Whenever I start becoming consumed by outcomes and find myself forgetting to focus on the process and enjoy the journey, I pull out my Bible and read all four chapters of Philippians. This is a habit I began in 1996 when I was in the midst of my one and only Cy Young season. The book of Philippians became my bedside companion that season, helping to keep me anchored and focused in what would be a 24–8 season.

I would suggest that the next time you find yourself getting carried away—with either success or failure—take a few minutes and read this letter from Paul, chapter four, verse four, which reads in part:

> *Rejoice in the Lord always. I will say it again: Rejoice! Let your gentleness be evident to all. The Lord is near. Do not be anxious about anything, but in everything, by prayer and petition, with thanksgiving, present your requests to God. And the peace of God, which transcends all understanding, will guard your hearts and your minds in Christ Jesus.*
>
> *Finally, brothers, whatever is true, whatever is noble, whatever is right, whatever is pure, whatever is lovely, whatever is admirable—if anything is excellent or praiseworthy—think about such things. Whatever you have learned or received or heard from me, or seen in me— put into practice. And the God of peace will be with you.*

Have dreams and chase them. Don't be afraid to fail. Learn how to rally, and trust that you have the ability to find your own measure of success in life. If an accordion-playing kid from Michigan can do it, believe me, so can you.

And finally I would say, in all moments, look up.

Acknowledgments

A book like this would not have been possible without the contributions of a lot of people's energy, hard work, dedication, assistance, and support.

First and foremost, my family has been great through this whole process. My kids were willing to give up a little "dad time" so that I could work on this, and my wife, Kathryn, has been a great proofreader.

I also want to thank my parents, John and Mary Smoltz, and my siblings, Mike and Bernadette, for sharing their stories and memories—and for not embarrassing me too badly. A special thanks goes out to my dad for pulling together a lot of the photographs for this book as well.

I would also like to express my sincere thanks to my longtime agents Myles Shoda and Lonnie Cooper. Yes, I have two agents, which is certainly not an ideal situation for them, but it is for me and they have been *essential* in helping to manage my career. To give you an idea of how much I implicitly trust these men: I would be completely comfortable leaving my children with them.

Ian Kleinert, the agent for this book, was absolutely fantastic. I was reluctant for a long time about writing a book but my mother-in-law really encouraged me to do it, and Ian made the process as painless as possible, so I owe them both a big thank you.

Adam Korn, my tireless editor, was indispensible and did what I think is a pretty darn good job of making this thing turn out logical and readable. Many, many thanks.

I also found several resources to be especially helpful in reconstructing certain scenes and checking numbers. The good folks at Baseball-Reference.com run a top-notch site that not only posts player stats but also has features like an online video about how to read a play-by-play. It is an awesome resource for any baseball fan or sportswriter.

I also want to credit several books, such as Jim Bouton's *Ball Four,* Tom Glavine's *None but the Braves,* Buzz Bissinger's *Three Nights in August,* Michael Lewis's *Moneyball,* and John Feinstein's *Living on the Black.* These books were all helpful sources as well as good examples of how a baseball book should read. The MLB rule book was also helpful in clarifying several points. Additionally, Mark Bowman at MLB.com, Jayson Stark at ESPN.com, Hal Bodley at *USA Today,* and Buster Olney at *ESPN the Magazine* provided some great articles and analysis that were very helpful in pulling this project together. And as a shout-out to Atlanta, Jeff Schultz's columns in the *Atlanta-Journal Constitution* were fantastic. I would be remiss if I didn't also thank Patty Rasmussen, formerly of *Chop Talk,* who inspired the title of the book.

Thank you to Dr. Joe Chandler, the team physician, who spoke with me for this book. Thanks also to Richie Hughes, Tim Cash, Chris Verna, and Chuck Cascarilla, who took the time to chat and share their insights. I greatly appreciate their time and willingness to help out.

This book would not have been possible without the insane level of dedication from Sarah Woodman Kansteiner. Her attention to detail, exhaustive research, and turn-of-phrase were indispensable. I can't thank her enough for her sheer willpower to get this done on time and done right. I don't know if she picked that up from her time in the Marine Corps, but it was impressive. The way that Sarah worked with my coauthor, Don Yaeger, to pull this all together was truly impressive.

Finally, I want to thank all of the baseball fans out there—especially the ones in Atlanta—who have followed me and supported me throughout my career highs and lows . . . and lowers and highers. Baseball is America's pastime, which makes you all America's fans. Thank you for the cheers, the prayers, and the support. I can never thank you enough, but I hope this book serves as a small token of my appreciation for everything you've offered me over the years.

Last, but not least, I am forever grateful for the hand that God has had in my life. To understand that I am truly loved and cherished by Him whether I am an All-Star baseball player, a struggling father, or a guy down on his finances or luck, to know that He is in control has given me a peace beyond anything I deserve. I hope I can continue to do His work.

Index

Go behind the scenes with John Smoltz in the enhanced eBook!

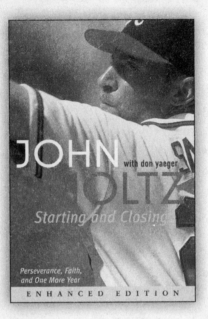

In the enhanced eBook edition of *Starting and Closing*, baseball legend John Smoltz goes on camera to give readers exclusive video interviews. Now fans can:

- Watch Smoltz in action
- See demos of his trademark pitches
- Find lists of his favorite and most feared competitors
- And much more!

Enhanced eBook • ISBN: 978-0-06-221569-7 • $16.99

WILLIAM MORROW
An Imprint of HarperCollins*Publishers*
www.harpercollins.com